CARPE MAÑANA

RESOURCES BY LEONARD SWEET

11 Genetic Gateways to Spiritual Awakening

A Is for Abductive (with Brian McLaren and Jerry Haselmayer)

AquaChurch

Communication and Change in American Religious History

A Cup of Coffee at the SoulCafe

FaithQuakes

Health and Medicine in the Evangelical Tradition

The Jesus Prescription for a Healthy life

Quantum Spirituality: A Postmodern Apologetic

SoulSalsa

SoulSalsa audio

SoulTsunami

SoulTsunami audio

Strong in the Broken Places:
   A Theological Reverie on the Ministry of George Everett Ross

Learn about these resources at
http://www.leonardsweet.com

CARPE MAÑANA

Is Your Church Ready to **SEIZE TOMORROW?**

LEON@RD.SWEET

ZONDERVAN™

GRAND RAPIDS, MICHIGAN 49530

We want to hear from you. Please send your comments about this
book to us in care of the address below. Thank you.

GRAND RAPIDS, MICHIGAN 49530 USA

WWW.ZONDERVAN.COM

ZONDERVAN™

Carpe Mañana
Copyright © 2001 by Leonard I. Sweet

Requests for information should be addressed to

Zondervan, *Grand Rapids, Michigan 49530*

Library of Congress Cataloging-in-Publication Data

Sweet, Leonard I.
    Carpe mañana : is your church ready to seize tomorrow? / Leonard Sweet.
        p. cm.
    Includes bibliographical references.
    ISBN 0-310-25012-9 (softcover)
    1. Church and the world.   I. Title.
BR115.W6 S95 2001
270.8'3 — dc21   2001026971

All Scripture quotations, unless otherwise indicated, are taken from the *New Revised Standard Version Bible,* © 1989 by the Division of Christian Education of the National Council
of Churches of Christ in the United States of America. Used permission of Zondervan. All
rights reserved.

Other Scripture quotations are from *The Revised English Bible* (REB), © 1989 Oxford
University Press and Cambridge University Press; *Revised Standard Version* (RSV), © 1946,
1952, 1971 by the Division of Christian Education of the National Council of Churches of
Christ in the United States of America; *The New English Bible* (NEB) © 1961, 1970 Oxford
University Press and Cambridge University Press; and the *King James Version* (KJV).

All rights reserved. No part of this publication may be reproduced, stored in a retrieval system, or transmitted in any form or by any means — electronic, mechanical, photocopy,
recording, or any other — except for brief quotations in printed reviews, without the prior
permission of the publisher.

Interior design by Nancy Wilson

Printed in the United States of America

02 03 04 05 06 07 08 / ❖ DC/ 10 9 8 7 6 5 4 3 2 1

For DayStar

*By the tender mercy of our God,
the dawn from on high will
break upon us
to give light to those who sit in
darkness and in the shadow
of death,
to guide our feet into the way
of peace.*

Luke 1:78–79

Contents

Acknowledgments

On my first preaching mission in Nassau, I quickly learned something: If I planned on going anywhere in this former British colony, I had to master driving on the "wrong" side of the road. My Bahamian host Carl Campbell gently reminded me, of course, that when he visited the states, he also had to master the art of driving on the "wrong" side of the road.

If you are going to go anywhere in the world, whether as an immigrant or native, one has to learn how to "go native." Sometimes that means learning how to drive in a whole new way. Gil Gilbert (Hosanna) and Wayne Cobb (St. James), two Lutheran pastors in Concord, North Carolina, challenged me to hone my skills at driving on the other side to the point where I could write this book. Up until 1987, I was a total Gutenberg Man, so my naturalization process has had to cover a lot of territory. I need all the help I can get.

Twenty Drew students in an online January-Term 2000 course first heard some of these ramblings. Their threaded discussions braced me to keep poking my nose into some fearsome fields. Lex Rivers of Bellingham, Washington, gave me the ending to the book, and my executive assistant Lyn Stuntebeck gave me the beginning. My editor at Zondervan, Lyn Cryderman, conceived the project and challenged me to undertake it. Senior editors Bob Hudson and Jim Ruark kept me believing in the book even when I lost faith.

This book's title is outright thievery. Ernie Fitzpatrick returned from a mission trip to Venezuela in early April 2000 and preached a sermon on "Carpe Mañana" at the multicultural, nondenominational Liberty Revival Church in Houston, Texas (for a tape of the 2 April 2000 sermon call 281-444-6346). Ernie is an apostolic inspiration to many of us immigrants who are trying to get to know natives and think as they think. Thanks for letting me use your sermon title, Ernie, as the title for the expanded version of the ebook that came out under the original title *The Dawn Mistaken for Dusk*.

This book was largely written during Holy Week 2000. In the space of that one sentence hangs some hoary, gory tales. Thank God, my family and friends are not telling. My wife, Elizabeth, was always there with a word or lift when I ran out of steam. Landrum Leavell III kept me laughing and "proofed" the manuscript. My research assistant Betty O'Brien checked a reference and corrected any mistakes as quickly as I wrote a sentence and footnoted it. How she did it is beyond my comprehension. After reading the book Betty is not convinced she wants a visa to begin with, but she hosted a party in her home that gave me the idea. She can't wash her hands of the book completely.

Introduction 1

What It Is

We will forever be at the beginning of a new level of civilization. And this is fortunate, because a beginning is a fascinating and exciting place to be.

▶ Douglas S. Robertson[1]

BUG ATTACKS

Millennium Three began with bug attacks. The most feared and hyped was called "The Millennium Bug." It was brought to us courtesy of computer programmers and other professionals who failed to provide four digit spaces for year 2000. Millions of dollars were spent in inoculation, millions of pounds of groceries were hoarded in preparation, and millions of people shuddered in anticipation of power-outages, missile launchings, plant explosions, etc. By the time the New Year's Eve ball in Times Square hit bottom, thousands had made good on their threats of "buggin'out," as they headed for the hills and other remote sanctuaries in fear of The Millennium Bug.

Nevertheless, the Y2K bug was a dud.

A second bug attack blindsided planet Earth and brought it to its knees. It was called the "Love Bug," and nobody saw it coming.

Where did it come from? A couple of Philippine college students living in a slum section of Manila decided to test out some software codes they had written for a computer course. With a few strokes on their home keyboards — computers cobbled together from recycled parts — they shut down government agencies, brought global portals to a grinding halt, and created billions of dollars worth of damage to corporations and individuals around the world. The CIA's official estimate of damage amounted to $4 billion, but some unofficial estimates go as high as $60 billion. A thousand NASA files were harmed or destroyed.

The Love Bug story is but one of many, some of which are being played out as you read these words.

The February 2000 "denial-of-service" attacks against Amazon.com, Yahoo!, and CNN.com, costing tens of millions of dollars, were launched by a 15-year-old Canadian kid known as "Mafiaboy."

Cameron Johnson lives in Roanoke, Virginia. In early 2000 he set up his second company called SurfingPrizes.com, which now averages $15,000 a day in revenue. Cameron Johnson is 15 years old.

26,000 credit card numbers were recently stolen; among them was one of Bill Gates's card numbers. Two Welsh teenagers were arrested.

The most heavily guarded code in the world, as secure as Fort Knox, is the Microsoft software code. A breach of security occurred in the fall of 2000. No one has yet been caught, but teenage hackers are the main suspects.[2]

Michael Furdyk set up a company with an Australian chat room friend called MyDesktop.com. Within a few months it was making $30,000 a month in ad sales. Teenpreneur Michael is seventeen. The friend he has never seen? Sixteen.[3]

Shawn Fanning was a college dropout. In 1999 he and his buddy Sean Parker started a company called Napster. Within one year the service reached 20 million users (by comparison, it took AOL ten years and who-knows-how-many discs in the mail to reach the 23 million subscribers it has today), and it shook the music establishment like nothing else in music history. Downloading MP3 files surpassed cruising sex sites as the most popular activity on the Net. Millionaire Fanning was 19, and Parker was 20.[4]

The main rival to Microsoft Windows, an open source system called Linux, was written by a University of Helsinki college student, Linus Torvalds.[5]

A 13-year-old Pennsylvania girl is rich today. Her Harry Potter website was so compelling and the traffic so one-way that a "West Coast dot-com" bought it and linked it to the official Potter site. The only other recourse was to sue the girl for copyright infringement.[6]

From these stories, and many more like them, I have learned three hard lessons.

(1) We are living in a world where, for the first time in history, children in all places on the planet — Philippines, Mexico, Norway —

can do the harm that only governments and generals could do in the past.[7]

The damage that the Love Bug did used to be called "war." Yet in the Philippines, where less than 2% of the population logs onto the Internet, where one-third of the people are farmers, where the government does virtually nothing to promote Internet use, where a computer costs more than most families' annual income, and most computers are powered by generators, a college student is able to control the planet.[8] We are now living in a world where the Cold War may have ended but the next world war has already begun. In fact, 30 nations are now preparing for the Info War (Information Warfare).[9]

(2) We are living in a world where, for the first time in history, children do not need authority figures to access information. Our children have new and different ways of acquiring and accessing, deciphering and digesting information.[10]

Try this experiment. After church engage a five- or six year-old Sunday school kid in conversation. Begin by asking them to explain Pokémon to you. Better have a couple hours handy. Not only will they be able to name you each of the couple hundred digital creatures (Charmander, Rattata, Geodude, Odish, Snorlax, ad nauseam), but they will also want to tell you something detailed about each of their strengths and weaknesses. When you cannot take it any longer, change the subject and ask them about some other stories and characters: Shadrach, Meshach, and Abednigo; Samson and Delilah; David and Goliath; Jonah and the whale; Peter; Paul; Ruth; Esther; John the Baptist; the Good Samaritan, etc. There is a reason why our kids know what we do *not* try to teach them, but do not know what we *do* try to teach them.

(3) We are living in a world where, for the first time in history, children *are* the authority figures, and adults have to come to them to get help. Children have knowledge their parents do not.[11] Why is your VCR not blinking "12:00"? How did you get more memory installed on your computer?[12] Who do you ask to hook up or fix your electronics?

Children are now contributors not just copiers of existing knowledge. Rather than empty vessels into which big jugs pour information, the little jugs are themselves sources of learning. Is it any wonder 26% of age discrimination lawsuits are now launched by people in their forties, up from 18% in 1986?

Once you understand one simple fact, you get fresh insights into everything. If you do not get this one simple fact, it is like trying to make a credit card call from a rotary phone.

The simple fact is this: If you were born before 1962, you are an immigrant. If you were born after 1962, you are a native.[13]

Some of us are aboriginals.
Some of us are auslanders.
Some of us are indigenes.
Some of us are foreigners.

The natives, the aboriginals, and the indigenes are no longer the exception, but the rule.[14]

I know where I fit into this scenario. I rediscovered my immigrant status not too long ago when I moved offices and opened old boxes. One of them was a forgotten cache of papers written for my Ph.D. degree. After the dust and mites had settled, I turned into an archaeologist. Stacked on top were 3 x 5 index cards, some with metal tabs, all color-coded, and a shoebox to keep them in. When I dug underneath the shoebox I pulled out thin onion-skin paper with black smudgy typeface and pencilled-in corrections that looked like chicken tracks. Digging even deeper I discovered typewriter paper with a rare artifact called "white-out" dabbed all over it. As I excavated the farthest reaches of the box, I suddenly turned into a paleontologist: There was something called carbon paper and, at the bottom of the box, mimeographed copies of papers I had written and distributed (in a variety of colors) to other members of my class.

> **Kids have the skills that adults need to run the world.**
> ▶ Queensland-based education expert Dale Spender[15]

As I stood back up and stared at the box, I thought, *Sweet, these are the remains of a defunct civilization.* These artifacts belong to a vanished world—an age as recent as "Yesterday" (The Beatles' song) but as antique and dead as ancient Rome. Yet this box contains the remains of my civilization. It is the world I grew up in. It is the world I was trained to think in and do ministry in. It is also the world I feel most comfortable in.

But it is a world that has come to an end in my lifetime. Much of what I learned no longer works in this new world. The challenge of my ministry is to get it "out of the box."

The world has come to an end. But I am still here. Or, in the words and the title of an REM song, "It's the End of the World As We Know It (And I Feel Fine)."[16]

With every ending there is a beginning. The "I Feel Fine" portion of the "End of the World As We Know It" song beckons us to the dawning of a startling new world out there. What a wonderful time to be to be alive.

With this new world comes a fresh vision of living that has massive consequences for art, literature, music, spirituality, and other manifestations of the human spirit.

But in this new world, some of us are immigrants. Some of us are natives.

Not to understand this one little fact is not to make it in — if not into — the future.

This book is written to help you put your face, not your back, to the future. Do you have designs on the future? Are you looking the future in the eye? Most institutions (especially churches) are more focused on inculcating memories of the past than on designing visions of the future. How many toil and moil for the future? No matter how much there is about the future that sets our teeth on edge, can we still set our face to the future?

Prepare to feel obsolete. It's the first step to moving ahead.

▸ youth culture writer
Elizabeth Weil[17]

The future presents itself to us in surprising ways.

▼ ▼ ▼

A man entering a country store saw a sign on the door: Danger! Beware of Dog!

Inside was a harmless old hound asleep on the threshold. "Is that the dog we're supposed to beware of?" he asked.

"Yep," said the proprietor.

"Well, he doesn't look dangerous to me," said the man. "Why the sign?"

Said the proprietor, "Because, before I posted that sign, people kept tripping over him."

▼ ▼ ▼

In many ways, our biggest dangers come not from getting bitten by the future but by tripping over it.

ECCO DOMANI — HERE'S TOMORROW[18]

A shift of major importance for 21st-century ways of life is the emergence of the future as the primary time zone for living. If the dominant time zone of the modern world was the present (before that it had been the past), the dominant time zone for postmodern culture is the future.

More and more of us are living in the future, which is why more and more newspapers are basing their coverage from the future backward. An unnoticed massive change in news coverage is taking place: "Stories no longer report on the past; they report on the future."[19] Next time you are reading the paper, notice the switch. Articles are based on predictions about what movies or stocks will do well, with subsequent articles based on which ones did not "live up" to the expectations.

In the fall of 2000 Intel announced a 19% profit. Immediately its value plummeted by 20% and it lost 80 billion dollars in an hour. What happened? What is wrong with that kind of profitability? Intel's performance "didn't meet Wall Street expectations."

If you want to buy a swimming suit, when do you go to the store to buy one? If you go in July, you will go away with mittens and a coat. To find swimming suits you must shop in the dead of winter.

Natives live in the FuturePerfect Tense. More and more students are demanding the future as a part of their education.

> Not long ago, junior high school students in Utah staged a protest because they were being forced to learn their history from social studies textbooks printed in the mid-1980s that failed to anticipate the revolution in personal computers and still wrote about Ronald Reagan, the Berlin Wall, and the Soviet Union as if they were significant factors in the students' lives. . . . So damaged did they feel by the experience [of a school not preparing them for the world that was actually out there] that they actually staged a strike against public authority in the most authority-conscious state in the union.[20]

In the analog world of modernity, it was enough to Carpe Diem — "Seize the Day" or "Seize the Moment." If there ain't no future living in the past, to paraphrase baseball manager Sparky Anderson, there ain't no future living in the present either. By the time you Carpe Diem, it is already too late. We need to learn how to, in the words of a live not dead language, Carpe Mañana ("Seize Tomorrow" or "Seize The Future").

In the digital world of postmodernity, the world is going so fast that if you Carpe Diem, you will end up seizing air. Only those who Carpe Mañana will end up with anything in their hands. Just as in skeet shooting, you have to lead the target. If you aim your gun at the target, by the time your bullet gets there, the target has moved. Aim at today, and you will be caught up in the daily and miss the mission. Aim at tomorrow, and you will hit the mark of God's high calling.

There is hope for your mañana, but only if you seize it with this awareness: Some of us are natives, and some of us are immigrants.

> **Think of life today as being lived in the pressure tense (*present + future*) because that's what it is, and that's where you are.**
> ▶ Watts Wacker and Jim Taylor[21]

THE NEW ELLIS ISLAND

If any culture should be able to understand this one little fact, it ought to be the North American one, the largest immigrant culture on planet Earth. Since its early settlement, more than 55 million immigrants have arrived in USAmerica, 20 million in the last 20 years (that's right, an average of 1 million immigrants to the US per year). The last time the Census Bureau asked the question (1992), immigrants owned 1.5 million US businesses (one out of every 12). The figure has likely doubled since then.

Economist Barry Edmonston has estimated that a third of the people residing in USAmerica in 1990 were either born in another country or were the descendants of immigrants who arrived in the 20th century. Another third he figures derived from immigrants who arrived in the course of the 19th century.[23] That leaves only one out of three USAmericans who have family roots that extend back to the days of George Washington and Thomas Jefferson. In a short time the average USAmerican will trace their descent not to England, Germany, Ireland, or Italy, but to Asia, Africa, and the Latin worlds.

> **I never felt closer to the experience of immigrant forebears than I do now. They sailed from old world to new. Now it's my turn.**
> ▶ Tom Ashbrook, Homeportfolio.com[22]

Scholars like to say that the immigration of people to the United States represents "the largest movement of human beings to any one place in the history of mankind."[24] Is this accurate? Well, yes and no. Yes, if one defines "immigration" as the move from one geographic area to another. No, if one defines "immigration" as the move from one cultural and economic arena into another.

The largest immigration has not already happened — it is going on right now. Cultural immigrants from the *modern* world are moving into the primitive new *postmodern* world. Long before the year 2025, immigrants from the world that is presently coming to an end will constitute only a fraction of net population growth, as the swelling number of natives take charge and control of a dawning world bursting into bloom.

DEGREE OR KIND?

"But aren't you a historian?" you ask. "Surely you should know above everyone the pastness of the present. Doesn't every age look in the mirror and see itself? Isn't the historical norm continuity over rupture? Who would deny that we have experienced stomach-churning changes? But to argue that they constitute a fundamentally 'new' cultural order?"

You are right about the need to put the past into perspective before moving into the future. Pope John Paul II's historic third millennium document made this plain: "Memory and Reconciliation: The Church and the Faults of the Past."[25] When even the Pope talks about the church's encounter with the past being "rich in perfomative efficaciousness," it behooves us to remember that an AncientFuture faith melds the old and the new. It remembers and recapitulates the past. Faith is both retro and innovative, redolent and recent. An AncientFuture faith has Augustine of Hippo, Bonhoeffer of Breslau, Catharine of Siena, Xavier, Yves, and Zwingli still alive inside it, not just museum relics outside it.[26]

Perhaps the historical truism that the past is past in ways yet present keeps us from seeing the kind of world that is actually out there. It is true: The past is not just one foreign country; it is many foreign countries where strange things happen. How many of us would want to emigrate back to a past where

> an average of 550 ships were wrecked annually on British shores at the end of the eighteenth century. By the 1830s, there were more than two wrecks a day.[27]
>
> Anne, queen of England from 1702 to 1714, had 18 pregnancies, 5 live births, but not one child who survived into adulthood.
>
> as recently as 1850, half of everyone born in Britain was dead by the age of 25.[28] Paris registered only 21,000 live births in 1780. Of these 21,000 births, only 5% of the infants were nursed by their own mothers.[29]
>
> in 19th-century Cairo, women trying to get pregnant would drink the mixture of blood and water in which the bodies of beheaded criminals were washed before they were buried.[30]
>
> as late as the 19th century, doctors practiced "laudable pus" and would spread it from one patient to another in the belief that some pus could heal.
>
> soft lavatory paper was invented in Walthamstow (England) in 1942, though it took an awful long while to reach the rest of the world.
>
> the first traffic lights blew up like bombs.
>
> the first hairspray sometimes set the hair on fire, turning the body into a human candle.
>
> early vacuum cleaners spooked horses to the point of running away, which was a problem as the machines were so bulky horses were required to haul them.
>
> the pop-up toaster was invented in 1926, but had to wait until the invention of sliced bread in 1928 by Otto Frederick Rohwedder. For 26

years Rohwedder had been working on a slicing machine, which finally went into production in 1928 in Battle Creek, Michigan.[31]

Yet the difference between the world of the immigrants and the world of the natives is not one of degree, but of kind, a difference not of *differentia* but of *genus* itself.[32] Stewart Brand of *Whole Earth Catalog* and Global Business Network fame figures in engineering terms that a tenfold quantitative change yields a qualitative change.[33] Hans Moravec argues that a fourfold quantitative change in the scientific world issues in a qualitative change.[34]

> **Life was better before sliced bread.**
> ► banner of the Neo-Luddites, as found on their website www.luddites.com

The very fabric of life, the very essence of reality, is changing all around us as these quantitative changes pile up and create qualitative change. In every arena there is this sense of being enveloped by a great historical event, of living at the crux of human history.

In less than 60 years we went from flying in hot air balloons, prop planes, and jets to landing on the moon on 8K of RAM.

In 1999 Sears, Chevron, and Goodyear were replaced on the Dow Index by Microsoft, Intel, SBC Communications, and Home Depot.

You can now buy a wristwatch (Casio Computer Company) with a built-in Global Positioning System indicator that links to 27 satellites so that you will never be lost.[35]

250,000 people every year become cyborgs. The boundaries between the born and the made are blurring on a mass scale with one little implant called a pacemaker.[36]

The average person of today living in a developed country is richer in many respects than Cornelius Vanderbilt.[37]

The world of matter is becoming animated, and the world of animation is materializing.

At this dawn of a new millennium, either you are making history or you are becoming history. If there were ever a time for on-the-edge, over-the-top, out-of-the-box leadership, it is now.

Everywhere we look, the landscape is being reshaped from the ground up. The old formations and damaged infrastructures remain visible while periodic "waves of creative destruction" (economist Joseph Schumpeter) are surging through modern cultures, sweeping old constructions away and drowning those who cannot swim.[38] In *The Road Ahead* (1999), Bill Gates, history's soon-to-be first trillionaire, argues that "We are watching something historic happen, and it will affect the world seismically."[39]

Gates is "thrilled" to be able to squint "into the future and catching that first revealing hint of revolutionary possibilities" at this "beginning of an epochal change,"[40] the most massive economic shift since the Industrial Revolution.

Is Bill Gates as right as Francis Fukuyama is wrong? In his *The End of History* (1992), Francis Fukuyama argues that with the victories of Western liberal democracy around the globe, history would cease to be interesting.[41] We are living in perhaps the most interesting times in history. The Web is rattling the world to its core, with each day shucking something unprecedented, something "historic."

READY OR NOT

Some things are simple but not easy.

At the end of his life philosopher Aldous Huxley confessed that "after a lifetime devoted to studying the human condition, it is a little embarrassing to find that one has nothing more profound to suggest than 'try to be a little kinder.'"[42] Like "try to be a little kinder," the phrase "some of us are immigrants, some of us are natives" is a simple thing to say, but not a simple thing to live. The difference between "native" and "immigrant" is more than metaphorical; it is more than the difference between updated and upgraded relationships with families, communities, and God. Living in a "foreign country" is not easy.

No one should know this more than religious leaders. It is not by accident that, according to psychologist Richard Blackmon, "pastors are the single most occupationally frustrated group in America."[43]

> **There will be a time when you believe everything is finished. That will be the beginning.**
>
> ▶ western writer Louis L'Amour

On Millennium Eve, *Newsweek* featured a story about a 26-year-old ultra-Orthodox Jewish man named Noam who decided to live his faith in secular Israel. It was only a few miles from his old home Mea Shearim, a gated enclave of ultra-Orthodox Judaism. But the distance measured in terms of mind not miles was light years away. "I'm like an immigrant trying to learn a new culture," he confessed to the reporter.[44]

This is my confession. Like Noam, I am an immigrant trying to learn a new culture. I am having Ellis Island experiences every day. I now find myself on a barely known universe, in an almost unknown culture, where I must discover and create new strategies for survival and success daily.

All ministry today is cross-cultural ministry — except the "cross" is across my dining room table. For instance, I am learning

> a new language (more than just the netspeak of *gigabyte, mega-hertz, spaming, downloading*)
> new customs (email, website, e-vangelism, e-commerce, crashing — I have even been "demmed"[45])
> new sights (.com, .gov, .edu, .mil, .org)
> new rituals (networking, chatrooms, hyperlinking, surfing)
> new technologies (CD-ROM, Jaz Drive, Zip Drive, Pentium III)
> new hieroglyphics ("/." and ":)" — to name two

I have even shown my immigrant status when I used the word "titanic" in a negative way. In a world where "bad" now means "good," "titanical" means "awesome" and "agreeable."

Little Ones to Him Belong

Like all immigrants, I feel most comfortable in protective enclaves of people who share a similar cultural background and customs. But also like all immigrants, I learn the most from my children.[46] Of necessity, immigrants build strong relationships with their kids. It is our children who can translate the cultural cues and clues, not to mention (in my case) free us from digital ignorance and homelessness. Where is it we have heard "A little child shall lead them" and "Let the children come to me ... for the kingdom of God belongs to such as these?"[47]

If the human four-stage life-cycle has its cultural equivalents — first we are our parents' children, then we are our children's parents, then our parents' parents, and finally our children's children — children are now their parents' parents, as pimpled or prepubescent pundits instruct their "dazed and confused" elders.[49] Without native teachers, immigrants could not stop saying "Duh" and staying in the dark.

> **Last year's words belong to last year's language.**
> ▶ T. S. Eliot[48]

Does this make us feel uncomfortable? Ezra Pound mentored writers Eliot, Hemingway, and Yeats (among others). Eventually, Yeats became Pound's own writing teacher. The best teachers always learn the most from their students and expect to become their best students' students.[50]

What It Means

*"What do you want me to do for you?" Jesus
asked him.
The man replied, "I want to see again."*

▶ paraphrase of Luke 18:41

THE 'HOOD

"In the kingdom of blind men," as the old saying goes, "the one-eyed man is king." I like to compare futurist Tom Sine to that one-eyed man. Sine is like a giant satellite dish that pulls in information, turns that information into Christian wisdom, and then looks for various channels in which to distribute it.

Sine observes that almost overnight "we have moved into a new neighborhood, and virtually no one in the church seems to have noticed."[1] John 1:14 says, "The Word became flesh and blood and moved into the neighborhood" (Eugene Peterson's rendition). Whatever the 'hood, the incarnation takes place. Have you noticed any changes in your neighborhood recently?

The little brown church in the wildwood no longer exists, except in Thomas Kinkade paintings.[2] Those who can see this no matter how dimly — the tribe of the one-eyeds — are rounded up and shouted down. In a church blind to the world it is in, where it mistakes the dawn for a setting sun, those with open eyelids must reconcile themselves to the role of either seeing-eye dog or bloodhound, even if they are immigrants like Sine.[3]

The theologians and historians of the church have failed us if the first task of any scholar is to give as accurate a picture of reality as possible, to portray not the reality of desire but the reality of truth. How leaders of the church can sleepwalk into this future is beyond comprehension. How many church leaders are on the short list of people who are changing the world? How many church leaders are hoping to keep things going the way they are until they can retire and not be bothered?

Of course, it is not only the church's leaders that have mistaken the dawn for dusk. Is there a periodical that has not reviewed either Jacques Barzun's scan of the last five centuries called *From Dawn to Decadence* (2000) or John Lukacs' *A Thread of Years* (2000)?[4] Everywhere these two historians look, everything is on the downward slope. Decadence and decline rule the day. Barzun concludes that "the time of vast original conceptions that cause a readjustment of accepted ideas" is over.[5]

What rock has he been hiding under?

THE GOOD, THE BAD, OR THE POSTMODERN

For many, the word *postmodern* sticks in the throat—making the new world out there so hard to swallow, they cannot get it down inside them. One Florida retiree was so incensed by my use of the word "postmodern" that he went on a letter writing campaign denouncing me and anyone else who would use a word that was a non-sequitur and non-existent in the dictionary.

> **The first man in history to reach out and voluntarily touch lepers didn't die of leprosy. He died at the hands of religious leaders who wouldn't have touched a leper on a bet.**
> ▶ Jimmy Allen[6]

I wrote back to the gentleman explaining that I call this radically different civilization we are mutating into "postmodern" for the same reason the first cars were called "horseless carriages."[7] In other words, this new world out there is not modern. We have no word for it as of yet, so we call it in terms of what it is not. I never heard from him again.

Faith's dimmer switch turns in either of two directions: towards optimism or pessimism. I know immigrants who are temperamentally allergic to good news, their brooding spirit broken from the obsoletizing changes around them. I also know immigrants who believe that all things are possible.

At a time when 70% of USAmericans are optimistic about the nation's future, and 82% are optimistic about their own futures and that of their families, a frightened church whines, wails, and withholds an invitation to an enlarged experience of who Jesus is.[8]

At a time when the culture is about equally divided between those who are excited about their kids' futures and those who are not — half of us are optimistic about the future, and half are pessimistic; half marvel and dance, half beat their breast and rend their tunic — the church has issued an almost unanimous thumbs-down report on the world and its prospects.[9]

At a time when postmoderns have "discovered" the future as a main-spring of merit and values, projecting into the future implications of choices made in the present and correcting actions accordingly, the church has lost that future feeling. It draws direction and guidance "absolutely and unreservedly from the past."[10]

At a time when science and technology are having an adrenaline rush, few in the church get IT (with IT referring to Information Technology). The notoriously technophobic mainline (then oldline) church has drifted beyond the "sidelines." It is best described as the offline church that willfully refuses to get IT. In fact, the whole church is best described as offline.

MUTATION OR MUTILATION?

For the vast majority of Christians, the sunset version of what is happening ("The world has come to an end") eclipses the dawn version ("It's a whole new world out there"). Much of the religious world is archaistic rather than futuristic in tendency; it abjures innovation, mourning the moment, and caressing the status quo or the status quo ante. It has no interest in powering the future with anything but the present. As novelist E. L. Doctorow portrays so powerfully in his novel *City of God* (2000), organized religion has become utterly incapable of addressing the biggest moral and intellectual questions of the day.[11] There are now companies who have more desire to change the world for good than the church does.

> I couldn't wait for success, so I just went ahead without it.
> ▶ comedian Jonathan Winters

As Karen Breslau put it, "Everybody acknowledges that there's a radical new order."[12]

Everybody, that is, except the church. Either the church is blind to the changes that are dragging us into the unknown, or our blinkered vision is causing nail-biting and hand-wringing, washing us from any responsibility in bringing about the new horizonless world. Our narrowed eyelids and sober survey of what is going on out there makes us more concerned about how to help people make it through the night than how to help people make it through tomorrow.

Will a sense of hope and trust pump new blood into this awakening future? Or will a fearful, fogeyish view of the world prevail? Will the fear of living be stronger than the will to live?

Jesus existed in time. When God became incarnate in Jesus of Nazareth, God did not just enter human history. God entered the creation story — God entered the history of this planet as well as the history of its people.

God was willing to submit the Godhead to cultural conditions — that's the Incarnation.

And we aren't?

God so loved the world.

And we won't?[13]

The church is trying to get *out of* what God is trying to get *into* — the world.[14] "We have churches full of people who love Jesus," New Zealand evangelist Brian Medway claims, "but who don't love what Jesus loves."[15]

> **The world is deaf, the world is blind, I dwell apart among my kind.**
> ▶ deaf poet Ellen Glasgow[16]

Doris Lessing relates her thematic thread throughout her novels to a Sufi admonition: "Be in the world, not of it." Actually it is a Jesus admonition, one that Paul and other early Christian leaders upheld by not withdrawing into the desert, but staying in the cities and countryside and incarnating the gospel in their everyday lives.[17] In order for the church to change the world, there must be a change in the way the church sees the world. The church must love what Jesus loves. The Incarnation is not over. It continues today, and the body of Christ is a historical community that is God's continuing incarnation.

To be *conformed* to this age is to live from the outside in. To be *transformed* is to live inside out. Christ reworks us from the inside out. That is true metamorphosis or transformation. But it is also a continuous metamorphosis, an unceasing transformation, an ongoing incarnation. In worship, the church recreates the world, in forming and transforming it into the image of God. Will we incarnate the transforming gospel in this emerging "postmodern" culture, this post-Norman Rockwell world?

Will you be a messenger of morning?

Too few in the church have eyes to see a dawn and not a sunset. And because of the sullen dusk air, the words may be true. But the music has stopped.

God will be in this future, with or without us. As God and history have shown repeatedly, even the irreplaceable can be replaced.

The church does not define its mission. God does. It is God's mission in the world that concocts the church, not the other way around. In fact, the word "church" and the word "mission" are almost synonymous. Adrian Hastings, a Roman Catholic historian at Oxford University, puts it this way:

> In truth it is because of the mission that there is a Church; the Church is the servant and expression of this mission. The mission consequently dictates the nature of the Church and in so far as the Church fails to live up to the demands of mission, it is effectively failing to be the Church. In this perspective it is quite misleading to say that the purpose of the mission is the expansion of the Church; in the fullest sense of mission the Church cannot possibly be its end. Rather, it is the Church called into being by mission for the sake of salvation.[19]

> **God never called you into the church. God called you into the mission field.**
> ▶ Tom Bandy[18]

Authors/consultants Bill Easum and Tom Bandy put it more succinctly. They define a Christian as "those who do God's mission."[20] One of my favorite activities while preaching is to look the congregation straight in the eye and say, "The greatest sin of the church today is not any sin of commission or sin of omission, but the sin of. . . ." At this point I hesitate, waiting for someone to finish the sentence. Never has someone not spoken the words, "No mission."[21]

No mission, Easum and Bandy say, no church.

No Christian, either.

An "Acts 29" movement is afoot. Its motto is "The history of the church is still being written. Be a part of it." This new world is being created by multinationals, consumerism, and new media. Why not by the church? A new world is being built from scratch without the church's schooling or support because the church refuses to rehear the gospel in anything other than the mother tongue of immigrants.

Church youth ministries are primarily "ministries to youth," as if youth needed to be "fixed." The church loves blue hair until it walks through its doors on a 16-year-old kid. An immigrant

> **We have visited the mission field and it is us!**
> ▶ Brad Cecil, founder of Axxess Learning Community, Arlington, Texas[22]

church needs to be fixed as much if not more than its native youth loves its crosses and other artistic renderings of a body-pierced Jesus, but recoils in shock when someone shows up who looks like they just fell out of a tackle-box. I have seen churches go to any lengths and spend any amount of money, as long as they didn't have to go native.

VISA OFFICE

The government divides geographical immigrants into two categories: Those who achieve permanent residence status and those who have limitations, of which there are three kinds: family-based, employment-based, and diversity immigrants.

This book was written to provide you with the documents you need — passports, birth certificates, baptismal records, other civil documents — to make sure you do not become a public charge in this new world.[23] Each chapter constitutes a quick class in naturalization. Together they comprise a crash course in postmodern naturalization.

Some of you may want to read this because your employment situation is forcing you to get employment-based immigrant visas. Others of you may read this because you have family members you love but do not understand and would like to pursue family-based immigrant visas. Others of you are mere tourists, exchange visitors who will read this book and run back home as soon as the trip is over. Some of you are natives already and want to probe deeper into what is already happening in you and around you.

Then there are those of you who will take this course to indigenize your leadership in this new native culture. If Peter Drucker has taught us one thing, it is that every organization exists to serve people outside the organization. When it exists to serve people inside the organization, it dies. Maybe it is time for the church to retire that unwelcome wagon it has rolled out for natives.

INTERACTIVES

 Discuss this confession by business guru Tom Peters:

Somebody once asked me what I want my epitaph to say. I want it to say, "He was a player." It wouldn't mean that I got rich, or that I was always right. It would mean that I participated fully in these fascinating times.

The most awful thing that I can imagine doing is sitting on the sidelines. Because whatever this "new economy" thing is, it is reinventing the world of commerce, the world of politics, everything. It is reinventing fundamental interaction.[24]

"The more we come to understand our future, the more we alienate ourselves from the present and those who live in it."[25]

Do you agree with futurist Watts Wacker about this? Have someone read and review John Foxe's *Book of Martyrs*. Is there a role for martyrs in the transition from modern to postmodern as there was from the medieval to the modern.

 Journalist Robert Kaplan makes the case that our country today is filled with optimists because our founders built a government on pessimism. Contrast that with the French Revolution. Here was a country founded by idealists and dreamers, and look what happened. Total disaster.

What is the biblical position about human nature, political structures, church bureaucracies, etc. Do we have grounds for optimism?

 In a world of doomsayers, how can the Christian be a doomslayer, one who has, in G. K. Chesterton's words, "hardened his heart with hope" and sings and slings that heart at a lost world?[26]

 Canadian theologian Douglas John Hall has defined "contextual" in the following fashion.

> Contextuality in theology means that the *form* of faith's self-understanding is always determined by the historical configuration in which the community of belief finds itself. It is this world which initiates the questions, the concerns, the frustrations and alternatives, the possibilities and impossibilities by which the *content* of the faith must be shaped and reshaped, and finally confessed. Conscious and thoughtful involvement of the disciple community in its cultural setting is thus the *condition sine qua non* of its right appropriation of its theological discipline.[27]

Is he saying here that the world sets the agenda for the church? If not, what is he saying? Do you agree or disagree?

 Biologist/atheist Richard Dawkins writes that "if you wish, as I do, to build a society in which individuals cooperate generously and unselfishly towards a common good, you can expect little help from biological nature. Let us try to teach generosity and altruism, because we are born selfish."[28]

How does this concept of a "selfish gene," which places violence and vice at the heart of human nature, compare with the Christian doctrine of "original sin?" Why is one acceptable and the other not?

 A Bahamas-based company now offers human cloning services for $200,000.[29]

Texas A&M has accepted 22.3 million dollars to clone a dog named Missy. They are now accepting money to clone other animals. Check out www.missyplicity.com.

Is it true that anything that can be done will be done?
Is it true that money can buy anything?
If either or both are true, what does this say about the future?

8   Join a discussion zone for Gerard Kelly's book *RetroFuture* at communities.msn.co.uk/FutureLeader&naventryid=106 (accessed 29 November 2000). Do you agree with the comment "Gen Xers aren't coming home. The temptation with short-term generational labeling is that we simply wait for the latest generation of rebels to grow up, come to their senses and rejoin the society and culture of their parents. . . . If Generation X says nothing else to us, it says, 'Life will never be the same again.' "[30]

9   Discuss novelist Salman Rushdie's observation that "in the real world the present is always imperfect and the future is (almost) always a religion of hope . . . the idea of the future [is] as a potential Star Trek utopia in which technological marvels . . . arrive hand-in-hand with a universalist, brotherhood-of-man philosophy of human relations."[31]

10 Have people bring from home and their friends some of the definitions of "optimists" and "pessimists" they have heard. Some of my favorite definitions of an optimist include:

An optimist is a man getting married at age 75 and looking for a home near a school.
An optimist is one who takes four pounds of steak, five pounds of charcoal, and one match to a picnic.
Optimists are parents who have three teenage children and one car.
An optimist sees the glass as half-full. A pessimist sees it as half-empty. The engineer sees the glass as twice as big as it needs to be.
But my personal favorite: An optimist is one who has been captured by the love of Jesus.

11 Biologist Midas Dekkers is the Stephen Jay Gould of Europe. In trying to explain why so many of our elders are having a hard time of it in this culture of change, he contends that "to learn something new, one first has to unlearn something old. So learning is twice as much work for an old person as it is for a person with no experience."[32] Does this thesis have any merit?

Introduction

It's a WWW World

*It is easy to miss Him
at the turn of a civilisation.*

▶ Anglo-Welsh poet David Jones[1]

WORLD AC OR WORLD BC

Tidal forces have crashed over every corner of culture.[2] The challenge of leadership today is to call people to a moral and spiritual way of looking at and being in the world at a time when that world itself has developed a whole new way of being and thinking.

Cubans talk about *Cuba AC* and *Cuba BC (After Castro, Before Castro)*. Perhaps it is now time to talk about *World AC* and *World BC — After Computers, Before Computers*. Early natives came to computers in high school and college. More recent natives came to computers in primary and secondary schools. Digitalists are computer literate before they even enter school. They are born into a globalized, Internet culture.

Whether or not "The invention of the computer is the most important event in the history of technology, if not in history, period,"[3] the computer is an even more significant technological development than the invention of the printing press in the late 1400s.

There was a time when the world was basically divided into *AB* and *BB — After Book* and *Before Book*. When the printing press was invented, there were only 15,000 "manuscript books" in all of Europe. The product we now know as "the book" was at one time the highest and costliest expression of print culture. John Harvard got a college named after him because he donated 400 books to it. In 1776, Adam Smith's *The Wealth of Nations* was the equivalent of $615.38. When the industrial revolution was getting under way, the cost of a book was the equivalent of one month's income, the average cost of a computer in the 1990s.[4]

But can one technological innovation split history into BC and AC? The fusing force of computers (whether unifying or dividing) is revealed in a Digital Citizen 2000 study that found the "very wired" and the "somewhat wired" have more in common with each other than do Democrats, Republicans, male, female, white, black, or any other demographic breakdown.[5]

One reason why computers are being touted as not just as important as the invention of writing, but as important as the invention of language itself is because the computer ushers in a technological revolution that manufactures other technological revolution.[6] A computer is designed to become other machines, hitching itself to biology, physics, and economics to generate untold other revolutions including a "bioterials" revolution.[7]

> **Fifty years from now our grandchildren will look at early PCs and say, "Isn't that funny, they thought computers should look like typewriters."**
>
> ▶ Hal Varian, dean of the School of Information Management and Systems, UC Berkeley

What is more, the "computer revolution" itself is revolutionary in that it creates a revolution in every discipline it touches. Douglas S. Robertson states, "Never have so many revolutions occurred all at once."[8]

The computer is still a relatively raw technology. The first true computer was built at Manchester, England, in 1945. The first programmable computer weighed 30 tons, with 18,000 vacuum tubes and occupying 1800 square feet of space. Think about that with your three pound laptop.[9] And while you are looking at the CD in your laptop, realize that a gram of dried DNA can hold as much information as a trillion CDs. DNA computers are more than a parallel processing pipe dream. Living cells have already been turned into logic computers—proteins are the wires, genes are the gates. And this is only the beginning. DNA spelled backwards is AND. DNA technology is a conjunctive technology—it adds AND to everything.

The highest expression of computer culture to date is not the Furbee (although one Furbee has four times the microprocessing power of all the computers combined that got the first men on the moon). It is the Internet. The social revolution created by the Internet is an even greater story than the technological revolution.

The shared memory and intelligence of the Web is placing everything up for grabs, whether it is human concepts of "community" or our understandings of "truth." Natives are beginning to think in brand new ways, which are creating whole new experiences. Just as print technology brought about momentous changes in the structures of society, whether in business or in education or in religion, in an emerging World Wide Web Society we are seeing a similar massive shift in cultural formation from rational to experiential (E), from representative to participatory (P), from word-based to image-based (I), and from neither individual nor communal to a hybrid of both called connective (C).[11] I call this native consciousness EPIC.

> **I don't know how really useful this will be.**
> ► John von Neumann, after inventing the modern computer[10]

Immigrants let their fingers do the walking. Natives have web feet. They don't go anywhere without first going to the Web. At the same age I built structures out of Lincoln Logs, natives are constructing websites out of digitized data. As Anne Hird's research has demonstrated, "Internet Age" kids are crossing oceans and continents before they can cross the street.[12]

The invention that is fashioning the future is the Internet, the fastest growing technology the world has ever known. It began in 1968 as a decentralized computer network created by the US Department of Defense called ARPANET (Advanced Research Projects Agency), but expanded beyond its military and scientific uses in 1990 when the World Wide Web (WWW) was invented and launched at CERN (the European Center for Nuclear Research), the high-energy physics lab in Geneva, Switzerland.

WWW has gone from something nobody took seriously ten years ago to the driving force of the dawning world. Think what the next 20, 50, 75 years will bring? Though the WWW was invented in 1990, the Internet Age did not really begin until April 1994, the month Marc Andreessen filed the papers incorporating Netscape, the company that made the WWW accessible to the masses. By 1996, the Internet had just under 100,000 sites. By 2000 it had nearly four million. In 1995, 14.9 million USAmerican households were online; in January 2000 there were 46.5 million households online. By 2004 it is predicted there will be 90 million. In 1998, 42% of Americans were online and by 2003 it is estimated between 62% and 67% will be online.[13]

You do the math. In the last 24 hours, there were 2 million new web pages, 196,000 new Internet-access devices, and 147,000 new web users added. "By 2002, there will be more web pages than people on the planet."[14] Internet use is doubling every 100 days. In 1999, when the US Postal Service delivered 100 billion pieces of mail, the Internet delivered four trillion. Within the next half-hour, 154 million email messages will be sent. Within the next half-hour, 2,800 people will log on to the Internet for the first time, adding to the ranks of the quarter billion worldwide Internet users.

WHATEVER YOUR 'HOOD

The transition from immigrant to native is taking place in Asia, Africa, and Latin America as well. In fact, in the same way the biggest opposition and obstacles to globalization come from developed countries, not developing countries, some of the most hard-core modernist hubs are in the most flush and plush places. Sundry non-Anglo cultures are addressing postmodern changes through fiction and the arts more than through science, philosophy, technology, etc.[15]

> Scandinavian countries boast higher Internet penetration than USAmerica, while Great Britain and Germany are closing the gap fast.[16]
> The first vote for president via the Internet was not cast in Arizona but in Croatia. Even though Croatia had only 3–4% of its population online in 2000, both presidential candidates had outstanding websites, more fully developed than any US primary hopeful.
> Chile has wired all 1,263 of its high schools and half the country's grammar schools to the Web, insuring web access for students at all economic levels.
> Brazil's level of Internet use is high, thanks partly to nonprofit organizations providing computer courses and Internet connections even in slum areas.[17]
> Twenty percent of Singaporeans are connected to the Internet. The censorship-prone government, instead of trying to curb its growth, has decided to make it a matter of public policy to connect every citizen with high-speed Internet access in an attempt to make Singapore Asia's electronic-commerce hub and to maintain its status as the most competitive economy in the world.[18]
> As of 2000, 60 million Chinese are using the Internet — a figure that will increase by 50 million a year for the next 5–10 years. Soon China will have the largest Internet population in the world.

If truth be told, historical immigrants are helping create this cultural immigration in ways we have yet to recognize. Nearly half of all Silicon Valley companies were founded by Indian and Pakistani entrepreneurs.[19] In almost every country, the Web is growing exponentially, doubling every nine months to a year. But in India, it is tripling every year. By 2001, India will have put in place an information superhighway that will not only connect universities to each other at extremely high bandwidth speeds, it will also bring broad bandwidth to remote villages. Once in remote villages, local doctors will be able to learn how to perform surgeries via video; local farmers will have access to databases about insects, farming practices, feed supplies; and new forms of online learning can be tested.[20]

In the Western world we normally think one person for every machine. But one machine per village suffices in the attempt to connect every man, woman, and child to the Internet and the farthest reaches of the planet. In fact, in many places around the world there is a new village well. For the cost of a postage stamp or less, you can spend 15 minutes talking to relatives around the world. In Peruvian villages, families line up with balloons in a festival-like atmosphere of singing and dancing, waiting for their global connection. Eighty miles above the Arctic Circle in Canada's Yukon Territory, where the preferred means of transportation for its 31,000 residents are dogsleds and snowmobiles, where the glass cracks from the cold and there are no Starbucks or McDonald's, what the people *do* have are 50 computers hooked up to the Internet at high-speed bandwidths.[21]

A META-MIND

The planet is getting wired. The globe is wiring itself like an entity, creating a body or at least a meta-mind. WWW is creating a social space that will connect everyone on the planet in 10–20 years. A new global consciousness is emerging. Defining the meaning of globalization should be at the top of the church's agenda. Does it mean, as it is usually defined, the "increasing international economic integration and, more broadly, the contested advance of market forces in the world economy?" Or does globalization mean increasing interdependence and common consciousness? If so, will this global consciousness have a conscience?

Ever since Martin Luther "posted" (that is the word he used) his 95-point sermon on the door of the Wittenberg Church, Protestantism has reinvented the church around the book. The Reformers started with the Bible as a book, but quickly saw how the technology of print could be used as a major delivery system for learning and faith development.

The technology of the book altered Christian spirituality in momentous ways. Spirituality is shaped by technology. Always has been. Always will be. The book revolutionized evangelism, liturgy, architecture, even the pastor-parishioner relationship.

Don't believe me? Try this experiment suggested by British chaplain Andii Bowsher. Try to disciple people without any Bible to use and without any assumptions of literacy. How well does your mentoring survive in such a context?[22]

Imagine trying to do ministry in the past 500 years and saying, "I don't need to learn how to read."

Imagine trying to do ministry in the next 50 years and saying, "I don't need to learn the Web." Like the printing press before it, the Internet is forcing us to rewrite the rules of every game. It is giving natives a whole new headset. Native culture is creating new keys, new questions, new answers, new rules.

NEW NATIVE ECONOMY

This is no more apparent than in the radical economic restructuring taking place in every arena. Even Alan Greenspan is now talking about the "New Economy," and admitting that the old economic yardsticks cannot really be used to measure a networked, dot com economy where. . .

a whopping half of all USAmericans now own stock—a totally unprecedented figure.

companies are now competing with one another to see what percentage of their employees they can make millionaires—Scient's executives want to create more millionaire employees than Microsoft's one-third.

Yahoo employees are almost all millionaires who wear t-shirts, eat pizza, and have to be forced to go home.

"Dellonaires," a name coined in Austin, Texas, refers to those Dell Computers employees who have witnessed dramatic increases in their stock value.

up-start corporations are snatching up old, established organizations: AOL buys out Time Warner; two-year-old Bermuda-based telecommunications start-up Global Crossing acquires Frontier Corp. and the undersea wire-laying business of Cable & Wireless; US West merges with three-year-old Qwest and becomes Qwest; and an upstart Hong Kong Internet company buys a huge Hong Kong telecom company.

A new dot com economy has surfaced with an entirely new set of economic rules and arrangements. The farm/factory worker of the Agricultural and Industrial Ages, nine-to-five office workers in their business life, are being replaced by the forager workers of the Knowledge Economy, hunter-gatherers in their business life. Immigrants read *The Organization Man*. Natives are reading FreeAgent.Com.[23] Business schools are putting in place endowed chairs in e-commerce, although they are having trouble finding people with the academic vesting to fill them.

Dell Computers' pioneering build-to-order system is setting the pace for everyone else. The Dell model turns everything on its head:

(1) new building strategies and competitive advantages (no longer geographic, but values, brands, networks, talent)
(2) whole new relationship between buyer and seller called "mass customization":
  (a) no longer fixed price
  (b) no longer buy what is available, you design what you want and need; in the future even restaurants will not order #1, #2, #3 from the menu, but will create your own meal
  (c) the customer pays for the product before it is made (no cash flow problem)
(3) no inventory (inventory defined as "bad information")
(4) no plant; much of its work is in cyberspace, making it a virtual corporation

Ten years from now natives will be as unconscious of the Internet as immigrants are unconscious of electricity.[24] Can you imagine buying a house and saying, "I want it with electricity." Power companies ARE electric companies. All companies that exist will be Internet companies. There will be no putting "e" in front of everything (e-commerce, email, e-tailing, ebooks, etc.) because everything that is anything, everybody that is anybody, will be driven by the online infrastructure.[25] Every device will have web-readiness. Already Ford and General Motors have introduced cars that read your email, check your stock portfolio, and access online city maps.

You are not on the Web? You will be. Natives migrate from the terrestrial to the virtual and back again as effortlessly as we walk in and out of doorways. Natives live in the dot coms and connect the dot coms. Natives can navigate the streets of the Internet better than immigrants can navigate the streets of their own neighborhoods. Natives are discovering virtual experiences so rich and expansive, we can only begin to glimpse the cyberspatial potential for human growth and self-expression.

The Internet is bringing the best libraries, museums, and artists of the world into homes, businesses, churches, or wherever we are. The David Rumsey Collection is making available to the residents of planet Earth some 150,000 original 18th- and 19th-century maps and charts of the Americas. To date over 2,000 maps with detailed notes can be found at www.davidrumsey.com.[26]

What the Internet is doing that is radically new, however, is twofold. First, it is connecting knowledge sources to one another in real time at speeds that defy imagination.[27] As one unknown expert puts it, when the

Internet Revolution and the Information Age came together, "knowledge and information exploded in a virtual 'Big Bang' that created a new universe — cyberspace." Two million new web pages of pavement are being laid every day, a superhighway transporting a global renaissance of innovation and invention. The number of patents issued in USAmerica alone are nearly twice the level of a decade ago.[28] In the words of John Seely Brown:

> The Internet is a technology that amplifies our ability to borrow what others have done and build on it. In this way open source is a kind of bricolage. If you look at how most systems today get built, they get built not from the ground up but by borrowing fragments of other people's work, cobbling it together, and then looking at what happens.[29]

Second, the Internet is connecting people with similar interests to one another on a global scale in a shared communication structure that is open.[30] No matter how quirky or unique your interests (there are numerous sites for octopush — underwater hockey — as well as sites for illegal sports like cockfighting), the Web promises to connect you to kindred spirits in a communications network with a potential we have only begun to comprehend.

The file-sharing technology that MP3 has made famous is as significant an online development as the introduction of the browser. The Napsterization of learning will make everyone a teacher and everyone a student. For good reason some are calling the new economy the "nude economy" because the Internet makes everything more distinct, everyone more diaphanous.[31] As of this writing the two biggest ethical issues of the Web are privacy and piracy. But the very concept of privacy as a personal right at the core of individuality is derived from the history of reading and print culture.[32]

John Perry Barlow of the Electronic Freedom Foundation argues that in web culture, "privacy is not a possibility" in the same way that anyone who has ever lived in a small town knows that privacy is a myth. True, small-town togetherness can mask a lot of small-minded bigotry. But in Barlow's words, "MAD (Mutual Assured Destruction) assures our survival. You dare not rattle the skeletons in any closet. You rattle mine, I'll rattle yours. I know your secrets. You know mine. Opaque institutions," Barlow insists, "are the future."[33] With the WWW, might we be coming into a world where Luke 12:3 is literally true: "Whatever you have said in the dark will be heard in the light, and what you have whispered behind closed doors will be proclaimed from the housetops"?

Whatever the case, the Web is the armature and metaphor of the future. Any leader or any church that fails to come to terms with the Web is putting its future service at risk. Peter had a net. And it became a worldwide net. It is not enough to add a website to your church or business, to dump stuff online (called "shovelware"), or to turn the Internet into a new switchboard. Your whole ministry, your whole business needs to be redesigned and e-constructed around this new delivery system for learning, communication, and faith development.

THE SALINGER SYNDROME

My favorite story about the differing worlds of immigrants and natives is the announcement by Pierre Salinger of his discovery of what brought down TWA 800 from the skies and into the waters off the Atlantic Coast — a test missile fired by US military went astray and blew up the aircraft.

Salinger called a news conference to announce his discovery. Because it was Pierre Salinger — former presidential press secretary, ambassador to France, etc. — the news media showed up in full force. CNN carried his press release live, and I watched incredulously as Salinger passed out the "proof" for his findings that a misguided missile exploded TWA 800.

After skimming one document quickly, a news correspondent asked, "Where did you get this?"

"I downloaded it from the Internet."

"Where did this document come from?" asked another reporter.

"I got that from the Internet too."

Within a few long minutes, it became apparent that all of Salinger's "proof" had been collated from various websites.

Salinger grew up in a book culture where, if information made it into print, it had been juried, refereed, cross-referenced, edited, copyedited, and reviewed by critics. Unless something was self-published by some "vanity" press, you could trust the information.

Salinger unwittingly found himself an immigrant in a world where everyone is an author, everyone a publisher, and everyone an expert. The mistake of applying one medium's standards to another medium is known as the "Salinger Syndrome." The blessing of the Internet is that it contains everything. The curse of the Internet is that it contains everything. Natives need bibliographic and hermeneutic skills in grade school that immigrants did not need until college and graduate school. Natives may be able to *access* information without intermediaries, but they need more help than ever in *assessing* and *processing* that information.

The Salinger Syndrome is a component part of an embalming bias that is best described as categorical imperialism or "incommensurability."[34] Historians learn not to judge one historical period by the categories, language, or values of a previous or later one. Not to respect each culture on its own terms is to imperialize the standards of one culture on another. The problems this has caused in the history of missions needs no retelling here.

MAINLINE MISERABILISM

Why have mainline denominations like the one I am a part of (United Methodist) been so slow to respond to the Web? For the same reasons that "legacy businesses" like Wal-Mart and Borders were slow to jump in. Those who invested the most in the previous model are the most likely to resist change.[35]

Now is the winter of mainline discontent. Mainline denominations have failed to find a place much less become a player in this new world order of electronics and screen. Like the Janet Frame character who confesses, "We were all walking inside ourselves . . . touching the brown picket-fences of our minds," mainline churches cannot see the future's picket signs for its picket fences. We know everyone's speech ahead of time.[36]

Once a heady brew, the mainline brand has now lost its flavor and a new brand of mainline evangelicals has emerged partly because of their willingness to embrace digital technology. The merger of what's left of old-line Protestant bodied into one disagreeable unity is inevitable without radical changes in their ecclesial and spiritual armatures.

But it does not have to be that way. In fact the exact opposite could have been true if mainline Protestantism had spent as much time unraveling this new world as yearning for a lost world. Rather than obliterating the old, a new technology might very well reinvent it.

The process of technological change is mostly one of binary fission. This is why the way forward is not looking ahead so much as looking around, peering at the peripheries and social contexts in which information matures and materializes.[37] No longer is 20/20 vision enough to survive in a native world. We now need 360 degree vision.

> Now that more and more companies are shifting sales to the Web, the sales representative has not been liquidated but upgraded as a "consultant," an "educator," and an "evangelist" with less paper, more responsibility, and more challenges.[38]
>
> The US Postal Service now moves a record 200 billion pieces of mail a year. But what kind of mail are they moving? Packages from e-commerce.[39]
>
> The paper consumption of offices is expected to double from 1996 to 2003.[40]
>
> I carry with me on the road both an electric razor and "old" disposable razors. In fact, I am using the latter more than ever.
>
> Cambridge University Press reported a profit of 10.2 million pounds for 1999. Why the "spectacular growth"? They attribute it to Internet booksellers and the "proliferating websites devoted to college students."

He "died among his books" is one of the best ways I can think of going. My study, where I already live among my books, sings with voices from old and new friends. When I write I rehearse our conversations and overhear their prayers. I harbor unsanctified thoughts of jealousy towards Karl Marx, who was free to read from nine in the morning until seven at night in the British Museum. Asked by his daughters in 1865 what was his favorite occupation, he replied, "Bookworming."

The highest honor an author can receive today? It's not a Pulitzer Prize or a Booker Award, but an Oprah. A television celebrity has rejuvenated the Book Club and doubles as a book peddler. The number one dot com (Amazon.com) is devoted to hawking books. The number two dot com (Ebay.com) has revived the barter economy. Internet chat rooms have brought back the party line.

Unlike mainline miserabilism, Main Street Mom-and-Pop stores are finding the Internet their salvation. A 400 town survey by the National Trust for Historic Preservation revealed that 84% name the Internet as "a key factor" in their economic growth.[41] Some experts are convinced that the greatest impact of the "new" economy will be "to make the 'old' economy more efficient."[42]

When hundreds of millions of people (and soon billions of people) interconnect via the Web, it is more than business as usual with a new customer base. The Web totally changes how we do business, how we do church, and how we conceive of the "body of Christ."

Like every prior technology—beginning with the roads of Rome, which Paul creatively utilized to communicate the gospel—the information superhighway is bringing the church new metaphors resonant with spiritual meaning—even new benedictions and blessings. An ad for Mind-Spring shows a surfer smiling as he looks out at the waves, with these words:

> May the road rise up to meet you.
> May the wind be at your back.
> May your Internet dial-up number never be busy.

IT'S A WWW WORLD

"There's the bit where you say it," admits J. L. Austin, "and the bit where you take it back."[43] Now that I've said it, let me take it back a bit.

Being a "native" or being an "immigrant" is more a mind-set than a matter of chronology; more psychographics than demographics; more a spirit, not so much a matter of geriatrics and pediatrics. In fact, the Internet is really the biggest heirloom of boomer immigrants. It was invented and designed by former Flower Power children of the 1960s, most of whom never profited from its discovery. In fact, the early architects of the Web were opposed to any commercial uses of their creation, which was loosely organized in good commune fashion. They believed in "open source" movements, and commercial application was not an "acceptable-use policy." The Internet was developed and commercialized by the native children of idealistic immigrants (Bezos, Yang, Andreesen), who made fortunes where their parents made fantasies.[44]

I know of some 80- and 90-year-olds who have more of a native headset than some 20- and 30-year-olds. Or using the words of Santana in the second song on his Grammy-winning CD *Supernatural,* they've *put* their lights on and their grandchildren and great-grandchildren didn't *leave* their lights on.[45]

A *Wired* magazine interview with Lee Iacocca asked him "Why not just retire?" Iacocca answered, "My kids ask me that all the time. . . . Why not play golf? I've played enough golf. The world is changing and I want to keep talking to young people and see all these wonderful new markets and inventions."[46]

In 1999 Rupert Murdoch, speaking in Singapore at a forum on 21st-century media, scorned the Internet and warned that the Net will "destroy more businesses than it creates." In one year Murdoch did a flip flop, investing over a billion dollars in Internet infrastructures and regretting that he did not value web culture years earlier.[47]

> **I didn't go to religion to make me happy. I always knew a bottle of port would do that. If you want a religion to make you really comfortable, I certainly don't recommend Christianity.**
> ► C. S. Lewis[48]

Contrast Murdoch's immigrant-to-native headset to the three biggest names on Wall Street, all of whom have at the time of this writing the mind-sets of immigrants on the way to becoming fossils: Alan Greenspan, Peter Lynch, Warren Buffett.

When the President speaks, the world listens politely and tries to stay awake. When Alan Greenspan speaks, the world sits on the edge of its seat and pores over every dense word that comes out of his mouth. The saxophone-playing, tennis-obsessed economist lost money on the stock market in 1998. In one of the biggest bull markets the world has ever seen, the "first great American of the 21st century," as some have called him, lost money in a bull market and confesses that his trusted maps and instruments don't work like they used to.[49]

Peter Lynch brags that he doesn't know how to turn on a computer. So he takes his own advice not to invest in something you don't understand. He has no tech stocks.

Who cannot help but like the Sage of Omaha? Warren Buffett disarmingly calls his private jet "The Indefensible" because he admits no one can justify the luxury of a corporate

E or Be Eaten
headline in *Fortune*[50]

jet. But Warren Buffett doesn't understand this new world he is in. He announced at a Berkshire Hathaway annual meeting in 1998 that he will not buy tech stocks because he cannot figure out how to value them: "We will never buy anything we don't think we understand."[51]

Some of our greatest musicians stand to get their visas revoked. Bob Dylan wrote an immortal anthem to change "The Times They are A-Changin'" (1964) that inspired the title of the first volume in my postmodern trilogy *SoulTsunami* (1999).

Come gather 'round people
Wherever you roam,
And admit that the waters
Around you have grown.
You'll be drenched to the bone,
If your time to you
Is worth savin',
Then you better start swimmin'
Or you'll sink like a stone
For the times they are a-changin'.[52]

Dylan's newest hit is the featured song for the soundtrack to Curtis Hanson's film *Wonder Boys* (2000, starring Michael Douglas and Tobey Maguire). The song is a devil-may-care musing on this new world out there called "Things Have Changed":

People are crazy and times are strange. . . .
I used to care, but things have changed.[53]

Some of our greatest writers risk losing their rights of residency. Tom Wolfe writes words that every parent of a child knows from personal experience to be false:

I hate to be the one who brings this news to the tribe, to the magic Digikingdom, but the simple truth is that the Web, the Internet, does one thing. It speeds up the retrieval and dissemination of information, messages, and images, partially eliminating such chores as going outdoors to the mailbox or the bookstore, or having to pick up the phone to get ahold of your stockbroker or some buddies to shoot the breeze with. That one thing the Internet does, and only that. All the rest is Digibabble.[54]

Some of our greatest management gurus have travel visas that are about to expire. Both immigrants and natives owe much to Peter Drucker. Business culture is deeper in his debt than church culture because it has listened to him more when he has said such things as "We are preaching, teaching and practicing policies that are increasingly at odds with reality and therefore counterproductive."[55]

But as Horace says, "Good Homer sometimes nods." In his refusal to write on a computer, Homer seems to be nodding. Unlike Pope John Paul II, who confessed in 1998 that "the computer has changed my life," Drucker says the computer is too fast, so he writes on a typewriter.[56] His pick for a growth industry in the first third of the 21st century? Fish farming (a good tip, by the way).

Some of our best media correspondents have passports that are out of date. Peter Arnet, CNN's war correspondent, assured the National Press Club that the Internet would never replace the news media's role of selecting and interpreting the news for people. One wonders what world Peter Arnet is covering. The information middleman has been eliminated by the Web through e-editors and copylefts (the opposite of copyrights), open source computer programs that are owned by the public and can never be owned privately.[57]

Some of our bow-tied universities are looking at the world through pince-nez glasses. Stanford University's study "Internet and Society" (released 17 February 2000 by the Institute for the Quantitative Study of Society) discovered several interesting statistics—a few revealing, one disturbing, and some downright stupid. On the revealing and disturbing side, they found that 20% of wired adults spend five or more hours a week online. Of those who use the Internet more than 10 hours per week ("heavy users"), 39% spend less time reading newspapers and 59% spend less time watching TV.[58]

On the stupid side, the Stanford's study's "sophisticated" probes into the social implications of increased Internet usage concluded that "increased social isolation" and antisocial tendencies were the biggest trademarks of Internet usage. People who spend five hours a week or more online spend less time, for example, talking to friends and family on the phone. The Stanford name is now associated with other "reports" that blame the Net (like television before it) for everything but the bombing of Hiroshima. In 1995 it was "porn" (Marty Rimm). In 1997 it was "net addiction." Now in 2001 it is the decline of social networking and increased isolation.[59]

> **The only sense that is common in the long run is the sense of change ... and we all instinctively avoid it.**
> ▶ E. B. White

What's wrong with this scenario? Ask any native over six. First, the phone line is the family's modem to the Internet.

Second, what are people doing online, even according to the Stanford study itself? Doing email, chatrooms, and other forms of cyber socializing in the natives' combined version of a town square, listening post, watering hole, and wailing wall.

Third, why are they spending less time watching TV? Because they've replaced the passivity of the boob tube with the interactive tangles of the Web.

Much of the "innovative" church movement is in name only. Its idea of "innovation" is giving the old jalopy a new paint job or mass-producing franchised spiritual experiences like McDonald's and Starbucks mass-produce franchised fast-food and quality-coffee experiences. Seeker-sensitive worship is often high-modern, native-insensitive worship. One of my doctoral students talks about the seeker-sensitive model as dated and "out of step" with postmoderns ("*Saturday Night Live* meets David Letterman meets Zig Ziglar").[60] The boomer generation's preference for topiaried worship, with highly sculpted performances and Broadway-trimmed productions, is native-numb. What God worth his Pearly Gates would call this worship, they ask themselves? Little wonder postmoderns are increasingly distant from both traditional and innovative churches.

> **The Christian life is but a constant re-beginning, a return to grace every day, sometimes even every hour, through Him who, after each failure, pardons so that all things should be made new.**
> ► Robert Schutz[61]

The Old World's vehicles no longer carry happy fares; the Old World's keys to success no longer turn; the Old World's doorways to meaning no longer open; the Old World's sanctuaries are increasingly empty.

INTERACTIVES

 On the Internet there is circulating an anonymous poem entitled "Not So Long Ago."

An application was for employment
A program was a TV show
A cursor used profanity
A keyboard was a piano!

Memory was something that you lost with age
A CD was a bank account
And if you had a 3 1/2 inch floppy
You hoped nobody found out!

Compress was something you did to garbage
Not something you did to a file.
And if you unzipped anything in public
You'd be in jail for a while!

"Log on" was adding wood to a fire
"Hard drive" was a long trip on the road
A mouse pad was where a mouse lived
And a backup happened to your commode!

Cut — you did with a pocket knife
Paste — you did with glue
A web was a spider's home
And a virus was the flu!

I guess I'll stick to my pad and paper
And the memory in my head
I hear nobody's been killed in a computer crash
But when it happens they wish they were dead![62]

What other "not so long agos" can you come up with?

2 There are two competing nominees for patron saint of the Internet. One is St. Isidore, born in Seville in the sixth century who compiled a twenty-volume reference work. The other is San Pedro Regalado, a 15th-century Spanish priest and expert navigator who appeared in multiple places at once.[63]
Which one do you think it should be? Why?

3 Munther (age 23) and Muzhar (age 22) Badir are blind Palestinian brothers who grew up in an Arab village north of Tel Aviv called Kafr Qassem. Their village hardly had running water and indoor plumbing, much less computer equipment. Their first access to a computer didn't come until Munther was 13 and Muzhar 12. Once exposed to computers, however, the world of these two blind Palestinian brothers changed dramatically. Still teenagers, the two brothers started a computer consulting firm. Their first creation was software for the blind. They built an electronic empire that eventually yielded them $10,000 a day in cash.

A couple years ago the Badir brothers broke into Israel's security-minded computer systems, tapped into Armed Forces Radio, and invited

Palestinians in Gaza City to call anywhere in the world at the expense of the Israeli armed forces. A 10-member Israeli police force took 15 months to figure out what they were doing and bring charges against them.[64]

What does this one story tell you about the 21st century?

4   Do you agree or disagree with philosopher Ludwig Wittgenstein's position that "Nothing is so difficult as not deceiving oneself." Give real-life stories to back up your position.

5   Bring some natives and immigrants together to watch the movie *Time Code* (2000), where four screens follow four different narratives simultaneously. Get both groups to discuss the experience of watching the movie (not whether they "liked" it or not).

From Manual to Digital

The four stages of revolutionary ideas
(1) "it's nonsense, don't waste my time"
(2) "it's interesting, but not important"
(3) "I always said it was a good idea"
(4) "I thought of it first"

▶ science fiction writer Arthur C. Clarke

Immigrants are products of a Manual Age — a world of radio, TV, type-writer, film. Natives are products of a Digital Age — a world of comput-ers, fax machines, cell phones, and WWW.

Today's brag factor is not the biggest wooden box, but the biggest bandwidth.

I grew up with a screen pet of Lassie.

Natives grew up with R2D2 and digital friends like Pokémon, pocket monsters that pop out of oval computers.

The sexiest women on TV when I was growing up? Mary Tyler Moore. The sexiest women on TV in the '90s? A borg (*Star Trek Voyager*, 1995) or an alien (*3rd Rock from the Sun*, 1997).

When I grew up, kids blew up things in microwaves — where micro-waves were the size of an oven and sold for $1,000 (GE sold the first microwave in 1956).

Immigrants blow up things on screens operated by play stations so pow-erful they can be used in military engagements to actually deploy missiles.

I grew up in a brick-and-mortar world of rotary dials, seven-inch reel-to-reel tape recorders, teletype machines, and long-distance phone calls.

It took a while, but the Museum of Modern Art finally admitted film into the realm of art. I think in terms of "switches" that turn on and off. How several million switches can function in a microprocessor the size of a fingernail is beyond my imagining.

Natives inhabit a point-and-click world where satellites are now routinely launched every week. My daring act on the typewriter was to leave the letters and go explore the numbers. Natives camp out on my unused upper shift number keys where only the cartoon character Bazooka Joe dared go: !#%^&*~/ — awaiting the imagination of one of ARPANET's creators, Ray Tomlinson, who put the "@" in email.

There is an old cartoon that shows a boy totally engrossed in reading a book. The father walks by, and growls: "Always reading. Ain't you got a mind of your own?"

For natives it is not the book but the screen that comes trailing clouds of glory.

AS SEEN ON TV

I was in the midst of an address to a youth convention, and it was not going well. Even when I moved to a more karaoke style of presentation and walked the audience while engaging them in dialogue, my feet felt like they were slogging through a quagmire. Just when the sacrament-of-failure stage started kicking in and I begin shuffling my feet ("When they fail to receive you, shake the dust off your feet," Jesus said, "and move on"[1]), an orange-haired member of the audience chimed in, "Sweet, don't you have this on video?"

"Yes, I do. How did you know? . . . Would you like to see it?" A giant sigh of relief rose from the congregation, and I headed for my virtual office (a brain bag and book bag goes with me wherever I go). As I unzipped the leather case to pull out the video, I thought to myself — *But you have me! Why do you want a video when you have me?* — but I gave the video to the minister of sound at the mixing table, sat down, and for the next ten minutes watched myself on screen.

When the lights went on and I stood back up, I faced an entirely different audience. The energy of the place was electrifying. "Surf's up!" I said to myself as I breathed deeply and dived in. For the next 30 minutes I surfed their spirit, surfed God's Spirit, and the waves of excitement and engagement gushed out of that room like the breaking of a big kahuna.

What happened? What made the difference? I had been legitimated by the screen. This group of natives (Gerard Kelly and others call them "screenagers"[2]) had only known me as a book person. For immigrant book culture, this was all the credentialing one needed. For natives, many of whom have graphicacy skills before they have literacy skills, the screen is what credentializes you. If you can't speak to them in their native tongue, they don't really listen to you. That phrase "As Seen on TV" is more than a tag found on advertisements, or a chain store found in malls.

The musical group Lost and Found confirms my story from their own experience. At a Youth Specialties event, the lead singer pointed out how the youth had rushed up to the mosh pit to get physically as close to the musicians as they possibly could, only to have them spend their whole time up front, at best an arms length away, looking at the big screen.

I am a card-carrying "chirograph," a person of print, a product of a textbook culture. We who are immigrants found meaning in texts and words more than stories and symbols. In some ways, as J. Leslie Houlden notes, from its beginnings Christianity was "bookish" —

> copying and circulating its productions — and using not smart scrolls, but papyrus notebooks, where you wrote on both sides of the sheet, creating sets of pages. Modern Western Europe may be less sure than it was that Christianity brought us salvation; it can, however, be grateful that (even if the future is shaky) it, largely, gave us "the book."[3]

Books still have the power to enchant (witness Harry Potter). But ubiquitous screens are shaping natives and immigrants alike in ways we have yet to understand. One study reveals that 88% of USAmerican households now claim at least two televisions. The same study also shows that "the average American kid lives in a household with three televisions, two VCRs, three radios, two tape players, two CD players, a video game player, and a computer."[4] In China as of 2000, "96% of city families own a color television; 78% have telephones, 48% have seen an American movie, and 11% have owned stocks."[5] The typical American child spends an average of more than 38 hours a week consuming media outside of school — the equivalent of a full-time job.[6]

The human spirit paid a steep price for television, one of the most dehumanizing inventions of the modern era. Unaccounted for but equal in importance to the television is the remote control, which alters television from a passive consumption of what someone else is dishing out to a participant sport. Remote controls enable all of us to create our own TV programming. We design and improvise our own shows, turning the television experience from something highly representative to something highly participatory — a participation which the Internet takes even further.

> **No wonder so many look for love in all the wrong places. Those are often the only places left.**
> ▶ congressman J. C. Watts Jr.[7]

Novelist Bruce Sterling, in his preface to the anthology *Mirrorshades* (1986), noted how technology has changed from "the giant steam-snorting wonders of the past: the Hoover Dam, the Empire State Building, the nuclear power plant" to a technology that "sticks to the skin, responds to the touch: the personal computer, the Sony Walkman, the portable telephone, the soft contact lens."[8] Soon to be on the market is the techno-bra. It is a bra that uses miniature electronics and conductive fabric to monitor the wearer's heart rate. With a sudden change in pulse, it radios a distress call to police and identifies the bra's location. In case it is a good change in pulse, there is a cancel button on the front clasp.

FROM CODEX TO CODEC

But the screen is in many ways only a membrane to a whole new future filled with holodecks, cyborgs (already here: artificial hips, contact lenses), teleporters (already here: the fax), and who knows what else. Hard as it is to imagine, some people did live before the elaboration of chemistry's periodic tables. Hard as it will be for our descendants to imagine, we immigrants lived before the elaboration of biology's periodic tables — the human genetic code.[9] It cannot be denied: There is a DNA that rough-hews our ends. But it can never be forgotten: Human personal identity is something that transcends our genetic identity. Family influences, personal choices, cultural conditioning assert themselves to chip an original off the DNA bloc.

The Human Genome Project (the attempt to identify all of the approximate 30,000 genes in human DNA) is the equivalent of the development of the periodic tables for chemistry. And that is with the past leaking into the future more than the future entrancing and enriching scientists' approach. The Human Genome Project has, for a number of interesting reasons, been hostage to history and to immigrant understandings of the human body as a machine that can be deciphered by taking it apart and reducing it to its most basic level.

Biotechnology, the most important science of the next hundred years, is going to make a lot of people angry. It will also make a lot of people rich. It will create social and epistemic changes yet unimaginable. Thanks to genetic engineering, robotics, and nanotechnology (notice there are no raw materials in this new technology, only knowledge), double-edged swords have never been sharper. With every step we take there will be downsides and upsides, good geniuses (chemist Mendeleyev and monk Mendel) and bad geniuses (Dr. Mengele) separated by only the curl on a pig's tail.

These series of "double-edged swords" that natives will face require a moral vision and deftness of discernment that makes the ethical dilemmas immigrants faced in the modern world look like layups. Natives will need to be innocent as a dove, shrewd as a snake, and as alert for wolves in sheep's clothing as a watchdog.

Why? Biotechnology puts us at a threshold for the genetic design of everything. We will be able to breed people for excellence in certain areas—enhanced athletic, musical, and dance ability. We will have the capability of reinventing nature and ourselves. We will struggle with new definitions of individual identity and untold other challenges unveiled by this new technology.

What will happen when natives take over biology's genetic tables? As the life sciences merge with the computer sciences, how will humans be redefined? How will natives shape "life," "nature," "human" into spiritual significance? Who will be the natives, and who will be the immigrants in the posthuman world of our 22nd-century grandchildren?

> **Our prayers accept, but judge us not through our prayers; grant them with mercy.**
> ▶ 19th-century Jewish prayer from a Babylonian rite used at Yom Kippur

Raymond Kurzweil, inventor of reading machines for the blind and electronic keyboards, predicts that "we will have the computing power of the human brain—about 100 billion neurons and 100 trillion connectors—in a $1,000 PC by around 2019."[10] Hans Moravec, another computer scientist and pioneer of mobile robot research, argues that the human species, through research in artificial life, artificial intelligence, nanotechnology, virtual reality, genetic algorithms, genetic programming, optical, DNA, and quantum computing (as well as other areas not yet conceived), may be obsoletizing itself as the highest point of creation.[11]

> The human brain has only a short time left as the smartest thing on earth. The speed and complexity of computers will continue to double every 18 months through 2012. By then the density of computer circuits will have jumped 1,000 fold, and the raw processing power of a human brain will fit into a shoe box.[12]

Are we passing the "spiritual baton to software minds that will swim in virtual realities of a thousand sorts that we cannot even begin to imagine," as cognitive scientist Douglas Hofstadter asks it?[13] Are your children and mine the last to experience the true "human condition"? Are our children's children destined to be posthuman?

All these questions do not even posit the existence of quantum computers.

The quantum computer has implications as revolutionary as any piece of technology in history. If such a machine could be built, it would transform not just the computer industry, but our experience of physical existence itself. In a sense, it would lead to a blending of real and virtual reality.[14]

Theoretical physicist Paul Davies has further calculated that "a quantum computer with only 300 electrons would have more components in its superposition than all the atoms in the observable universe!"[15]

Douglas Hofstadter invited a blue-ribbon panel of experts — Ray Kurzweil, Hans Moravec, Bill Joy (chief scientist at SUN microsystems), John Holland (inventor of Genetic algorithms), Ralph Merkle (nanotechnology scientist), Kevin Kelly (*Wired* editor), Frank Drake (radio astronomer), John Koza (inventor of genetic programming) — to address this question: "Will Spiritual Robots Replace Humanity By 2100?" The symposium was held on 1 April 2000 at Stanford University to an overflow crowd. The scientists differed widely over the whens, hows, whys, and dangers of self-replicating computers. But whether or not we would have intelligent, emotional, "spiritual" machines in our future was a given.[16]

> **Truth, however disenchanting, is better than falsehood, however comforting.**
> ▶ Albert Schweitzer

So far our machines are emerging along a path that is still controlled by us. But for how long? In the last century computers became so sophisticated, they passed beyond human grasp. "It's becoming more like our relationship to nature," contends Danny Hills. "It's a digital jungle. We've created this jungle which we planted the seeds for but which we're not totally in control of any more."[17] The movie *Bicentennial Man* (1999) is a native parable as is Stephen Spielberg's *AI* (2001). Native culture has already created computers so complex, so complicated that they can only be programmed by other computers, computers that are literally beyond any human brain's comprehension. . . . At what point beyond any human being's control?

Anyone who doesn't have qualms and forebodings about the merger of the born and the made is a fool. But a lot of the church's fear of technology is about as perceptive as the Midwest resident's protest of a proposal to locate a biomedical research laboratory within the community. Her complaint? "They're trying to bring DNA into my neighborhood!"

FAIRCHILD'S MULE

Mr. Fairchild was a London nurseryman who died in 1729. He published the classic *The City Gardener* (1722). But he is best known for crossing a sweet william with a carnation. The result was the first man-made hybrid known as "Fairchild's Mule" — the first of the thousands of hybrids that we find in every garden.

Fairchild was so worried about his tampering with God's order of things that he left in his will a fund for a sermon to be preached annually at St. Leonard's Church, Shoreditch (East End of London). The sermon had to be on one of two topics: "The Wonderful World of God in the Creation" or "The Certainty of the Resurrection of the Dead Proved by the Certain Changes of the Animal and Vegetable Plants of the Creation." These sermons are still preached today.[18]

We ought to be no less concerned than Mr. Fairchild. Genetic Modification (GM) is neither inherently hazardous, nor inherently safe. GM happens naturally throughout creation. It has also happened artificially ever since plant breeders like Fairchild took Mendelian theory and made hybrids. As Fairchild intuited, we need to be careful and proceed with caution. But there is an antiscience streak to postmodernity, especially its Fundamentalist and New Age strain, that would lock creativity into modern, old-science modes. Before we can come to terms with the ethical dimensions of these new technologies, we must do a lot of epistemological, ontological, and theological homework.

The transforming work of the Holy Spirit is posthuman. The doctrine of sanctification helps us think in radically new ways about what we are and what we are to become. It is part of the "gift" of the Spirit that we can transcend being human; that we can morph more perfectly into the image and likeness of Christ; that we can think and move beyond our humanity.[19]

However, in his acceptance speech as the winner of the 2000 Templeton Prize, Princeton scientist Freeman J. Dyson quoted Sir Francis Bacon, one of the founding fathers of modern science: "God forbid that we should give out a dream of our own imagination for a pattern of the world."[20] Dyson is warning us of what I call the Frankenstein Syndrome. Remember Frankenstein? Science begetting monsters is a vision Mary Shelley had at the start of the 19th century through the story of a scientist who pursued his own dreams for the world, not God's dream for the world, and who sought in godlike fashion to create another person in his own image — a clone of himself. And Frankenstein, and Hitler, and Stalin, and . . . was the result.

In God's house there are many rooms. In the Devil's house there is only one.

To continue God's creativity, you need diversity and distributed control. This is why all centralisms are collapsing: Centralism opts for monopolistic values and control over variance and choice. To make the world safe for democracy is to make the world secure for difference. If health is in the diversity, the days are long gone when churches can "target" homogenous sectors of the population. Our "target" should be the least, the littlest, and the last first.

Then anyone with a heart that beats.

THE SKY IS THE LIMIT

Some years ago the Denver Zoo was given a large polar bear, but it had nowhere to put the bear. The zoo officials accepted the gift of the bear on the condition that their capital campaign be altered to provide for a natural habitat for the bear.

During the construction of his new home, the polar bear was put in a small cage. The space was so small that the bear could only take three steps, turn around, and then take three steps, and so on. For reasons of delay and design defects, the construction took three years.

The new home for the polar bear was almost as spectacular as its natural habitat, filled with waterfalls, caves, wind, lots of space. When the bear was released into its new home, it looked around, took three steps, turned around, took three steps, turned around, took three steps, etc.

> You were set on the cross,
> just, for the unjust,
> good, for the wicked,
> blessed, for the cursed,
> sweet, for the bitter.
> ▶ St. Afra's prayer

That polar bear needed the roof taken off his consciousness of what his limits were. But even with the roof off, his arctic home still had limitations. The earliest story in the Jewish-Christian tradition revealed that there are limitations imposed on our use of this Garden Planet. When we do not respect the limitations God has placed on us, we go out of kilter—with our outer and inner environment.

A conference took place called "The Unlimited Human." There are no limits, but there are limitations. Or as it is written, everything is possible, but not everything is permitted.

Human possibilities are endless, but the privileges have bounds. There are limitless horizons, but the horizon does have limitations. For Albert Einstein, it was the distinguishing mark between genius and stupidity to know what the limitations are. Learn no limits, but learn your own speed limitations. Every one of us travels at different speeds; every one of us must learn our biological limitations. Including the species called *homo sapiens*.

The uncharted and unchartable expanses of the Internet and the boundless biotech culture sanction an ideal of unconstrained liberty. But freedom is not the absence of limits, or pursuing infinite possibilities. True freedom is choosing and acquiescing in limits, and connecting oneself to good, true, and beautiful possibilities. The composer Igor Stravinsky explored creation and limitation, and came to this conclusion: "Whatever diminishes constraint diminishes strength."[21]

Complete freedom is the end of freedom. Without limitations there are no demarcations, which is what makes me me and you you. Our talents are either disciplined or dissipated. We are made more free by working within constraints as finite, contingent, and creative creatures.

Humans are called to tend and

> **These days, Americans think less about who is leading them and more about the prospect of leading themselves. Events are outpacing the system's keepers, and traditions are breaking down.**
> ► Karen Breslau[22]

till our Creator's creativity, not embark on our own selfish, nightmarish dreamings. Christians are called to tend and till Jesus' thoughts first presented 2,000 years ago, not to trust our own unfettered imaginings.

Will alarmed immigrant churches, trapped in the analog world of the past, abandon conversations with natives altogether? Or will the soul of Jesus live in us in a native biotech culture?

CLASS #1 INTERACTIVES

1 One of my favorite portions of Len Wilson's book on *The Wired Church* is his disavowal of what he calls the "AV mentality" or in another place, "the shoving of rounded mouths into square screens." In the AV mentality, according to Wilson,

> [the] use of electronic media is an afterthought, an add-on, or something less than an integral ingredient in worship and church life. An AV mentality is one in which the new communication form's primary use is to communicate themes and messages still centrally located, developed and implemented within old communication forms such as mass print culture. . . . Video, audio and graphics become merely support pieces for the primary communication tool of text.[23]

Which mentality dominates your church's use of media? How can the screen become a primary text in your community?

2 Graham T. T. Molitor, President of Public Policy Forecasting, condemns religious leadership throughout history for its inability to come to terms with the future.

As human intervention in creating or ending lifeforms evolved, religious leaders always have done so [fought the future], each step along the way. Not so many years ago, hybridization of plant life by Luther Burbank was denounced as blasphemous by church leaders. Centuries earlier, human dissection was blocked on grounds it was sacrilegious, cruel, immoral and obscene. Obstacles encumbering advances in biotechnologies, genetics and life sciences will be overcome. Eradicating genetic diseases, extending life expectancy, increasing food production, improving pharmaceuticals, and contributing overall to extraordinary advances in the quality of life are too important to be denied.[24]

Can you come up with examples from church history that contradict this litany of resistance? What "scientific progress" have religious leaders fought that should have been denied? Is all "progress" truly progress?

3 According to Mark Gerson, co-CEO of the GLGroup (New York),

The current technological boom is the second greatest explosion of creative genius in US history. The first was in Philadelphia in 1787, when men named Washington, Franklin, Madison and Hamilton created a system of governing that remains the envy of the world centuries later.[25]

What other "creative explosions" can you think of? What "creative explosions" are going off in your life right now?

4 Immigrants are in need of help in accessing the Internet. How might natives help render their immigrant parents and grandparents less isolated and give them a new lease on life?

5 One woman working at the MIT labs reportedly quit because the robot COG responded appropriately and emotionally to her so much better than her husband that she felt she had to quit, or get divorced. She could not suffer the comparison between her inferior husband and the superior COG.[26]

What are some of the new issues natives will be facing as we move into this biotech world?

6 Sixty-four percent of USAmericans say they trust CEOs of technology companies more than elected officials to make the right decisions about the future.[27]

Where do you stand in this survey? Who do you think should lead the way forward? Who should blaze the trail into the future? Business? Government? Or something else?

7 From your experience, evaluate the following observation: Immigrants think in terms of stock dividends; natives think in terms of share prices.

8 The US Constitution prevents "search and seizure." In other words, the government can't willy-nilly dispatch federal agents to inspect your home. What do you think the Fourth Amendment may say about digital agents sent to inspect your computers?

9 Discuss Douglas Robertson's contention that computer technologies remove the "two fundamental limitations of musical performances": the limitations of the instrument, and the limitations of the performer.[28]
Do you think he is right that digitized music will one day replace orchestras?

> It may be a good thing that we have high-quality recordings of some of the greatest violinists, pianists, trumpet players, and other instrumentalists now alive, for future musicians may have little incentive to devote the years of effort that are required to master these instruments. They are as likely to be found in musical performance in the future as the dulcimer and sackbut are today.[29]

10 Your grandchildren will have kids whose medical life history can be predicted at birth (excepting accidents, of course). Would you choose to be given this information? Or would you want to know to better prepare and circumvent?

11 Benedictine monks at St. John's University in Collegeville, Minnesota, have commissioned the first illuminated Bible since the printing press. For an update on how Welsh artist Donald Jackson is faring, see *www.saintjohnsbible.org*.

12 Send your group into a local bookstore. Open up books in the business section at random. See who can be the first to find a book with two facing pages of uninterrupted text—i.e., without subheads, graphics, sidebars, etc.

13 Those between the ages of 45 and 64 are the fastest-growing segment of web users. At Sun City's 17 retirement communities, computing has replaced theater and investing as the residents' favorite activities.
What do you think is motivating this group of people to enter cyberspace? Check out SeniorNet. Also Elderhostel *(www.elderhostel.org)* and Jupiter Communications *(www.jup.com)*.

14 In an attempt to bridge the digital divide in Argentina, anyone who is employed can obtain a subsidized loan of $1,000 to purchase a computer and Internet connection.

Would this work in North America? What more can be done to see that everyone can become a participant in this new economy?

15 We are now living in a world where each person can create their own world. Do you share the same media life as your children? What about you and your spouse?

What are the implications for faith of living in a world where everyone inhabits different realities?

16 In light of the last question, how do you appraise Oprah Winfrey's confession, "I don't take for granted one moment having a platform where I know thirteen million people around the world are watching and we are all feeling the same thing at the same time."[30]

17 Discuss Lutheran theologian Ann Pederson's lament that "The church . . . has chosen to remain ignorant, blissfully so, about the scientific and technological questions that our world faces."[31]

From Linear to Loop

The soul's motion is not direct.

▶ philosopher Plotinus

Immigrants think straight, in cause-and-effect linear fashion.

Natives think loopy, in hopscotch, hyperlink, field fashion.

M. Scott Peck argues on the first page of the first chapter of his book *Golf and the Spirit* (1999) that "golf is probably the most nonlinear pastime on the face of the earth."[1] Peck thinks this is part of why golf cuts such a wide swath through multiple generations. I think it may be exactly the opposite. In such a loopy world as the one we are in, a linear activity like golf balances the scale.

Write on your computer or on a piece of paper these three words:

Cough
Dough
Tough

Can you say them? Have you any idea how difficult it was for you to learn the pronunciation and meaning of these three English words? Just ask Desi Arnez. In a classic *I Love Lucy* episode, Lucille Ball tries to teach her Hispanic husband the various "ough" sounds starting with "through." It almost causes a divorce. Specific areas of your brain developed in certain ways to decipher these words. If you spoke another language, these areas of your brain would not have developed in this fashion, and you could not say or hardly see the differences in these words.[2]

There are culture-specific ways of organizing knowledge that shape brain functioning. Cab drivers develop the navigation area of the brain.[3]

Musicians have different brain structures than nonmusicians. We are only beginning to appreciate the plasticity of the brain to mediate diverse processing systems.

Anthropologist Clifford Geertz has shown how common sense is a cultural system. What is common to one culture is uncommon to another. Jocelyn Penny Small's book *Wax Tablets of the Mind* (1999) shows that different technologies produce different ways of thinking and learning. This does not mean that writing on a papyrus roll on your thigh is any inferior to writing on a codex or sheet of paper on a desk.[4] But brain development depends on all sorts of cultural factors, including technology, language, customs, music, etc.

"Mind and culture orchestrate reasoning," says Richard E. Nisbett of the University of Michigan at Ann Arbor. "An indefinitely large number of presumably basic cognitive processes may be highly malleable, rather than hardwired into our brains," Nisbett asserts.[5] An unexplored question that natives will pick up is whether the spiritual practice of prayer might rewire our neurological functioning into more suprarational, supernatural directions.

First to make the case for culture-induced neuroscientific changes was Canadian theorist Marshall McLuhan. McLuhan argued that new media altered human consciousness by literally changing the "unified sensorium" of the central nervous system.[6] Mainstream cognitive psychology has denied this, insisting instead that "people everywhere possess universal modes of thinking." Now scientists like Nisbett, Kaiping Pen (University of California, Berkeley), Incheol Choi (University of Illinois at Urbana-Champaign), and Ara Norenzayan (University of Michigan) are adopting McLuhan's multiple systems philosophy.[8]

> **Our writing materials contribute their part to our thinking.**
> ▶ Nietzsche[7]

Brains are wired differently, depending on the different cultures. Culture shapes how people think, and reasoning patterns differ dramatically in East Asian and Western cultures. For example, a variety of 20th-century studies of nomads in central Asia, Kepelle of western Africa, and Itzaj Mayans of the Guatemalan rain forest are accumulating evidence demonstrating that social structures cultivate different mental processes.

In July 1931, Russian psychologist Alexander R. Luria led a scientific expedition to central Asia to probe the minds of nomads who lived in that harsh, mountainous region. Luria wanted to explore whether members of what scholars at the time ranked as "primitive" communities could reason logically, like inhabitants of modern European and North American societies.

He got a rude shock. Upon hearing the scientist describe carefully phrased problems designed for simple, logical analysis, one nomad after another balked. They looked at Luria as if he had just asked them to run naked through a snowstorm.

For instance, Luria told one man that "all bears in the North are white" and that a friend who lives in the North "sent me a letter saying that he had seen a bear." Luria then asked the man to name that bear's color.

> **Typewriter: It types *us*, encoding its own linear bias across the free space of the imagination.**
> ▶ J. G. Ballard[9]

It seemed like a no-brainer to the intrepid scientist. Logic compels one to conclude that if a person sees a northern bear, then that creature must sport an ivory-colored coat.

"How should I know?" responded the man. "Ask your friend who saw the bear."[10]

NEW NATIVE NEUROLOGY

Natives and immigrants access and process information differently. Immigrants think in cause-and-effect, linear ways. Natives think in nonlinear, laminated, loopy ways (hence their low boredom thresholds). Once the modern world discovered that the world was round, it did everything in its power—intellectually, scientifically, spiritually—to make it flat again.

The postmodern world is making the world round once more.

The phonetic literacy of the alphabet shaped western culture and human thought patterns in revolutionary ways. Thought patterns made possible by phonetic alphabets (in which letters represent sounds) as opposed to logograpic writing systems (in which pictures or characters represent words) generated abstract terms like matter, motion, change, time, ratio—concepts that enabled classification and analysis. Without linear thought processes (abstract, analytic, rational, etc), Western science, logic, and codified laws could never have been possible.[11] The Chinese actually invented the printing press. But their language needed over 2,000 symbols. For its printing press, the West needed only 26 symbols plus a few for punctuation.

These two ways of thinking, the linear and the nonlinear, the phonetic and the logographic, the square and the round, are being combined because of the computer's format.

The invention of writing led to the dominance of the left side of the brain and an eclipse of right-brain values. Print culture fostered divisional disciplines and linear outlines. Governance meant mainframe command-control and closed systems, which was taken to an extreme in communism, one of history's great experiments to create a closed society — an experiment that ended between 1989 and 1991. Of course, other experiments in creating closed societies are ongoing, and the church is home for many of them.

Digital culture has ushered in a world of surgical rethinking and recircuiting of all our brains. When an unknown middle-aged man introduced something called a "mouse" before a crowd of mathematicians and hippies gathered in the San Francisco Auditorium in the fall of 1968, he invented something more than a pointing device. He conceived a laser surgery that rewired the human brain. With the interface called the "mouse," Doug Engelbart changed the course of history and the channels of consciousness.[12] In the words of Steven Johnson, who has shown how the interface medium has become a truly new art form:

> The term *computer* is something of a misnomer, since the real innovation here is not simply the capacity for numerical calculation. . . . The crucial technological breakthrough lies instead with the idea of the computer as a symbolic system, a machine that traffics in representations or signs rather than in the mechanical cause-and-effect of the cotton gin or the automobile. . . . The interface makes the teeming, invisible world of zeros and ones sensible to us. There are few creative acts in modern life more significant than this one, and few with such broad social consequences.[13]

The mouse bias is towards an open society and open systems. Native governance is distributed empowerment and, tapping into the creative energy of every associate, is based on EPIC values of speed, networking, systems thinking, chaos theory, spirituality, and nonlinearity. Nothing is private. Expose yourself before others expose you. The native rediscovery of the labyrinth — there is now even a labyrinth in the San Jose county jail — is a perception of life as a nonlinear maze where one finds the center only by walking a winding path.

In Russia, it is impossible to predict the past.

▶ Russian joke inspired by decades of "revisionist" history reflecting Communist Party doctrine

Natives don't watch TV in linear fashion (hence "roaming"). Natives don't watch movies in linear fashion either. Some of the most successful movies of the last century actually began in the middle, then looped to a backstory or prequel (*Star Wars* film saga, *Pulp Fiction*, etc.). Even immigrants are getting the hang of being loopy — volume two of Margaret Thatcher's memoirs came out before volume one.

Why aren't we in Gopherspace right now instead of web cyberspace? "Gopher" was a pioneering browsing technology invented in

1991 at the University of Minnesota (whose mascot is the digging rodent) that allowed people to surf from a home page to content sites anywhere in the world with just the click of a mouse on a link or bookmark.

Where is Gopher today? Gopher made civilian use of the military's ARPANET first, and enabled computer users to find servers and files on the Internet. So why did the Web win out over Gopher? The Web was developed by another research lab at the University of Illinois (NCSA — National Centre for Supercomputer Applications), building on a browser developed a few years earlier by British engineer Tim Berners-Lee at CERN, the European particle physics laboratory that employs half the world's particle physicists.

> **Consider God's handiwork; who can straighten what he has made crooked?**
> ► Ecclesiastes 7:13 NEB

Only one difference separated Gopher and the Web. Gopher was straightforward and upheld its linear bow, while the Web was loopy and allowed you to click on links anywhere in the document. Gopher insisted on a menu of links that returned you to plain documents. In the words of Mark McCahill, one of the developers of Gopher, "We were coming from a library perspective. . . . We were trying to maintain some hierarchy of information, not those spaghetti links of the web."[14]

The academics could not get looped. The physicists, who needed new ways to collaborate, could. Not to get looped is to be left out of the loop.

If "systematic theology" — where the Christian story is broken down and divided up into rational categories or is presented in linear fashion with beginnings, middles, and ends — does not become systemic theology or parabolic theology — where the Christian story is an organic holistic body of thought or a sumptuous banquet of narratives — the future of "professional" theology will be no different than Gopher.

Natives have brains that are wired differently than immigrants. Immigrant brains are wired to be queens on a chessboard — to move in straight lines all over the board. Native brains are wired to be knights and queens — to move sideways and across as well as up and down. There is a famous road sign in the rural South that reads: "If you want to get to heaven, turn right and go straight." If you want to get to heaven in a native culture, turn around and go curved. If you want natives to experience God, don't think straight. Think in circles.

It isn't that natives cannot focus. Watch a six-year-old play Nintendo, and you will see a focus of steel for hours on end. Natives just can't focus on text media like immigrants can. Natives do not have short attention spans; rather, it is more accurate to say that natives process information so much quicker that they need increased levels of stimulation, which is why they talk in shorthand and snappy idioms. "If I tell a girlfriend, 'That guy is just out for himself; be careful 'cause he just wants to sleep with you,' that would take too long," says Immaculata Reynosa, a nineteen-year-old from Rhode Island. "If I say, 'He's the Mack,' she'll know what I mean."[15]

Natives are voracious learners. But they prize ideas less for their content or "truthfulness" than for their vortex of energy, vitality, joy, and their ability to tickle the soul. Making the grade means more than making good grades. They aren't interested in keeping "in step" with mentors, but they are interested in keeping "'n sync." "You're out of step" is one of the worst things that can be said about an immigrant. "You're out of rhythm" is one of the worst things that can be said about a native. Rhythm is everything.

Immigrants grew up in a lecture-drill-test learning environment of classroom and chalkboard. The native learning environment could not be more opposite. In fact, for them the educational method of "lecture-drill-test" is the equivalent of the dental practice of "drill-fill-bill." Natives learn not by sitting still and listening, but by interacting and doing — game learning, team learning (this used to be called "cheating"), electronic learning, etc. Native learning is eye-popping, ear-ringing, nose-tingling, mouth-watering, finger-licking learning.

> **The things we have to learn before we can do them, we learn by doing them.**
> ▶ Aristotle[16]

The primary verb for web activity is "browse." However, what we are really doing online is playing.[17] In *The Republic*, Plato insisted that "Knowledge which is acquired under compulsion obtains no hold upon the mind. . . . [Therefore] do not use compulsion, but let early education be a sort of amusement."[18] In other words, children should be educated the way they educate themselves — through play. The creation of a play-based education system ("Lifelong Kindergarten") is more natural and normal than the highly regulated work environment of modern pedagogy.

It is named *PlayStation*, not *WorkStation* for a reason. Toy companies are now making instructional games and PlayStations (Sony's PS2) for our children that are sophisticated enough to launch land-based missiles and guide submarines. Export controls were slapped on Sony's PS2 game machine because the Japanese government called it a "general-purpose product related to conventional weapons." What spooked them was a North Korean submarine captured by the South Koreans in 1998. Its radar and global-positioning equipment were built from joysticks, gamepads, and gadgets made by Japanese consumer-electronics firms.

Native pedagogy now demands conversation and interactive learning rather than silence and note taking. Immigrants designed libraries to be centers of silence when they are conceived to be centers of scholarship. I went to the library to hide out and find a quiet place to study. Natives go the library (if they go) to work together and access information.

Even if the philosophers are wrong, and the anthropologists are wrong, and the scientists are wrong about the architectural changes now taking place in the neurological structure of the brain itself, no one can argue against the fact that we are undergoing a cognitive metamorphosis that is breaking out of biological memory systems that fit a "lecture-drill-test" world.

> **For every expert, there is an equal and opposite expert.**
> ▶ anonymous, sometimes attributed to science fiction writer Arthur C. Clarke

We decry television for turning our kids into couch potatoes, but that is precisely what our dominant educational system does. The notion that how you learn "US History 101" is by setting up a schedule where you go to a classroom for three days a week, an hour-and-a-half a day, for 13 weeks where you sit still, watching a head talk and a body sprinkle itself with white chalk will seem as silly in a few years as the citizens of Königsberg, Prussia, bragging about being able to set their clocks at 4 p.m. when Immanuel Kant began his afternoon walk.

Why do you think it is true that the more we spend on our children's education, the worse they do on standardized tests?[19]

Here is a 10th grade social studies objective from the Virginia Standards of Learning program:

> The student will analyze the regional development of Asia, Africa, the Middle East, Latin America, and the Caribbean in terms of physical, economic and cultural characteristics and historical evolution from 1000 AD to the present.[20]

Here is what is expected of sixth graders in South Dakota:

> Students will analyze the geographic, political, economic, and social structures of the early civilization of ancient Greece with emphasis on the location and physical setting that supported the rise of this civilization; the connections between geography and the development of city-states, including patterns of trade and commerce; the transition from tyranny to oligarchy to early democratic patterns of governments and the significance of citizenship; the differences between Athenian or direct, democracy and

representative democracy; the significance of Greek mythology in the everyday life of people in ancient Greece and its influence on modern literature and language; the similarities and differences between the life in Athens and Sparta; the rise of Alexander the Great in the north and the spread of Greek culture; and the cultural contributions in the areas of art, science, language, architecture, government, and philosophy.[21]

There is a "rationality" to memorization and there is a "rationality" to "knowing where to find things."[22] Natives don't need to memorize facts (though they do memorize lyrics). What they do need to know is where to find out about Athenian democracy, how to conduct Senate proceedings, how to present images of various democratic theories, how to create projects about Greek culture, and how to perform philosophical debates.

No wonder immigrants feel compelled to give natives amphetamines to snap them back to alertness and straight thinking. The "diagnosis" of ADD or ADHD, and the 9 million Ritalin prescriptions written in 1999 alone, can most often be attributed to immigrant school systems reacting to native learning styles.[23] These natives (boys to girls ratio of 5 to 1) are seen as "deviant" or "challenged" children.

> **Oh, I can't do that. That's my bad side.**
>
> ▶ Yogi Berra, when asked to look "straight" into the camera

This is the silent atrocity of our age: The public school's administration of the chemical subjugation of our native children. As one teenager was swallowing his Ritalin, he asked his preacher mom, "Do you think they'll ever stop giving pills to kids who think in circles and not straight?" Neuropsychiatrist Sydney Walker, director of the Southern California Neuropsychiatric Institute and a child psychiatrist, calls attention disorders "symptoms of modern life, rather than symptoms of modern disease."[24]

Linear competence is single-minded. The teacher occupies center stage. Its "skill and drill" exercises stress memory retention, reduction of meaning, and creation of an ordered worldview with cause and effect and beginnings and endings. Its "workplace" is the classroom.

Nonlinear, digital competence is stacked. The student occupies center stage. It stresses rapid hand-eye coordination, mental ability to make quick connections, the ability to organize information, skills at accessing rather than memorizing information, and puts a "spin" on meaning rather than reduces it. Its "work space" is anywhere.

As Anne Hird has documented in her study of what happens when "cyber-savvy" students enter public school classrooms, natives learn to function in two worlds — an outmoded one where they are dependent and passive and they humor their elders, and their world where they are large and in charge.[25] No wonder so many natives have a sense of "something from another place," almost an innate sense of parallel universes.

> **The truth was not a line from here to there ... but rather trails of oscillating overlapping liquids that poured forth but then assumed a shape and life of their own.**
> ▶ Jeffrey Lent[26]

Some postmoderns will continue to prefer more linear, abstract, sequential learning modes. Some brains lean in that direction naturally. But just as the modern bias was toward linear modes, the postmodern bias is towards nonlinear modes — more imagistic, relational, concurrent modes of thinking. If truth be told, these are more organic modes of learning than linear ones.

Loopy is more natural, more cosmic than linear. In "superstring" theory, "string" is another name for "loop." The very building blocks of the universe, it turns out, are loops that vibrate. The more building design reflects nature, the more we will see great curves like in the VW Beetle and the Macintosh Aqua.[27]

Or the Guggenheim Museum in Bilbao, Spain. Artists like Frank Gehry are breaking out of the linear "box" that has limited artistic presentation in almost all the art mediums. Santa Fe artist Jim Vogel, for example, portrays landscapes that present themselves in nonlinear ways. "One day I realized — I don't see in rectangles and squares, why should I paint that way?"[28]

Look at nature. How many straight lines to you see? How many right angles? It appears that even God doesn't think straight.

24-7-365$^{1/4}$

The *Pensées* (1670) of mathematician/physicist Blaise Pascal is one of the most original and vigorous defenses of Christianity ever written. It has often been maligned because of the *Pensées'* obstructive disorder and flagrant fragmentariness — a nonlinear narrative propulsion attributed to Pascal's early death. But Pascal himself presents a different reason for the curvaceousness of his *Pensées:*

I will write my thoughts in no particular order but not perhaps in a confusion without any design to it. That is the true order which will always mark out my objective through disorder. I would be paying too much

> **So God led the people by the roundabout way of the wilderness.**
> ▶ Exodus 13:18

respect to my subject-matter if I treated it in an ordered way since I want to show precisely that it is incapable of order.[29]

The heart of the Enlightenment project was to control, to tag, to order, and to discipline: all in the name of science and reason. Scholars became "masters of disdain" (Charles Peguy), specialists who policed their fenced-by-discourse patch of professional ground and who disparaged all trespassers and all travelers in pursuit of larger horizons. This Enlightenment legacy is still with us in the fact that people who offer critique, aloofness, and sparse praise are viewed by others as more intelligent and expert than those who offer praise, encouragement, and affirmation.[30]

We learned a lot about our world from the linear dissections of "modern science." Part of our world is a whole equal to the sum of its parts. But it is a small part. Perhaps as small as 5% to 10%. A "new science" has arisen in the past few decades that corrects the modern bias against the nonlinear. Unfortunately, the church still clings to an outmoded scientific mind-set, one that is now thrown out by the very scientists the church is trying to please.

This "new science" instructs us in the sublimely chaotic spirit of the universe and the fractal untidiness of truth. In fact, for most of the world's systems (eco, human, social, economic), the erratic is more routine and more enlightening than the systematic. The simple, ramshackle interactions of parts generate a whole not only that is greater than the sum of its parts, but a whole that is constantly changing, a phenomenon of complex adaptive systems called "emergence." Complexity scientist John Holland (University of Michigan) defines "emergence" as "much coming from little," which means that mystery, marvel, and magic are built into the structures of the universe.[31]

There seems to be a consciousness at the most elemental levels of matter. It is not just that electrons and quarks are "enminded." Even more, the consciousness of the universe is embodied. This is what modern linear science failed to see and appreciate. The old linear scientific method cannot account for consciousness or for soul or for 90% of what the world is about.

To build a method of how we ought to live on the 10% of the universe that is linear and not on the 90% that is nonlinear seems rather stupid when you come right down to it.

No one lives a linear life.

No one has ever truly been "modern."

But no one lives a loopy life either — at least not for long without crashing and burning.

Centralized planning is a bad dream.

But self-organizing processes are unstoppable roller coasters full of sound and fury signifying nothing. God has front-loaded pattern and purpose into the system. How do we get to them?

Out of randomness, pattern and purpose can emerge—but only if you bring the linear and the loop together.

Then you get a spiral that goes upward.

CLASS #2 INTERACTIVES

 Why do you think USAmerican high school students rank near the top in reading skills around the world, but they rank near the bottom in math and science, beating only Cyprus and South Africa? To what extent are today's tests designed to measure skills relevant to an industrial age not a digital age?

 How applicable in your area is this assessment of our public school system?

America's education system is in the sort of crisis that Detroit's car industry faced in the 1970s, before Japanese imports almost destroyed it in the 1980s. Teachers and parents are uneasily aware that something is wrong but have little idea how bad matters really are. At fourth grade (ten years old), American children score better in reading and science than most pupils in 20 other rich countries, and are about average in mathematics. At eighth grade, they are still slightly better than average in math and science but fall behind in reading. By 12th grade, they are behind 95% of the children in other countries. The longer children stay in American schools, the worse they seem to get.[32]

 The National Association for the Education of Young Children, the primary professional organization for early childhood professionals, has taken a strong stand against the academic testing of young children. Besides telling us virtually nothing about what children know and how they learn, these tests harm a child's sense of self either by inflating it or deflating it. See their website at *www.naeyc.org*.[33] Do you think they are right?

 Laurence Lerner, the Edwin Mims Professor of English at Vanderbilt, asked in his farewell lecture on 19 April 1995 this elementary but elemental question:

How important *is* the teacher? . . . Is he an enabler, an oppressor, or a dispenser of knowledge? Is he needed? What, I would ask myself from time to time, have I really got to offer my students.[34]

What if every teacher started asking these same questions again?

 If shared projects and teamwork is the calling card of the future, is this a good or bad motto? "Copy others, and let others copy off of you."

6 Douglas Robertson has observed that the rectangular shape of the House of Commons reflects the British constitution's bent toward a two-party system, the government on one side, and opposition on the other. By contrast, the semicircular domed US Congress reflects the US founders' antiparty bias and preference for multiple perspectives around a common core.

Reflect on this thesis. Consult with a local historian about the views of the founders towards political parties. Are we seeing the emergence of multiple parties in USAmerica? Are the Democrats and Republicans about to become dinosaurs?

7 For some examples of game learning as it applies to corporate culture, check out The Stock Market Game, invented by the Securities Industry Foundation for Economic Education. It teaches kids in grades 4–12 the fundamentals of the American economic system, with kids putting together a simulated stock portfolio.

See also Kiplinger's newsletter *Dollars & Sense for Kids* as a model of how to interest kids in economics.

8 Check out the narrative found at *themoonlitroad.com*. What part of this story is linear and what part loop? Compare with *wudsup-God.com*.

9 According to Douglas Robertson, hypertext "allows the ordering of the text to follow the reader's cares and interests rather than the author's. These techniques could allow the entire process of both reading and writing to evolve into something totally different from the way literature has been thought of since the days of clay tablets."[35]

What might that "something totally different" look like?

10 One of Philip K. Dick's novels (he wrote 11 in one year alone), *Do Android's Dream of Electric Sheep* (Garden City, N.Y.: Doubleday, 1968), was made into the movie *Blade Runner* (1968). Explore what it means for unfeeling people to act more and more like machines, as machines become more feeling and more human.

Is the following statement a mark of postmodern culture? Breathing humans are being turned into objects while we create objects to become human and treat objects as human — sometimes better than real humans.

Rent *Blade Runner* (Burbank: Warner Home Video, 1993) and discuss it. Or read Dick's novel *The Simulacra* (New York: Ace Books, 1964) and discuss his metaphor of "schizophrenia." How can the church use the biblical language of "incarnation" and "embodiment" in an age of virtuality and collapsed boundaries between carbon-based life and silicon-based life? For those who would see a person as a large and complex multiprocessor, how important is embodiment to the Christian? Does spirit matter? Or are spirit and matter two separate entities?

11 Are big-box churches a thing of the past?

12 The 20th century proved communism a failed dream. What about capitalism? Did it "prove" itself? Edward Luttwak once said, "With the possible exception of nuclear weapons, capitalism is the most powerful of human inventions." Do you agree with him?

13 Anne Hird's important research on the changing roles of teachers and learners in the Internet Age reaches a number of critical conclusions, one of which is this: "The question that remains is whether educators will follow in the footsteps of the earliest ARPANET (as the Internet was first named) users and employ the Internet for collaborative discovery processes or will appropriate this technology to support continued information delivery as the primary mode of classroom learning."[36]

What stakes are involved in this distinction? How high are these stakes?

From Word to Image

Instead of living on the edge, Christian artists ought to go deeper into the heart of Christ and deeper into the real church. Most Christianity in America is heretical, and if you go into that church, you're not going into the heart of Christ, you're going into the heart of religion. But if you're going deeper into the heart of Christ, you can become more creative and more integrated. You will be stretched, but you won't become marginalized.

▶ recording artist John Michael Talbot[1]

Immigrants are word-based. Natives are image-driven.

Not that immigrants don't use visual aids. When I was forced to sit in a corner with my back to the class, I was being jailed in effigy for bad behavior. The Puritan who owned the only cow on board the Mayflower sold milk at the inflated price of two pence a quart. The preacher made this grifter sit up front as his glass-case exhibit in a sermon on usury.[2]

But modernity's print culture created a word-based literacy, which was severely allergic to metaphors and images. Say "image" to any immigrant, and they think superficial, shallow, and uncritical. Even though metaphor and symbol are the native languages of religion, the language of theology became in the modern world the language of abstraction and absolutes. Only recently are theologians realizing that abstracted principles "do not capture the sensory or linguistic richness of actual religious experience" and that "with theology's explicitness comes a loss of the sensual, the implicit, the 'layers underneath the surface.' In other words, it represents the loss of mystery, which seems to be a necessary ingredient of *authentic* religious experience."[3]

In the dialog between the verbal and the visual, who has the final word? The visual. The primacy of image over word is definitive. "Image is everything," as the saying goes.

GRAPHICACY

The chief literacy of natives is image driven (I call image-based literacy "graphicacy"). The way we interact with media shapes how we view the world and how we function in the world. I know natives whose first language is HTML, and who are better at exegeting and maneuvering symbols than entire advertising companies. In 1999, more video games were sold in USAmerica than books. In Japan, video-game characters are now bigger than rock stars and movie stars. So what is driving the sales of video games? Characters like Zelda, Donkey Kong, Lara Croft (the native version of Barbie — soon to be a billion dollar babe). For natives, moving images (movies, videos, streams) are metaphors on which they build their lives.

The dominance of images in this visualholic culture is forcing immigrants willy-nilly to get their green cards in graphicacy. One study of responses to personal ads in the classified sections reveals that ordinary men and women are "capable of refined and sophisticated utilization of a range of cultural symbols."[4]

Here's a little test:

Q: What do you think of when I say "Green Bay Packers fan?"
A: *Cheese hats.*

Q: When I say "Buddhist monk," what image comes to mind?
A: *Orange robes.*

Q: When I say "Bastille," what words pop into your head?
A: *Storming of the Bastille.*

Forget the fact that the Bastille was the home of seven old men who resented the disturbance, not the horrible prison that had to be "stormed." The image takes precedence over the reality.[5]

Why will you forget a name quicker than a face?

Why will you remember where a quote was on a page but forget the quote itself?

Because your visual memory is stronger than your textural memory.

Here is another test. Let me names some names: Michael Jordan, Sadam Hussein, Fidel Castro, O. J. Simpson, Barbara Walters, Billy Graham, John Madden, Mark Twain, David Letterman.

As you heard these names, did a visual picture of each of them pop into your brain? Do you know what that means? It means that each of these people are living in your mind. These people have taken up residence inside your skull. You hold all these images, from wildly diverse stations of "real life," in your mind at the same time.

Why are conservatives losing, and will continue to lose, on the issue of keeping the minimum wage low?

All the statistics are on the conservatives' side.[6] Only one in four low-wage workers resides in families in the bottom 20% of the income bracket. In other words, a lot of minimum wage workers are actually the kids of rich people. Less than one in five dollars of the additional earnings from increased minimum wages goes to families who rely on low-wage jobs as primary sources of income. And of the one dollar in five that does go to increase earnings, much of the increase is lost in taxes (Social Security, state and federal income tax). In short, minimum wages raise prices in an income-regressive manner.

> **A religious symbol does not rest on any *opinion*.**
> ▶ Ludwig Wittgenstein[7]

So why will conservatives lose the battle against raising minimum wage levels?

Because when an image of a minimum-wage worker clicks in our mind's camera, it is a poor family, scruffy kids, a run-down apartment that we see — not a Tommy Hilfiger-clad kid working for gas money for his Honda. You can't keep a good (or bad) metaphor down.

The power of graphicacy is enormously greater than the power of literacy. Why? The most primal and primeval intelligence is metaphorical.

ELEMENTARY

The basic categories of the mind and the most profound capabilities of humans are images, as our dreams instruct us every night. The earliest languages we have been able to trace back are in logographic script. The rongorongo script of Easter Island looks like children's paintings, not words.

Cognitive science has been split between those who argue the mind is basically a neural network of connections (connectionists) and those who view the mind as a place that manages and maneuvers symbols (theoretical linguists). Even if the connectionists didn't already know the smell of cooking goose, the theoretical linguists would be right.

Mark Turner, a scholar of the Center for Neural and Cognitive Sciences at the University of Maryland, has demonstrated that the mind is made up of stories, metaphors, parables, and projections. His term for our most elemental mind is "the everyday mind." His term for the human mind that is constructed of metaphors, stories, and parables is "the literary mind."[8] "The motivations for parable," he writes, "are as strong as the motivations for color vision or sentence structure or the ability to hit a distant object with a stone."[9] For Turner, language is not the mother of parable but its rebellious child. "Parable is the root of the human mind — of thinking, knowing, acting, creating, and plausibly even of speaking."[10]

ELEMENTAL — EINSTEIN'S BRAIN

In its 31 December 1999 issue, *Time* magazine named Albert Einstein the Person of the Century.[11] *People* magazine named him the Most Intriguing Person of the Century.

In 1955 at the age of 76, Einstein died of a ruptured abdominal aneurysm. The Princeton pathologist who did the autopsy, Dr. Thomas S. Harvey, walked off with Einstein's brain after the autopsy. He was given permission by the Einstein family to remove Einstein's brain and keep it for scientific study before he was cremated.

Shortly thereafter Harvey moved to Lawrence, Kansas, where he kept Einstein's 2.7 pound brain in two mason jars of formaldehyde in his office. Harvey and his students put the brain to every test conceivable. What was different about this brain? At first, the brain of the century's greatest genius seemed normal in every way.

> **I used to think that the brain was the most wonderful organ in the body. But then I thought, who's telling me this?**
>
> ▶ comedian Emo Phillips

It was the same size and same weight (maybe even a bit lighter) as every other brain, the story went. Einstein just used his.[12]

In 1996 an aging Harvey, after a bizarre car trip with Einstein's brain stowed in the trunk in two Tupperware containers, sent Einstein's brain to McMaster University (Hamilton, Ontario), one of the leading centers for comparative studies of brain structure and function.[13] As soon as it arrived, the McMaster scientists began conducting sophisticated studies on Einstein's brain using new equipment and evaluative techniques. Will these studies reveal any physical differences?

The results of their research are only beginning to be published. In terms of the gross anatomy, they found that Einstein's brain was not any heavier than anyone else's. The brain was the same as others with one exception. In Einstein's brain the parietal lobes were wider and the brain more spherical than the control group. A region of Einstein's brain called the inferior parietal lobe was about 15% wider than normal. In fact, the whole parietal operculum was missing in each hemisphere of Einstein's brain. Einstein's left parietal lobe was larger than usual, making it symmetrical with the right hemisphere (usually the sizes are asymmetrical).

What about these parietal lobes in Einstein's bulked up brain? According to an article in *The Lancet*, the inferior parietal lobule is

> **In both scientific and religious culture all we have finally are symbols.**
> ▶ sociologist Robert Bellah[14]

a secondary association area that provides for cross-modal associations among visual, somesthetic, and auditory stimuli. Visuospatial cognition, mathematical thought, and imagery of movement are strongly dependent on this region. Einstein's exceptional intellect in these cognitive domains and his self-described mode of scientific thinking may be related to the atypical anatomy in his inferior parietal lobules. Increased expansion of the inferior parietal region was also noted in other physicists and mathematicians.[15]

And what is there about this bicep on Einstein's brain that makes it so unusual? The inferior parietal lobe controls, in the words of neuroscientist Sandra Witelson, "visuospatial cognition, mathematical thought and imagery of movement." Or as Michael Lemonick explains it, "Einstein's impressive insights tended to come from visual images he conjured up intuitively, then translated into the language of mathematics (the theory of special relativity, for example, was triggered by his musings on what it would be like to ride through space on a beam of light)."[16]

Einstein's mathematical formulas derived from mental images. Einstein liked to talk about the gift of "fantasy" as being essential to the work he did. The most brilliant mathematical equation in history was born not in calculus but in pictures.

The highest intelligence is metaphorical. It thinks in images and puts complex thoughts into metaphorical boxes that vibrate emotionally when you pick them up.[17] The mind works, not by Boolean logic, but by metaphors and images. One of the thorniest problems in the field of AI (Artificial Intelligence) is this: How do you get machines to think in metaphors?

And if you can get such machines to think in images and then to tell stories in images, does this mean that they have come to consciousness? Neurologist Antonio Damasio defines consciousness in precisely this way:

> Consciousness begins when brains acquire the power, the *simple* power I must add, of telling a story without words, the story that there is life

ticking away in an organism, and that the states of the living organism, within body bounds, are continuously being altered by encounters with objects or events in its environment, or, for that matter, by thoughts and by internal adjustments of the life process.[18]

The most elemental requirement for a healthy and mature life is the ability to inhabit stories. What some are calling "the cooking process" of what it means to be you begins in the womb, where as fetuses we learn to listen to stories and are shaped by them.[19]

Mark Turner uses a story as his "touchstone text" for his thesis about the centrality of story: Peter Pan and the lost boys in Neverland.

The lost boys will always be boys, and always lost, as long as they don't know stories. They can't grow up because they cannot understand how to inhabit roles in stories, how to belong to categories of characters running across story spaces, how to have lives. Peter Pan persuades Wendy to go with him to Neverland exactly by telling her that the lost boys don't know any stories:

"You see I don't know any stories. None of the lost boys know any stories."

"How perfectly awful," Wendy said.

"Do you know," Peter asked, "why swallows build in the eaves of houses? It is to listen to the stories. O Wendy, your mother was telling you such a lovely story."

"Which story was it?"

"About the prince who couldn't find the lady who wore the glass slipper."

"Peter," said Wendy excitedly, "that was Cinderella, and he found her, and they lived happily ever after." Peter was so glad that he rose from the floor, where they had been sitting, and hurried to the window. "Where are you going?" she cried with misgiving.

"To tell the other boys."

"Don't go, Peter," she entreated, "I know such lots of stories."

Those were her precise words, so there can be no denying that it was she who first tempted him.

He came back, and there was a greedy look in his eyes now which ought to have alarmed her, but did not.

"Oh, the stories I could tell to the boys!" she cried, and then Peter gripped her and began to draw her toward the window.[20]

CULTURE JAMMING

Metaphor is not just more natural than word. Metaphor is also more spiritual than word. If cultures are systems of symbols — intricate, interwoven webs of metaphors and symbols — then natives' image culture is more like biblical culture (Genesis begins by describing God through images — wind, breath, spirit) and Jesus' oral culture than immigrants' print culture.

The Jesus Movement was performative and image based. Jesus picked up images like a magnet does paperclips. Jesus knew that images more than words could best bend the world to God's being, so he communicated most of his truths through visual images wrapped in sound.

Jesus was the original "culture jammer." Kalle Lasn is fed up with a culture where the stories are being told by people with "something to sell as well as to tell." He advocates turning the power of marketing against itself in a series of "demarketing" or "uncooling" campaigns that he calls "culture jamming."[21]

Jesus exerted leadership in the "public square" with a succession of "culture jamming" performance metaphors:

(1) rode on a donkey
(2) cleansed the temple
(3) fed five thousand
(4) raised the dead
(5) carried a cross on his back

The figure of Christ himself is the biggest culture jamming metaphor out there. That word "figure," from the Greek *schema* and the Latin *figura*, is fertile of feeling and thought. It means among other things "the image, likeness or representation of something material or immaterial; a metaphor or metaphorical mode of expression; a represented character, as in one acting a part; an image or similitude..." (Oxford English Dictionary). If the church is to present natives with Christ figures, it must learn to communicate like Jesus and his first followers did — through metaphor, image, parable, and icon.

The first Christian icon was a textless symbol — ICHTHUS (Iota, Chi, Theta, Upsilon, Sigma), a word symbol for fish. Picture in your mind the Mercedes-Benz icon. Notice how similar it is to the peace sign? Picture in your mind the Pepsi icon. How close

> **Fringe voices raise flags, blaze trails, and give perspective. They warn, they amuse, they cajole, often with wisdom. If we listen carefully to the voices that seem extreme today, we may glean what it would be like to live as peaceful human beings in a technologically dominated time.**
> ▶ futurist John Naisbitt[22]

is it to the yin-yang Chinese symbol? Now picture in your mind the Nike Swoosh. Flip it over and add it to another Nike Swoosh. How close is it to ICHTHUS?

If the church is to present Christ figures to natives, if the church is to become a Christ figure for the world, Christians had better start using their own images and icons before they are all stolen by a culture that preys upon the Bible's metaphorical power.

Because the worlds of church and media by and large do not mix, natives are on their own in paring down the media propaganda and distinguishing the good from the bad. They are without spiritual coaching in discerning what is precious from what is cheap.

Body by Jesus: Minds Molded, Bodies Inscribed[23]

Can you guess the #1 online discussions among native Christians under 20? Body modification, or "bod mod" for short—tattoos, piercings, body implants, etc. "Among some Christian teens," Andrew Careaga writes, "tattoos are the hottest Christian fashion accessory since WWJD bracelets."[24]

Body colors and cuts are predictable for two reasons. The first is cultural: In an image-driven culture, the image most under natives' control is their bodies. Since 1996, when 1.9 million USAmericans had some form of aesthetic surgery, the number of body modifications has exploded. Life stories are being written on the body through pierces and pigments. Natives live in a field of dreams that is constantly changing, revealing new ways for them to be a person.[25]

In many ways, body shops are already here. There are two million plastic surgeries a year in USAmerica alone, with male body tune-ups increasing every year. I had a call not too long ago from a highly placed woman executive in Manhattan. She wanted my advice as to whether she should have plastic surgery. It had become routine for her peers, but she had misgivings.

As someone whose only skill in counseling is to give take-it-or-leave-it opinions, I registered my theological misgivings at the concept of "physically correct" bodies. I noted the feminist consideration of plastic surgery to be as invasive and oppressive as female clitoridectomies. Plus, I wondered out loud, how come women who have more than one face-lift start looking alike? Joan Rivers no longer looks like Joan Rivers. Is this a new form of mummification?

When I concluded my dissertation, I asked, "So what do you think?"

"I think I'm going to do it," she replied (I told you I'm not good at counseling).

Before she hung up, I asked about her college daughter. "She's great. Thanks for asking. She's due home for break, and she told me just the other night that she has a surprise for me."

"What do you think it is?" I inquired.

"I think I know what it is. What I'm not sure about is whether it's a tattoo or a ring. Leonard, so help me, if she has either of these things, I'm going to cut her tuition payments."

> **Men with earrings make the best husbands. They're not afraid of pain, and they've bought jewelry.**
> ▶ comedian Rita Rudner

Wait a minute. Plastic surgery is a severe form of bod mod, which is okay, but piercings and tattoos aren't?

The second reason why body modification is predictable is theological: Christianity is incarnational, founded on the image of God in Jesus the Christ. If the ultimate theological image is Jesus himself, the penultimate theological image is the image of Christ in us. Postmodern pilgrims not only want a mind molded by Jesus and the Scriptures. They want a body by Jesus as well. As apprentices of Jesus, postmoderns want their apprenticeship to show up not just in their mental states but in bodily form as well.[26] They want to write the story of faith on more than sheepskin. Faith that is intellectual and not incarnational is a field without dreams.

In Flannery O'Connor's short story "Parker's Back," O. E. Parker starts getting tattoos when he is 14 because he does not like what he sees in the mirror each morning. Each time he feels that something is missing inside, he gets a tattoo. When that tattoo loses its power to make him feel better, he gets another . . . and then another, and then another.

> **Icons help keep our spirituality rooted in the world, and our world rooted in spirituality.**
> ▶ Charles Hoffacker[27]

O. E.'s name is really Obadiah Elihu, which means "servant of the Lord, who is God." But O. E. refuses to claim his real name and find God. His soul becomes more and more miserable. He marries a religious fanatic, who convinces him that what he needs to find is "religion." Finally he goes to a tattoo parlor to get a Bible tattooed on his back, but comes home with a picture of Christ tattooed on his back instead.[28]

The challenge of the church is to not denounce those with "permanent cosmetic applications" (the spa name for tattoos) and pierced body parts. Our challenge is to point those with pierced noses, tongues, and eyebrows to the inscribed body of the Savior of the world, to show them O. E.'s picture of Christ, whose pierced hands are reaching out to them.

The Most Valuable Diamond in the World

Michele Gold tells the story about a man "who gave his young daughter a simple locket and told her that it contained a valuable diamond sealed inside the locket, so if at any time she was ever in need she could crack open the locket, sell the diamond," and pull through.

The daughter grew up, but her life was far from cosy and rosy. She endured times of grinding poverty. But that secret diamond nestled inside the locket she wore around her neck kept her head up and her feet moving in the right direction.

After many years of surmounting hurdle after hurdle the woman became quite wealthy. She no longer had to worry about money and was curious about how much the diamond her father gave her was actually worth. The finest jeweler in the village agreed to appraise it for her. He picked it up, eyed the obviously cheap pendant with condescension, and smashed the little locket to smithereens with one swift blow. A small shiny object rolled across the table.

The jeweler held it up to the light. "Why, this is not a diamond, my lady, but a worthless piece of ordinary glass."

"No, kind sir," replied the woman with tears in her eyes, "that is the most valuable diamond in the world."[29]

The most valuable gems in the world are the spiritual values of faith, hope, and love. But they need images to convey their power. Jesus is our greatest jewel: the divine embodiment of faith, hope, and love—God with us, Emmanuel.

CLASS #3 INTERACTIVES

1 "If Pope Gregory said that icons were the Bible for the illiterate," Minister of Media Len Wilson writes, "then the screen is the Bible for the post-literate."[30]

Discuss this statement and evaluate its implications for your church and your ministry.

2 Gertrude Jekyll, the legendary British gardener, says that there are three phases a gardener passes through on the way to maturity of thought and garden:

(1) wanting to have a garden with one of everything
(2) wanting to have a garden that specializes in one family of flowers
(3) wanting to have a garden that paints a picture[31]

Which stage is your own personal faith in? How would you characterize the witness of your church?

3 Albert Einstein liked to refer to God using the Talmudic expression, "The Old One." He defined theology as "tapping into the thoughts of The Old One," and confessed to a pervasive sense of being in the presence of a mystery, "partly known, partly hidden." The work of a true scientist begins, Einstein argued, not in what he "sees," but in the "attitude" he brings to the subject. He argued that the "attitude" of wonder and awe ought to precede everything.

What are your attitudes? What are the attitudes that you bring to your choices? What are the attitudes that your church brings to its decision making?

4 In an information-overload society, how can you tell what is useful content, meaningful information?

Discuss the future of "portals" as information providers. The giant web portals in the near future (AOL, Amazon.com, Yahoo!, At Home, Go!) will offer free wearable computers, according to futurist Richard Worzel, to anyone who will check in with them before making purchasing decisions (a kind of consumer report).[32] Would you sign up? Why or why not?

5 Visit the home of A.L.I.C.E. She lives at *www.alicebot.org*. Try conversing with her. How different an experience is it talking to a computer who talks back?

6 A senior Coca-Cola executive is said to have declared that the company could survive the loss of all its plants, capital, staff, and access to raw materials, providing that it kept possession of the Coca-Cola logo. With that it would be possible to walk into a bank and receive sufficient credit to replace the entire global infrastructure.

Do you believe him? Is a logo that important? Does your church have a mission statement? Does it have an image statement?

7 If the cry of immigrants is "let's-make-it-relevant," might the cry of natives be "let's-make-it-real"? What does "real" mean to natives? What other cries are you hearing?

8 Revisit the debate between Socrates and Phaedrus on the relative merits of writing and memory.

Socrates (quoting King Thamus's conversation with the god Theuth):

The parent or inventor of an art is not always the best judge of the utility or inutility of his own inventions to the users of them. And in this instance, you who are the father of letters, from a paternal love of your own children have been led to attribute to them a quality which they cannot have; for this discovery of yours will create forgetfulness in the learners' souls, because they will not use their memories; they will trust to the external written characters and not remember of themselves. The specific which you have discovered is an aid not to memory, but to reminiscence, and you give your disciples not truth, but only the semblance of truth; they will be hearers of many things and will have learned nothing; they will appear to be omniscient and will generally know nothing; they will be tiresome company, having the show of wisdom without the reality.[33]

Socrates continues:

I cannot help feeling, Phaedrus, that writing is unfortunately like painting; for the creations of the painter have the attitude of life, and yet if you ask them a question they preserve a solemn silence. And the same may be said of speeches. You would imagine that they had intelligence, but if you want to know anything and put a question to one of them, the speaker always gives one unvarying answer. And when they have been once written down they are tumbled about anywhere among those who may or may not understand them, and know not to whom they should reply, to whom not: and, if they are maltreated or abused, they have no parent to protect them; and they cannot protect or defend themselves.[34]

To what extent is this critique of writing a debate on the relative merits of word vs. image?

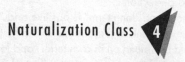

From Vast to Fast

It isn't good enough to be moving in the right direction — if you're not moving fast enough, you can still get run over.
▶ Will Rogers

If you are on the right track, you will get run over if you just sit there.
▶ Mark Twain

If the path before you is clear, you're probably on someone else's.
▶ Joseph Campbell

Immigrants think in terms of big and small. Natives think in terms of fast and slow. It is now fast over vast. Stand still, and you won't be still standing long.

Leadership is the ability to turn on a dime in a new direction. What is "new" in this New Economy is not a "speed" that does what you have always done except faster. Rather, it is doing faster than ever before things you have never done before.

Big can be either bad or good. But small is best. The average business of the future will be three people. Thanks to the Web, smaller voices can be heard over larger, institutional voices. A small shopkeeper in Calcutta is equal in marketing power and scope to Coca-Cola. The Web puts the globe into the hands of every human being. Literally.

Small is better than big when small is quality-fast and quantity-tailored. In this fast-off-your/think-on-your-feet world, it is not what or how much you know. It is when you knew it. Speed is everything. Speed trumps perception and perfection.

To an immigrant, "long-term" is positive and "short-term" is negative. Natives don't even think in these terms in the first place. But if they did, short-term would be valued on its own terms, and long-term would be really long — like the "art of the long view" as reflected in the 10,000-year clock and library *(www.longnow.org)*.

In the velocious living of postmodern culture, everything takes place in the itch of the instant, the ick of the moment, the fingersnaps of Internet Time (1 Internet year=2 dog years=14 human years).

A man went to his doctor for a checkup. The doctor finally emerged and told him the bad news. "You have only a short time to live."

"How long?" he asked.

"Ten . . ." replied the doctor.

"Ten what?" the man said. "Ten years? Ten months? Ten weeks? Ten days?"

". . . nine, eight, seven, . . ."

Time is now measured in seconds. Natives will only wait at most 8 seconds for a page to download before moving on. The average life of information on the Internet is 44 days.[1]

A new high-tech product hits the US marketplace every 17 seconds. The average job tenure in information technology in 2000 was 13 months, down from 18 months in 1998. Wall Street lunges and lurches in days what used to take weeks and even years. In March 2000 the Dow Index swung like a pendulum 800 points in two days. One woozy commentator shook his head and confessed that he could remember when the Dow *was* 800.

Data on the early US space program was lost when NASA replaced the technology on which it was stored. In my own academic career, quite a bit of my research and writing (including one whole book) has perished alongside the equipment needed to read it.

> **The combination of quick learning and deep remembering makes a civilization strong against shocks and profoundly adaptable.**
> ▶ Stewart Brand[2]

"REMEMBRANCE OF THINGS FAST"[3]

In native culture, it is the survival of the fastest, not the biggest or even fittest. "If things seem under control, you're not going fast enough." So says race car driver Mario Andretti. So says Tom Peters in his final paragraph of his final column for *Forbes ASAP.*[4]

In a world where the positive-feedback laws of bootstrapping and leapfrogging reign supreme, the monthly journal, weekly magazine, daily newspaper — all are out-of-date without online sites with information updated hour-by-hour, even minute-by-minute and linked. Keeping up to speed is now more important than keeping up to date. Can you find a television commercial or newscast that doesn't provide a web address for "updated information"?

The cadences of thought are racing at breakneck speeds. The norm of immigrant culture was the *status quo.* The norm of native culture is the *fluxus quo,* with almost apocalyptic change characterizing the fluctuations. The amoebic manueverings of church culture contrast sharply with the volcanic drive and cyclonic energy of native culture where things change overnight.

In my lifetime London, England, has become the most expensive city in the world and the most cosmopolitan city in the world. Over 300 languages can be heard being spoken in this one English city.

In my lifetime I have seen a restaurant start-up, sell its first franchise in 1952, and grow to the place where it feeds 0.5% of the world's population every day. In 1995, there were 8,600 McDonald's in USAmerica and 12,000 in the rest of the world.

In the last decade (1990–2000) about half the stadiums in USAmerica that house football, baseball, basketball, or hockey have been replaced — either to lure new teams to a city, or to prevent the home team from leaving town (e.g., Seattle or San Francisco).

In the last decade I have seen Salt Lake City go from being a joke to in 1997 the 26th ranked best place to live. In 1999 and again in 2000, it was voted the best place to live in North America.[5]

In the last decade Charlotte, North Carolina, has become the second leading banking center in the nation, with corporations hauling their offices to Charlotte faster than the city can hail them in.

In the 1980s, cell phones and private jets were status symbols of wealth and power. Today every cabbie talks on a cell phone.

Ten years ago, who would have predicted that people would be going to the malls for eye surgery, or swallowing a pill inside of which is a "gut-cam," a camera that takes pictures of your gastrointestinal tract and transmits images to a CD-player-sized detector worn on your belt.

In a few short years economists have gone from fretting over too much government debt to now worrying about too little debt (since government debt in the form of bonds and other securities plays an important role in the financial system).

As a child of the '50s and '60s, I grew up reading *1984* and *Animal Farm*. My fear was of a government that could spy on you and subvert the individual. I now live in a world where instead of one Big Brother, there are 6 billion "little brothers" that have the power to subvert the government and bring *you* down.

Nellie Holcomb Roeder (1888–1973) of Jefferson City, Missouri, used to say to her Methodist pastor, "I came here in a covered wagon. I've lived to see a man on the moon. Don't talk to me about changes."

But talk we must. For the changes Nellie saw were incremental, not exponential.

Exponential Change

I shall never forget the day the church I pastored in Geneseo, New York, opened up the time capsule deposited in the cornerstone of a church with which it had merged (Griegsville, New York). Local Evangelical and United Brethren leaders from the 19th century had placed in a metal box all sorts of treasures they thought might interest their descendants a hundred years hence.

> **Microsoft must continue to innovate because the fact is that we are always just two years away from extinction.**
> ▶ Bill Gates

Churches planting time capsules today can't make the same assumptions that these 19th-century Christians did. They assumed that the people opening the capsule one day would look like them and be like them. Of course, times would change. But change was linear.

This is no longer a safe assumption. When we think of 50 or 100 years from now, we can no longer posit incremental, linear change.[6] Change now is seditious. Change now happens exponentially in front of our face but beyond our comprehension or control. Paradigm shifts are taking place every decade. Here is an example of exponential growth: We did not have integrated circuits until 1956, or the Web until 1990. Some things are improving at double exponential rates—brain scanning.[7]

A favorite parable scholars use for explaining exponential growth functions, and why they can be so alarming, is this one: A king wished to honor a faithful servant. He invited the servant to make any request within reason, and he would try to honor it.

The servant, seeing the king playing chess with a courtesan, placed a grain of wheat on the first square. He then asked if the king would give him double that grain of wheat for each square on the chessboard — e.g., two grains on the second, four grains on the third, eight grains on the fourth — through the sixty-four squares on the chessboard.

The king, thinking he had been let off easy with a few bushels of wheat, quickly granted the request. And immediately went bankrupt. The amount of wheat he had agreed to give the servant was 9.233×10^{18} grains, or about 598 metric tons of wheat.[8]

In every arena of life, we are facing the inconceivable. Everyday existence has become a sci-fi chapter.

> **Impossibility is the only door that opens.**
> ▶ poet Les Murray[9]

In fact, science fiction can hardly keep ahead of reality. In the lifetimes of most natives and the lifetimes of their children, there will be raised the most stupendous ethical challenges and brow-knitting puzzlements ever faced by humankind. Life is now a moral chess game of enormous complexity.

▼ ▼ ▼

A tourist took a cab through the city of Washington, D.C. Driving by the National Archives Building, he saw the inscription:

THE PAST IS PROLOGUE

The tourist asked the driver, "What does that mean?"
The cabbie responded, "I guess it means, 'You ain't seen nothing yet.'"

▼ ▼ ▼

This is an anything-can-happen-and-probably-will world. When immigrants hear that Hillvue Heights Church or Hillsongs Church has "anything-can-happen-and-probably-will" worship, they shudder and make snide remarks.[10] When natives hear about an "anything-can-happen-and-probably will" church, whether it is in Bowling Green, Kentucky, or Sydney, Australia, it is like the smell of barbeque. They flock to it in droves.[11] The complacency of the expected is a new cardinal sin.

Only two things I can say for certain about the future. First, the unexpected happens. Second, the expected does not happen. There are two indispensable survival skills in such a volatile world: learning relationships and low viscosity.

> **If it's worth doing, it's worth doing wrong, fast.**
> ▶ Scient's motto[12]

LEARNING RELATIONSHIPS

Lasting relationships are now learning relationships. That old immigrant mantra, "There is no substitute for experience," is no longer true. Experience is no longer an asset. Only constant learning. The native mantra is, "There is no substitute for learning relationships." To plan the future by the past is a recipe for disaster.

Learning costs — even more than experience.

Natives can experience in one year of life what it took their ancestors a lifetime to accumulate. Five years ago online information was doubling every four years; it is now doubling every sixty days. Never before in history has learning played such a starring role in the fate of humankind.

A good example of the need for constant learning is a bankrupt Iridium, the world's first pan-national corporation from its inception, its board meetings conducted with simultaneous translation in Russian, Japanese, Chinese, and English. One of the costliest corporate boondoggles in history, Iridium sent up 66 satellites, spent $6 billion dollars to connect everyone on planet Earth, only to have everyone on planet Earth connected by land-based cellular systems, negating the need for Iridium in the first place. Iridium could only attract 20,000 customers to pay $3,000 for their global phones, many of whom immediately began complaining that the system could only handle analog voice calls and pages in a world swimming in digital data.

Natives can count on one thing about the future: How you did things in the past will not be how you will do things in the future. My-secret-of-success books are now how-not-to-do-things books. Learning is the key activity of postmodern culture. Without a learning culture, there can be no success in this new world.

Learning now is different from the past in a few ways. First, learning is now high-tech. In some sense it has always been. We just can't see that books and pens are high-tech. Second, learning now involves de-learning, or what the apostle Paul called "forgetting" ("forgetting those things which are behind. . . ," Phil. 3:13 KJV).

The world is moving so fast that even natives can quickly become immigrants without a steep learning curve. Some are calculating that knowledge is growing exponentially at such a rate that by 2010 knowledge will be doubling every eleven hours.[14] The word "career" originally meant a carriage

> **Put yourself at risk — every day. If you are not willing to risk your being — every day — then you are not committed to change that flies in the face of the establishment.**
>
> ▶ corporate consultant/author
> Tom Peters[13]

road—a clear path forward that takes you to the end of your journey.[15] There are no careers any more. The only thing that is predictable is that the average person can now anticipate eleven job changes during a typical working life. No matter what your profession or company, you will need to reinvent yourself at least every seven years.

This is where immigrants have one advantage over natives. Of necessity immigrants have learned the art of reinvention. When one has reinvented oneself once, it can be done again more easily than if one has never done it at all.

Whatever project you are working on, it is a new masters degree. I have never heard the case for continuous learning put more pungently than by Elliott Masie, President of The Masie Center:

> Higher education is the only business that has a ceremony for firing its customers. Colleges spend thousands of dollars on recruiting students, and then, after four years, those colleges make students dress up in a gown, march them across a platform, and then fire them. The only other time that happens is at an execution.[16]

If seminary education is ever to be seen as a system of lifelong learning, not a three-year event, it must break out of the classroom walls and get into the churches and communities where ministry takes place.

LOW VISCOSITY

Another survival skill is *low viscosity*. One of the key questions of any enterprise, according to Terri Lonier, is "What's the viscosity of this organization?" Low viscosity means things can move quickly. High viscosity means sludge and stagnation. A low viscosity church is a changing church and a high voltage church.[17]

When I was growing up the brag factors were "new" and "improved." The natives' brag factors are not "new" but "first"—the first trip to Europe, the first skydive, the first. . . "First" is impossible without low viscosity.

Low viscosity is hard for immigrants for a couple of reasons. First, we have been programmed to turn on/off lights, turn on/off TVs, turn on/off radios, turn on/off lifestyles. I am not programmed to leave things on. A pastor friend in Atlanta says that screensavers are the #1 nightlight in his neighborhood. I am not programmed to fathom things being left on—like computers. I have crashed more computers because I keep turning them on and off. My immigrant mentality of

> **Do you want it funny or do you want it Friday?**
> ►early Hollywood saying

"turn on/off" broadcast and "turn on/off" access can't comprehend "always on" broadband, "always on" access, "always on" lifestyles.

Second, low viscosity means a high failure rate. The immigrant mentality is expressed in the much quoted line from Apollo 13: "Failure is not an option." The native mentality is conveyed in the motto of IBM's founder, Thomas J. Watson Sr.: "The fastest way to succeed is to double your failure rate." What are you doing today to fail?

Trial and success has replaced trial and error. The church gets its leaders together, plans a program, and then rolls it out. After a conference, immigrants want to go home and implement some program. Natives want to go home and start a conversation and float some trial balloons. Better for leaders to try some initiatives, watch how things emerge, and go with what is taking off. Even a shot in the foot can become a shot in the arm. But only if the learning curve is always on.

And a double-loop learning curve at that. Single-loop learning, or lateral thinking, is all the rage among immigrants: focus groups, surveys, management-by-walking around. But the loophole in single-loop learning is its extrapolation of the present into the future rather than the opposition of the present.

> **I never wear a watch, because I always know it's *now*—and *now* is when you should do it.**
> ▶ Steve Mariucci, San Francisco 49ers head coach

In double-loop learning, there is respect for the organism as a complex adaptive system, with everything in a state of emergence and with unpredictability the norm. Simple interactions can alter the emergent order, which in turn influences the whole through successive feedback loops that spiral upward. In double-loop learning, you become smarter as you go along.

BUSY SIGNALS

Sierra Rivers is a nine-year-old Florida native, now living in Bellingham, Washington. She called her father Lex over to the phone not too long ago and asked, "Daddy, listen to this. What is it?"

Her father put the phone to his ear, and said, "Honey, have you never heard a busy signal before?"

Sierra had heard many sounds on the phone in her nine short years—answering machines, fax and modem buzzes, call waiting, multiple lines, dial tones. But never a busy signal.

Postmodern culture is getting busier than ever. But we are not giving busy signals. We are not telling people, "Sorry, I'm doing something else at the moment." We believe that it is a sin to acknowledge that we are busy. There is always room for one more thing, and we are not hearing life's recess bells.[18]

In the words of one endocrinologist, "You can have a 24-hour society, but you can't have a 24-hour body."[19] The more short-term the changes that are happening, the more long-term our consciousness and commitments need to be. Hence the project called the "Clock of the Long Now."[20]

It is a clock that ticks once a year, gongs once a century, and cuckoos once a millennium.

CLASS #4 INTERACTIVES

1 According to Graham T. T. Molitor, President of Public Policy Forecasting, we will be leaving the Information Age for the Leisure Era no later than 2015, when leisure will occupy over 50% of total individual lifetime activity.[21]

Do you think he is right? If so, does the predominance of "leisure" activity reflect a slowing down or a speeding up of the culture? Why has the "land of the free" had such a difficult time with "free time"? Are we getting any better at it?

2 "Enlightened trial and error outperforms the planning of flawless intellects." So argues David Kelley, founder and CEO of Ideo Product Development.[22]

Is your church deploying "enlightened trial and error"? If so, where? How dependent are you on centralized, permission-required planning models of movement? How "free" are you to be creative?

3 "Data Smog" is the name David Shenk has given the tsunami of information washing over us daily. "Just as *fat* has replaced starvation as this nation's number one dietary concern, information overload has replaced information scarcity as an important new emotional, social, and political problem. With virtually no effort and for relatively little cost, we can capture as much information as we want." He argues that "Data smog is not just the pile of unsolicited catalogs and spam arriving daily in our home and electronic mailboxes. It is also information that we pay handsomely for, that we *crave*—the seductive, mesmerizing quick-cut television ads and the 24-hour up-to-the-minute news flashes."[23]

What do you think about this?

4 There are over 340,000 churches in USAmerica. In 1900, there were 27 churches for every 10,000 of us. Now there are 11 churches for every 10,000 USAmericans.

How many of these churches do you think will exist in 20 years? Is the threat of "Change or Die" the best strategy for reaching these churches? One of the greatest rock climbers who pioneered ascents of Yosemite's big walls, Royal Robbins, used to say that the point is not to avoid death but to reach the top and keep on climbing. If all you wanted to do was avoid death, you should stay on the ground.

5 Check out this website for futuristic planners of meetings: *www.successfulmeetings.com.* One recent issue talks about "interactive" business and professional meetings instead of the old method of "come to be trained."

6 There are 180,000 political elections in USAmerica each year. This does not include other kinds of elections. What if you could vote online rather than in booths? When Election.com was hired to run the Democratic primary in Arizona, voter turnout soared by an unbelievable 600% over four years ago. "If you let young people vote in a medium they consider their own," contends Election.com VP Mark Strama, "they'll do it."[24]

7 Visit Election.com and discuss the potential impact of the Internet on political and governmental processes. For example, what if your local Division of Motor Vehicles went online? Or is it already?

8 Adidas has put together a website that doesn't sell sneakers but resources athletes in their training. It gives them ideas and exercises and resources for how to improve their agility, speed, and strength. Check out *www.trainingforsport.com.*
Where else do you hear natives saying, "Teach me how to get better at my sport, don't try to sell me something"?[25]

9 Samuel Johnson liked to say, "Studious to please, yet not asham'd to fail."[26]
What do you think he meant by this? Are most of us just the opposite of Johnson's motto—ashamed to fail, and indifferent about pleasing?

10 James Taylor sings, "Time may be money, but your money won't buy time."[27]
Which part of this refrain is harder for us to grasp? Or are we really understanding either?

11 "Online trading is like the Old West. The slow die first."[28]
Does this advertising slogan from Fidelity.com accurately portray the future for the church? Or can the church operate out of different rules?

12 In the business world, you used to get ten minutes to make your pitch. Now you get three PowerPoint slides to make your pitch. Which would you rather get? Can you conceive of the Gettysburg Address in PowerPoint?

13 Most of us are unaware that we go through life with a large blank spot in the middle of our visual field. Have someone research and report on this biological fact.

What are some other "blank spots" we often go through life not knowing about? Where are they?

14 Look up the Britannica website. Does anyone still have old Encyclopedia Britannica volumes? Britannica used to be the largest and most expensive mass-market publication in the world. It has reinvented itself as the largest free mass-market publication in the world. All of Britannica is now free on the Web.

So how do they make ends meet in this new economy?

15 Discuss this thesis from *The Visionary's Handbook:*

The reason a free-market economy failed in Russia was that the critical mass of Russian people were unprepared to redefine themselves: Their future is hostage to their history. The reason a free-market economy has prospered in the Czech Republic is that nearly everyone there was prepared to embrace a new definition of themselves.[29]

From "Make Sense" to "Make Sense"

For the joy of ear and eye,
For the heart and mind's delight,
For the mystic harmony
Linking sense to sound and sight.

▶Folliot S. Pierpont[1]

One of the highest compliments immigrants could pay was to say something "made sense." One of the highest compliments natives can offer is to say something as "making sense." But a universe of difference separates these two compliments.

For moderns, something "made sense" when it appealed to the intellect or could be perceived by reason. For natives, something "makes sense" when it can be experienced and felt, not just thought.

In this, natives are more "sensible" than immigrants. Up until the 18th century, "sensible" did not mean "rational" or "perceiving through the intellect" but "that which can be felt or perceived, perceptible by the senses."[2] Here is Dionysius about one of Demosthenes' speeches that "made sense:"

> When I pick up one of Demosthenes' speeches, I am transported: I am led hither and thither, feeling one emotion after another — disbelief, anguish, terror, contempt, hatred, pity, goodwill, anger, envy — every emotion in turn that can sway the human mind.[3]

This is one of the hardest things for immigrants to get through our thick skulls. We learned to dazzle people intellectually, but to dazzle people emotionally was forbidden. We learned how to be glamorous and glitzy with our reasoning, but not with our emotions. Our communication was artfully contrived in rational ways, and we were forbidden to let our minds keep step with our hearts.

Suddenly we find ourselves in a world that has returned to a more Aristotelian perspective where reason by itself is an insufficient guide to achieve wisdom without emotion and intuition.

Suddenly we find ourselves in a world where the President of Mazda Motors, James Miller, smiles at you in a television commercial (aired in Japan) and announces, "We are getting rid of three things — everyday thinking, meaningless rules, and the ordinary. Why? Because we want to move you with revolutionary ideas that stir your emotions."

Suddenly we find ourselves in a world where Cessna advertises its planes for those who don't want just to think outside the box but who want to "Live there."

Suddenly we find ourselves in a world where Sony refers to its 128-bit processor graphics chip as "The Emotion Engine," not because it can feel, but because it can generate games on the PlayStation 2 (PS2) so graphic that you will feel and relate to it emotionally.

Suddenly we find ourselves in a multimedial, multisensory world where natives learn through a rich sensorium of experiences: hearing, seeing, touching, smelling, and tasting, as well as thinking.

The triumph of writing meant the decline of nonvisual media like touch, smell, taste, and the belittling of nonverbal gestures like dance, image, and gesture. The monopoly of the written word — "Write it down," "Put it in writing" — led to the disassociation of the senses and the rational understanding of "sensible" worship.

This was not easy. Biblical religion is a participant culture featuring a unity of sensory expressions. Every Hebrew was a "performer" and "participant" who learned cultural fluency in five senses. Worship was spread across the sensory spectrum. All senses beckoned to the worship of God. God was not only heard. God was also felt, smelled, seen, and tasted.

In fact, a "make sense" world made transactions sensory. At Roman banquets, the evening was over when doves' wings were dipped in perfume from glass flasks and the doves were released. People of faith did not classify and split sensory experience; rather, they combined them synesthetically — hence, the "loud" colors, "sweet" smells, "sour" notes. In Exodus we read, "And all the people saw the thunderings, and the lightenings, and the noise of the trumpet and the mountain smoking" (Exod. 20:18 KJV). God was accorded a visual-tactile presence. Medieval supplicants felt and touched the religious image.

TEXT.TOAST

The "eye gate" and the "ear gate" are no longer enough. There must also be a smell gate, a taste gate, and a touch gate. Truth is not just for the ears, eyes, and hands. Truth is for the whole body.

Postmoderns enter the third millennium of Christian history with a high regard for feeling or sensibility and a fuzzy distinction between body and mind. Natives "feel" more than "think" their way forward. Even Harvard Medical School psychiatrists are telling of personal faith commitments in the new "make sense" terms. "My evidence for taking the fork toward faith is," writes Edward M. Hallowell, "emotional evidence. I *feel* God must be there, otherwise life makes no sense."[4]

Mine is very much an emotional relationship with what is beyond, rather than a cerebral one. I *feel*—and have felt since I was a child, listening to my mother tell me that God was everywhere—that a spirit surrounds us. I feel there *must* be a God. "Jesus loves me, this I know," the song says, and I do feel that love, but only when I let myself feel it. I have to pause and reflect for the feeling to find me. Stuck in traffic, I do not feel the love of God unless I remind myself of God. Stuck in sadness, I do not feel the love of God unless I remind myself of God. My awareness of God's love does not beat within me as automatically as my heart does, nor does it come as naturally as my breathing. I have to open up and let it in. *Then*, I feel it. But if I don't pray or reflect, I could go for days, years, probably the rest of my life without feeling the love of God. In my personal experience, God's messengers do not break down my door. I have to open the doors myself.

However, if I do open up, I feel a response. Call me crazy, as some of my friends do when I tell them how I feel about God, but I feel that the spirit, which I call God, is always near us, trying to connect.[5]

In contrast to political leaders and White House officials who mocked St. Brendan stories of dolphins protecting Elian Gonzalez, Princeton sociologist Robert Wuthnow begins his study of postmodern culture from an opposite perspective: "A contemporary sociologist like myself would never say that mystical experiences or angelic encounters are only a projection of our cultural understanding. There might well be something out there trying to communicate with us; we know we see through a glass darkly."[6]

One of my favorite historians, Simon Schama, has been criticized by fellow historians because "he seems almost deliberately to be trying to reduce historical writing to vivid impressions, appealing unabashedly to the senses instead of to the mind."[7]

Natives inhabit a new way of understanding the world and processing information about that world that is actually very old—65% of communication is received through channels other than words. Why fundamentalisms? Because they are stubbornly modern. The "old-time-religion" is big-time modernism.[8] "Old-time religion" makes sense in linear, logical, rational ways, not in EPIC ways.

The more complex our world, the greater the need for simplicity. Postmodern life is extremely complicated, and getting more so. Singapore now has "female female impersonators." The entire 1996 Canadian 4 x 100 relay team came from the West Indies. It is getting harder and harder for natives to fill out forms that ask . . . Home Address . . . Citizenship . . . Marital Status. . .

"Old-time religion" solves the double-ring riddle of simplicity and complexity by ridding itself of complexity and denying paradox in the pursuit of security through hard-and-fast doctrinal propositions. Fundamentalism is a backlash against the backlash.

COME TO OUR SENSES

Want the gospel to make sense to natives? Help natives come to their senses. Literally. For natives to savor the Spirit, they require rich emotional palettes that paint in all the colors and hit all the notes. Natives think with their eyes, ears, noses, mouths, and hands.

Copenhagen futurist Rolf Jensen has made the strongest case for the coming to our senses. Information, Jensen argues, is the domain of computers. The human language of emotion—which cannot be computerized—will become culture's most prized possession. Stories that evoke emotion will capture the hearts of the people. Stories that shun emotional resonance or what he calls "emotional jogging" will fail to move postmoderns.[9]

Companies will need to understand that their products are less important than their stories. And storytellers—specialists in the art of conveying human emotions—will need to have a voice in the design process. . . . Storytelling will even

> The best argument for Christianity is Christians; their joy, their certainty, their completeness. But the strongest argument *against* Christianity is also Christians—when they are sombre and joyless, when they are self-righteous and smug in complacent consecration, when they are narrow and repressive, then Christianity dies a thousand deaths.
> ▶ Sheldon Vanauken[10]

affect the way companies hire and retain employees. Companies will recruit people based on how they express their spirit.[11]

Alex R. Garcia-Rivera reaches back into the early history of the church in North America to offers us a parable about how to indigenize the gospel in a native culture where people live rich sensory lives:

> If Spanish became the lingua franca, the preaching of the Gospel would be unintelligible to the Mexican. On the other hand, if Nahuatl was adopted the precision of the Church's dogmatic precepts would be lost; their meaning quite possibly altered. The missionary solution to this dilemma was as creative as it was astounding. Dominican, Augustinian, Franciscan, and Jesuit missionaries all, in their own way, managed to merge Christian and indigenous signs and symbols via aesthetics. The missionary turn to an aesthetics of symbol aimed to communicate Christian concepts less with the precision of language than with the incision of the aesthetic sign. Drama, music, and paintings all were called into missionary service. As if responding to a genuine communication, the indigenous response was striking. Almost instantaneously, native Americans began to make such aesthetic and symbolic catechesis their own.[12]

What if the church was to return to a more aesthetic apologetics that soaks all the senses in the Scriptures, where the truth is conveyed through several media to several senses simultaneously? For natives the holiest moments are when ear, eye, nose, mouth, and hand come together on the same axis.

Altered Sociology of Taste and Smell

It was one of those misty Seattle days when the promise of rain permeated the air. A young woman drove up to a drive-thru fast food window and was waited on by a long-white-haired gentleman. As he handed the woman her order through the car window, he looked her straight in the eye and said, "Ah, the smell of Eternity is in the air."

The woman was struck by these words. Was the man a prophet? Were these words a revelation? Did he know something everyone else didn't? She hesitated long enough to hear the man continue to speak.

"Eternity," he repeated. "Aren't you wearing Eternity cologne?"

Pop artist Andy Warhol confessed to being a scent addict. Warhol would dedicate a particular cologne for a particular project or place, then switch to another when he moved. He saved a bottle of every scent he had ever worn. This way, every time he encountered a fragrance again, he could recall a particular time and place. "Of the five senses, smell has the closest thing to the full power of the past," Warhol wrote. "Seeing, hearing, touching, tasting are just not as powerful as smelling if you want your whole being to go back for a second to something."[13]

For apprentices of Jesus, a well-favored life is a well-flavored life. In the late middle ages it was thought that saints could be recognized by the sweet odor of their bodies. The savory media of smell and taste connect us to the spiritual resources that are our birthright.

We are selling that birthright for messes of pottage.

One advertising company has business cards with a scratch-off oval on the back that reads, "If we got you to do this, we'll get them to your site." How many scratch-and-sniff ads have lured you in? How many nine-pepper sirloins have you tried?

The eucharistic experience must bring together taste and smell in fresh combinations that can help natives "remember" their faith. In the sacrament of the Lord's Supper the five senses — sound, sight, touch, smell, taste — are in their most harmonious, melodic relation to one another.

Altered Sociology of Hearing and Seeing

An Ernst&Young ad devotes a full page to three words: "Hearing Improves Vision." From a biblical perspective, you hear a vision, you do not see a vision.

The Celtic way of evangelism was not to convert and then to join, but to join and then convert within the context of a community of faith.[14] Sanctuary Church in Santa Barbara, California, has a Celtic approach to evangelism. The pastor of this church used to be a roadie for AC/DC. Now he pioneers postmodern worship on Sunday nights from a local nightclub. "People are expected to BELIEVE, then they can BELONG," notes Barry Taylor. "At Sanctuary you BELONG just by showing up. Then we can work out and answer our questions together and perhaps you will come to BELIEVE."[15]

"Faith comes from what is heard," Paul insisted (Rom. 10:17). To disjoin hearing and seeing is to fragment faith.

The uses of sound and sight to shape spiritual experience are common throughout history, and especially common to postmoderns weaned on the screen. The kitchens of the first two decades of the 20th century were painted apple green, because color experts believed that apple green calmed the nerves and made people more placid and accepting. So why in the kitchens? Because wives were in these kitchens, wives that were being wooed away by suffragettes and social changes. That is also why in old houses under the sinks and in closets you'll see this apple green. Ditto for insane asylums and hallways of old police stations.

Altered Sociology of Touch

The lack of feeling in most of our worship experiences is palpable to natives.

It is as easy to take cheap shots at the way postmoderns are collecting things people have touched — books signed, clothes worn, artifacts used — as it is to satirize the annual hawking of wares at the Christian Booksellers Association meetings.[16] The co-owner of the Manhattan-based shop *Gotta Have It! Collectibles*, when asked why he bought a Marilyn Monroe dress for $1.3 million, said, "Because it wasn't $3 million, which we thought it was worth. . . . We stole it."[17] Displayed among the six football fields of "holy hardware" at a recent convention were bulletproof New Testaments, angel paisley neckties, the perfumed Fragrance of Jesus. In fact *The Door* issued a "Truth Is Stranger than Fiction" desk calendar containing some of the wackiest Christian products of the last 20 years — including Talking Patty Prayer Doll, Bible gum, crucifixes shaped like oil derricks (from Zales Jewelers), and Gold Cross Fragrant Pantyhose.

But any good thing can be taken too far. Devotional objects keep our faith breathing and vital; the divine becomes real through the five senses, especially touch. And natives are especially reaching for high-touch experiences that connect them to the divine spirit. Leaven has to touch something. Can anyone be healed without being touched?

How do we communicate with God? How do we savor the Spirit? With all of our senses, with the entire sensory spectrum that can express truth in multiple combinations of sound, touch, savor, and gesture.

When the bride and groom are toasted at weddings, there is the tinkling of the champagne glass because without the sound, the champagne experience would be limited to four senses. The tinkle of the glass completes the senses.

For truth to "make sense" to natives, they need that final tinkling sound.

CLASS #5 INTERACTIVES

1 Discuss this thesis: "As a culture, we are all suffering from attention deficit disorder — we are simply not getting enough attention."[18] Will "attention" — who gets it, who does not, whose websites are visited, whose are not — be a primary power currency in web civilization?

2 Jazz musician Miles Davis, when asked by a guest at the White House what he did to get himself invited, said, "Well, I've changed music five or six times."[19]

How can the church embrace change and still be itself?

Tom Bandy critiques immigrant worship in the following fashion:

Modern worship has become mere pastoral care. It is designed to attract needy, unhealthy people with low self-esteem who want experts to take care of them. Truly healthy people actually stay away from church worship in the same way that they avoid hospital emergency rooms and unemployment lines. They'll go if they must, but they don't want to do it. The liturgies are depressing, the preaching is condescending, and the people tend to be preoccupied with their own shortcomings . . . whatever that might be. The order of service prays for the needy, laments the collapse of social safety nets, promises visitation from the staff, and advertises programs to remedy personal complaints. The offering has become a monthly subscription to a dubious therapeutic technique that is not really respected by medical professionals."[20]

What part of this critique do you agree or disagree with?

4 I have a student who argues that the emerging native church will be part "coffee bar, part nightclub, part monastery, part movie theatre, part library, part playground."[21]
What do you think?

5 If the two primary constituencies of postmodern evangelism are the unchurched and the overchurched, a huge subcategory of the unchurched are those who hate church. Some examples of churches for those who hate church, called by Connie Cavanaugh "Believe It or Not Churches," are New Heights Community Church (Mission, British Columbia), Fraser Valley Baptist Church (Fraser, Colorado), and North Arundel Church (Glen Burnie, Maryland), and to these three, I will add Hillvue Heights (Bowling Green, Kentucky). [22]

Visit their websites:

New Heights (www.newheights.bc.ca/)
Hillvue Heights (www.hillvue.com/)

Or telephone for latest information:

Fraser Valley Baptist Church: (970) 726-8020
North Arundel Church: (410) 787-9893

What do they share in common? Where do they differ?

6 In church, a good cuppa' joe is hard to find. Why do you think churches are reluctant to offer their members and guests quality coffee experiences?

7   Check out the websites for alternative worship services worldwide as linked from *www.greenbelt.org.uk/altgrps/altg.html* or *www.church Net.org.uk/listings.html* (accessed 25 July 2000).

Why are there not more USAmerican churches listed? Are churches failing to take advantage of readily available electronic promotional opportunities?

8   Exegete the 1999 Virginia Slims ad: "The Eyes are the messenger of the Soul, but the Voice reveals the Spirit."

Is this a spiritual thermometer of native culture?

9   View the CD-ROM from *The Prodigal Project: Journey into the Emerging Church* by Cathy Kirkpatrick, Mark Pierson, and Mike Riddell (London: SPCK, 2000).

What new approaches to worship make you most uncomfortable? Are they the ones that appeal to natives or immigrants the most?

10   Watts Wacker talks about The Soul Catcher Project which has already proven that by "attaching a silicon chip to the optic nerve you can take a moving picture of everything a person sees throughout his or her entire life. The same can be done with smell, taste, touch, and feel. In effect, total recall is now a total reality."

Wacker goes on to "expand" the project "a small step." What if we were to "download that totally recalled conscience into a host human form." These are his questions. How would you answer them:

(a) "Are we now an alien memory occupying its body, or are we a continuation of ourselves in that new human form?"

(b) "If we are the latter and if we can repeat that downloading time and again through the centuries, layering conscience on conscience on conscience, haven't we escaped this mortal flesh and achieved immortality?"[23]

Does the Bible teach "immortality" or "eternal life"? What's the difference?

From "Who Am I?" to "What Is to Be Done?"

One half of the world cannot understand the pleasures of the other half.

▶Jane Austen, *Emma*

The question of "Who am I?" which immigrants answer in terms of what they buy, has been replaced with the question of "What is to be done?" which is answered in terms of how you invest your time and how you spend your life.

This distinction is more than the well-rehearsed comparison between luxury defined as how you spend your money and luxury defined as how you spend your time, the most prized currency in postmodern culture. The knowledge economy is an experience economy. But the ultimate experiences in life are dreams, emotions, and service, not commodities and products.

That is why the question of "Who am I?" is forged for natives in the crucible of "What is to be done?" Natives sense better than immigrants that what God wants from us is not admiration, not even imitation, but habitation and animation.

Canadian theologian Douglas John Hall has created a composite conversation out of his lifetime of students at McGill University:

"I'm not in the least interested in getting to heaven," the student says. "In fact, I'm doing everything I can to avoid it! So when I hear 'saved' people talking and singing and shouting about how great it will be when they are dead and in heaven, I have to wonder: What they must think about this life if they're so enthusiastic about wrapping it up . . . I'm also not worried about hell . . . and I don't feel all that guilty."

Professor Hall asks: "What do you feel? What do you worry about?"

The student responds: "Well, fairly often actually, [I feel] superfluous . . . Who needs me? . . . Does life have any meaning?"[1]

I am not convinced Professor Hall retrieved that last sentence as accurately as he might have. "Meaning" echoes immigrant noises. "Purpose" would be much more native. A Yankelovich survey of what we would ask of God if assured of getting a direct and immediate answer yielded 34% asking, "What's my purpose here?"[2] Just right. The difference between "Does life have meaning?" and "Does life have purpose?" is the difference between "What should I think?" and "How should I live?"

Socrates says in Book One of the *Republic of Plato*, in his discussion of the Greek word usually rendered in English as "justice" *(dikaisoune),* the just society and the just soul are, in some sense, one. In other words, "How should we live?" and "What is the just society?" are one and the same questions. What is to be done? What is my purpose here? How should I live?

Natives are answering these question in surprising ways:

Build a better neighborhood
Build better relationships
Build better families
Build a better world
Build a better environment
Build a better you

Of the three things immigrants were told never to talk about in public ("politics, religion, sex"), religion (along with sports and entertainment) trips off the native tongue at a moment's notice. Politics is not seen as worth talking about in public or private, and "sex" has been replaced by "money" as the taboo topic. Immigrants sometimes accuse natives of being apathetic or passive about justice issues. The truth is just the opposite. Natives are passionate about human betterment, but they do not see much help coming from government.

Natives are postpolitical, distrustful of political answers or structures. The assertion that "Government is the means by which we citizens express our considered judgment about our identity, our values, and our purposes back to ourselves" most likely elicits not just "Huh?" but also "Duh?"[3] Ask any broadcast manager in the country. They will tell you what they are hearing most from natives — interest in government and politics — is not what it used to be under their parents' polling. The civic habits of natives tend toward economic conservatism and libertarianism, especially cyber-libertarianism.

A bumper-sticker war says everything about the differing civic orientations of immigrants and natives. One bumper sticker announces "[Crap] is Caused." Another says "[Crap] Happens." Moderns come out of a cause-and-effect mind-set where everything that happens has a source: hence blame, guilt, and no-fault protections. Natives come out of a chaos mind-set where things happen either because of chance or for reasons that are beyond our grasp. Natives are not prone to finger-point, alibi, or play the victim. They accept personal responsibility for their choices and are disinclined to blame the social structures for the problems of the world. Technology has given them a confidence and an optimism that bursts forth in fix-it self-reliance and repeated start-ups. The fastest growing employer in the USAmerica today? Self.

Globalism has a greater impact on natives' lives than governments. In contrast to their indifferent or negative outlooks toward politics, most natives display a pragmatic outlook toward corporations as places of research, risk, and creativity. For them dollars speak louder than diplomats or guns. CEOs and dot com entrepreneurs are now more respected than presidents and senators.

Some companies are luxuriating in their new role as the primary drivers of positive social change in the world.[4] Social audits are almost as inspected as financial audits. In short, what the nation-state was to immigrants, the market-state and global city-states (New York, London, Singapore, Berlin, Paris, etc.) are to natives.[5]

Immigrant radicals feared the intrusion of government (CIA, Defense Department) into civic and university life. When I was in college there were street protests of ROTC on campus. Native radicals still protest on the streets (the washouts in Washington State and Washington, D.C.), but the protest now is focused on universities and cities finding themselves in bed with multinational corporations and international agencies and agreements.[6] One challenge of the church today is the reconception of "the language and understanding of Christian religion" in terms of its "scope and role in today's economic life."[7]

Partly because they take for granted an adequate standard of living, natives are redefining "wealth" and "success." The standards of wealth and symbols of success are less and less a corner office, silver jet, platinum card, or golden parachute. The biggest ingredients of "wealth" are relationships, values, service, justice, character, etc. What natives expect from leaders, especially religious leadership, is the communication and coaching of inner wealth, and help in distinguishing *zoe* from *bios* — the "raw material" of life (DNA) from the "good life" of beauty, truth, and goodness.

IDENTITY SIGNIFIERS

The importance of identity signifiers in this reinvented definition of wealth cannot be overemphasized. Some of these identity signifiers of wealth are:

(1) Service Mission

Fast Company insists it is not a magazine, but a movement. Natives' ideal way of creating wealth is by serving others and living beyond themselves.

The materialistically exhausted soul of the West has taught them that when "goods" become "gods," life becomes hellish. Every generation needs to learn this lesson for themselves. But natives seem to be learning it faster than their ancestors, perhaps because it has now been statistically and sociologically proven that increasing real income does not itself make people happier.[8] In fact, the richer in substance, the poorer in spirit.

The impact of people like Leadership Network founder Bob Buford in turning people "from success to significance" has been enormous. It is only by a sleight of soul that we can convince ourselves any longer that money brings happiness. We eat better than ever. We dress better, we drive better, we live better. Be we are not happier than our ancestors were. We are not more noble than they were. We are not holier than they were. We are not even smarter about the facts of life than they were. We do not love better. We do not die better.

Gladness and happiness come to those who spend their lives serving, not being served.

(2) Play Large

"Life is a Game. Play it well." This motto of GameWorks could serve as the native standard slice-of-life. Where immigrants built the modern world on knowledge (science, technology) and work (commerce), natives are building this new world on love and play.

Yahoo!'s Jerry Yang recalls an early meeting with venture capitalist Michael Moritz:

> We were talking to our venture capitalist, Mike Moritz, and he asked, "What are you going to charge for service?" We said, "Actually, we thought we wouldn't charge anything." So he asked, "Then what are you going to charge for licensing?" We said, "We thought we'd give that away free. You know, more eyeballs, building traffic and brand." Moritz looked at us and said, "So how are you going to make money?" We said, "Gee, we don't know. We were hoping you'd help us with that."[9]

Play is the central human activity of postmodern culture. A play ethic is replacing a work ethic.[10] For natives, either work is play or it is not working. Immigrants think in terms of nine-to-five. Natives create their own flexible work schedules that integrate daily life.[11] Why would you spend your life doing something (work) that you dream of "get-aways" from or plan escapes from doing? Natives are insisting work be a fulfilling and life-enhancing experience — a place where souls are enriched and enthralled.

"Played large" is replacing "worked hard" as the ultimate compliment. Of course, to play large one has to work hard, sometimes even harder than moderns worked. But natives can work hard because they are not working — they are playing. The more chaotic the culture, the more play becomes the psychological response and spiritual mechanism for navigating one's environment.

Natives would rather toy with work than let work toy with them. They are not looking for the work of a lifetime, they are looking for life missions that can bring all of their gifts into play. To be sure, some are still conceptualizing out of the work paradigm. Christian Schumacher, son of E. F. Schumacher, has written a book arguing that the three divine functions of the Trinity are the same as those in work: planning, doing, and evaluating.[13] But by and large, metaphors of play have replaced work as the dominant postmodern pattern.

> **Good's not good enough.
> Play with the line. Turn it around, and see what happens. Try taking a stress away; change tense, loosen the rhythm. Shake the words up.**
> ▶ poet Sheenagh Pugh's advice to creative-writing students[12]

The poetics of postmodernity is a poetics of play.

(3) Aliveness

What's better than being rich? Being spontaneous, authentic, connected. Being alive. Being *you*. Half alive is half true.

Nike now stitches your own name on your sneakers, next to the swoosh where Michael Jordan's name used to be. Go to Nike.com. Pick the colors you want, and select the name (up to eight letters) you want on there. Reebok's Traxtar — a sneaker for 6–11-year-olds that features a microprocessor unit in the shoe's tongue — measures your personal running and jumping skills. When you accomplish goals you have set for yourself, lights flash and your sneaker tongue plays "Pomp and Circumstance."

You can even compete with other kids for gold, silver, or bronze medals, all showcased on the shoe's tongue.

Being alive and being authentically you are one and the same thing. Natives cherish idiosyncracies. Whatever is wild and whacky about you is part of your aliveness. You matter to God. You are unique. Your soul is unlike anyone else's in the universe.

No matter how raspy or nasal or grating, natives prize the authentic voice.

Julia Butterfly Hill spent 738 days living in the redwood tree Luna to protest the clear-cutting of old-growth redwoods. When asked about her impressions of someone who visited her to disagree with her, she replied, "I truly appreciated the fact that he was real, even if his reality was very different from mine."[14]

Natives expect others to be real, even if their reality is different or weird. Natives do not prize idealized images. They value images of real people doing real things. This is one reason network television is losing its native viewers. The combined share of television viewers ABC, CBS, and NBC can boast has plummeted from 50% to 23% over the past 20 years.[15] Hence the emergence of "reality" TV — documentaries, authentic soap operas, if you will.

Paul Wartman is the lead pastor of Winnipeg's The Meeting Place. In his welcome to visitors, he invites them to bring their coffee into the sanctuary: "We have coffee stains all over the carpet. Add yours to it." Authenticity and participation are cherished over appearances and arrangements.

The laughter of God's love is the most authentic voice of all. The average 5-year-old laughs about 150 times a day; the average 45-year-old laughs eight times a day.[16] Immigrants laugh until their sides split; natives laugh until their tatoos roll and their piercings ache.

The quest for "aliveness" is what is causing such a run on rural "Valhallas" and small towns. The shift of cultural gravity away from suburbs to rural areas and small towns is exemplified in the fastest growing cities in USAmerica — those with populations of 10,000 to 50,000. Mesquite, Nevada, grew from 1,871 in 1990 to 10,125 in 1998. Particular hot spots include Frisco, Texas; Fishers, Indiana; Lake in the Hills, Illinois.[17] The Red Hot Chili Peppers launched their 2000 tour in Minneapolis in March. But instead of going from there to other big cities, they camped out in the hottest real estate markets of the future — college towns (Madison, Wisconsin; Carbondale, Illinois; Champaign, Illinois; Columbus, Ohio; Amherst, Massachusetts; Albany, New York; State College, Pennsylvania; Roanoke, Virginia; Bloomington, Indiana).

In Santa Fe, houses on unpaved roads bring higher prices than houses on paved ones. In Phoenix, one housing development features a climbing wall, skating park, roller-hockey rink, children's railroad, four-acre fishing lake, and 30 acres of sports fields. Retirement is now to small towns or rural areas with another home in the city.[18] In the words of one native, "I have no plans to retire, ever, to that elephant graveyard for humans known as Florida, or to that bone-bleaching works called Arizona."

There is a Mexican saying: "La vida es corta, pero ancha." Translated into English, "Life is short, but wide."

> **Imagine there's no countries**
> **It isn't hard to do**
> **Nothing to kill or die for**
> **And no religion too**
> ▶ John Lennon, "Imagine," stanza two voted the most popular lyrics of the 20th century[19]

There is a lot more room in your life than you think. Natives want their lives to take up as much space as the room will allow.

(4) Global Wheeling-and-Dealing

Paul Wayland is one of the most faithful members of Royal Palms Baptist Church in Phoenix, Arizona. He seldom misses worship or Sunday school and serves his church in a variety of capacities. But Paul Wayland lives in Iowa. He drives to church in his 18 wheeler. His route brings him to Phoenix every weekend, and after services on Sunday night he hits the road for Yuma.

For people like Wayland, the world is their playground. Immigrants have been trained to think in terms of neighborhood and national sovereignty. Natives do not think national as much as they think global and tribal. When they do think national, it is less the United States of America and more the United States of the Earth. When they do think sovereign, it is the sovereign individual over the sovereign state.

The planetary interests of humanity in general are transcending national sovereignty. The growing rate of unifying international processes and institutions are leaving the separate, sovereign state behind.[21] In the European Common Market, nations gave up sovereignty for better economic status. The International Monetary Fund controls political agendas of nations while the UN and NATO intervene in internal affairs. Consider the pace of

> **Relations between nations can no longer be founded on respect for sovereignty—they must be founded on respect for human rights.**
> ▶ Bronislaw Geremek, Poland's foreign minister[20]

international interventions in northern Iraq (1991), Somalia and former Yugoslavia (1992), Haiti (1993–94), etc.

Centralized nation-states ruled by uniform rules of bureaucratic rationality are spinning apart, with the former Soviet Union now 15 nations split along ethnic boundaries. Pico Iyer says that the nation-state is giving way to the deracination-state—where refugees are one of the growth industries.[22] The decline of the politics of national identity is given graphic prominence in UNESCO's *World Social Science Report 1999*, which is organized according to regions not nations.[23]

The Millennium Eve television specials gave everyone an experience of how arbitrary those national boundary lines are on planet Earth.

In the future, it will not just be celebrities like Anthony Hopkins or Canadians who will enjoy dual (soon multiple) citizenships.[24]

Immigrants now come to Western countries, less to become Englishmen, Frenchmen, Canadians, USAmericans, but to become better residents of a global village. Politics is now personality-based, but the personalities are global and can become bigger than the politics. Phil Mickelson won a golf tournament. But the headlines read: "Tiger Woods Loses." Tiger Woods losing is bigger news than anyone else winning.

In a global culture, where CNN can be watched in over 200 countries, where Bart Simpson is a hit in Calcutta, *Wheel of Fortune* tops the charts in Nairobi, and *Who Wants to Be a Millionaire* is everywhere, there is the opposite end of the paradox of the One and the All: the hyper-tribal/hyper-individual.

The Sovereign Individual has replaced the Sovereign State. Buckminster Fuller predicted this decentralization of power into individuals and named it "desovereignization."[25] The power of one person, for good or ill, is not lost on natives.[26]

The nation-state is a modern construct, along with various "nationalisms." But tribal values like Irishness or Scottishness are longstanding. It was the nation that took over from the tribe to give expression to such feelings. Now it is devolving back to the tribe. Natives live more in tribes than in nations or neighborhoods.[28]

> **It is undeniable that the centuries-old doctrine of absolute and exclusive sovereignty no longer stands. A major intellectual requirement of our time is to rethink the question of sovereignty.**
> ▶ Boutros Boutros-Ghali, former Secretary-General of the United Nations[27]

The person living next to you may be from an entirely different world, literally. Immigrants were divided by geography and demographics.

Natives are divided without any reference to geography or proximity to each other. One's neighborhood (where one lives) and one's community (social circle) used to be the same. Now they are both decentralized. One lives in many places. One can be a part of many tribes.

Regional differences mean less and less. In its place are values, voluntary loyalties, and common devotions, means of locomotion in the world, brand names, "lifestyle markets," and consumption patterns. Emily Eelkema, former director of Experian's global micromarketing division, contends that

> There are neighborhoods in Manhattan that are more similar to ones in Milan than in Brooklyn. . . . The yuppie on the Upper East Side of New York has more in common with a yuppie in Stockholm than a downscale person in Brooklyn. The neighborhoods in Fargo, North Dakota, are very similar to Freisland in the Netherlands as well as Calabria in southern Italy. From a day-to-day perspective, their lifestyles, attitudes, motivations, and products are all very similar. They're more provincial and connected with family and friends.[29]

A native's social circle is in multiple geographic spaces, including online. There are over 400,000 communities on the Web, from antique cameras to jadite tableware to Rush Limbaugh lovers and haters.

USAmerica is becoming more diverse and more tribal than ever before. In California, whites are now the minority for the first time since the 1849 Gold Rush. Latinos now outnumber "Anglos" in Los Angeles, also known as "Mexico's second city." Yet Los Angeles also has a Salvadorean population larger than that of San Salvador.

Latinos now comprise 27% of Chicago's population. There are as many Latino people in the US as African-Americans. Already 200 US counties have a "minority majority" (i.e., their combined non-white and Hispanic populations exceed non-Hispanic white population). Thirty-two different languages are spoken by students at Hollywood High School. California Baptists worship in 55 different languages.[30] "Today, the country's new motto should be e pluribus pluriba," Michael J. Weiss contends: "out of many, many."[31] The melting pot has melted.

In a world where both diverse subcultures and a common global culture are replacing national cultures, natives will increasingly need to be both multilingual and experts in World English. There is the need for multilingualism in order for us to process diverse perspectives and insights. Fourteen percent of US residents age five and older speak a language other than English at home. There are now specialty telephone directories for non-English speaking citizens (Spanish, Japanese, Chinese, Korean, Hebrew) as well as for gays, women, African-Americans, military bases, universities, etc.

But there is also the need for a common universal language to facilitate connectedness and understanding. The three most widely spoken languages in the world are Mandarin Chinese, English (the world's most widely spoken second language), and Spanish. These are the three world languages of the future. As of today, World English is the language of the new global economy. More than half of the world's population (projected at 8 billion people) will have competence in English by 2050.[32]

English may be the new *lingua franca*, but we will all have local accents. Some of these accents will be geographic — Slovakian, Spanish, Mississippian, Minnesotan. Some of these accents will be cultural — a hip-hop fan speaks a different language than a punk-rocker, an art collector speaks a different language than a beanie-baby collector. These languages of local accents will be the *lingua* of art, literature, sports, etc. This will have far-reaching consequences, since ethnicity is now based more on language than on location.

There is no single blueprint for what it means to be human or to speak with a human voice. There is no single blueprint for what it means to be Christian and to speak with a Christlike voice. You recognize it when you hear it, but that voice is as different as everyone speaking it.

BRIDGE THE DIGITAL DIVIDE

Incomes of the rich are booming, while incomes of the bottom tier are flattening or falling. The wealthiest 20% of humanity is 135 times richer than the poorest 20%.[33] The 19th century began with a three to one ratio of real incomes per capita between the world's richest and poorest countries. By 1900, it was ten to one. By 2000, it had risen to sixty to one.[34] In a highly connected world, huge inequalities pose more dangers than they did in the past.

> **In that which we share, let us see the common prayer of humanity. In that in which we differ, let us wonder at the freedom of humankind.**
> ► Jewish prayer

Sudden Wealth Syndrome is an unprecedented problem. Never in human history have so many people become so rich so fast. USAmerican tax rolls now boast 300 billionaires and 7 million millionaires.[35] From 1982 to 2000, the USAmerica went from 2 million with household incomes over $100,000 to over 9 million. The masses are becoming rich. Housing costs are soaring to the point where an employed person making $60,000 in Silicon Valley can end up in a homeless shelter. More than half the 1,100 residents of the Emergency Housing Consortium in Cupertino, California, are employed.

When the rich and the poor are headed in opposite directions, one is venturing on a volcano. It is only a matter of time until social unrest erupts in violence. One can already hear the gasps from both sides of the gap:

We live in an insecure world, a world threatened by violence, lack, and spiritual malaise. . . . The world doesn't even work for the materially privileged. Increasing uncertainty, family violence, cancer, a polluted environment, and a diminished outlook for all of the world's children cloud the future for us all.[36]

In his acceptance speech as the winner of the 2000 Templeton Prize, Princeton professor Freeman J. Dyson asserted, "The great question for our time is, how to make sure that the continuing scientific revolution brings benefits to everybody rather than widening the gap between rich and poor."[37] The church's role in making "universal access" the rallying cry of the future, in ending "digital apartheid" and making sure that every person, every country, has a piece of the high-tech pie, looms larger with every passing day. The church must update Aristotle's definition of justice: Making sure that each child gets his or her due.

> **We cannot create a heaven inside and leave a hell outside, and expect to survive.**
> ▶ Clement Attlee

One restaurant in *Gourmet* magazine advertises a set-price meal for $860 per person and a shot of Bowmore scotch for $920 ($7,000/bottle if you prefer).

A visibly angry passenger next to me in Continental's Business First Class section uses his airphone to fire his travel agent because she did not put him in First First Class. Business First wasn't "first" enough.

The outcry of the poor will crescendo in the future until it deafens everyone.

What would "a world that works for all" look like? Sharif Abdullah proposes three criteria: enoughness, exchangeability, and common benefit.[38]

Enoughness

Does _____ have enough? Not an equal sharing of resources, but sufficiency for everyone? Not just "things," but love, life, oxygen, etc.

Natives are on the brink of building their world on a hydrogen economy like immigrants built their world on a fossil-fuel economy. Because they run on hydrogen from the air, hydrogen batteries run without recharging. And if natives can produce hydrogen using renewable sources like solar power, the only by-product is clean water.

Exchangeability

Would you trade places with _____? Since there is no national economy, only one global economy, how do we help the poor become "players" in the global market economy? Since those gasping for breath in the new economy will be forced to move into the 21st century slums — the suburbs — would you live there with them?

The biggest cause of the digital divide is the inability to read. In many cases the issue is less one of no access to technology, than one of no reading skills which prevents people from participating in the new economy. Three-quarters of 10-year-olds in the poorest public schools have not yet begun to read or write. The illiteracy rate among 17-year-old USAmerican youth is one in seven.

Would you send your kids to these school systems?

Ironically, the business world is more active in mentoring programs and literacy workshops than the church. Computer Clubhouse is where kids from the streets can learn from technology mentors. The Countdown 2000, Get Connected campaign conducted by the Urban League was enormously successful. What is your church's computer technology doing after office hours? Why not redeploy it to teach kids how to use computers? Make it into a computer lab.[39] Or why not make your office equipment available to members to use instead of having to go to Kinkos?

Common Benefit

Was the system designed to benefit _____? It is hard to find someone on the planet who has not gained from the new knowledge. But these gains have not been equitably shared. The Goldilocks Economy — rapid growth, low unemployment, and subdued inflation — is not universal, but everyone should benefit from it and our goal should be to make rising living standards universal.

> **Capitalism is to economics what democracy is to politics, the best of all possible inadequate systems.**
> ▶ Joseph Epstein[40]

If "stakeholding" is the master metaphor for the 21st century, the universal "stake" will be access to the Web.[41] Internet access is the new right of citizenship. It is not a privilege, but a universal right. In 2000 Ford Motor Company and Delta Air Lines took a first step in this direction. Both companies gave their employees (Ford–350,000; Delta–72,000) home personal computers and Internet access, thereby linking everyone around the globe in the first "boundaryless organizations."

A NONMONOPOLY GAME

One way immigrants have learned the ins and outs of capitalism is by playing the board game Monopoly. Few people realize that the game of Monopoly started out as a moral tale that critiqued the unfettered pursuit of capital. Monopoly's predecessor was The Landlord's Game, invented in Maryland by a Quaker woman Lizzie Magie who wanted to unmask, not to commend, capitalism. Magie's game sent greedy landlords who charged unfair rents straight to jail.

The new Monopoly version of The Landlord's Game was copyrighted by a heating engineer of Germantown, Pennsylvania, who originally used the names of streets of Atlantic City (with a notorious misspelling, "Marvin Gardens," for "Marven Gardens"). By the time the rights of Quaker Magie were bought out, Monopoly had become a parable not of a chastened capitalism, but of sheer financial success. As such it was forbidden in Nazi Germany and in Stalin's Russia. It is still banned today in China, North Korea, and Cuba.[42]

Perhaps it is time for a more "original" version of Monopoly that helps us set life in a more spiritual frame than Monopoly sees it. Perhaps it is time for a more humane capitalism that transcends the latest CEO's pet preferences or interests.

Let it not be said that those who can do the most did the least.

CLASS #6 INTERACTIVES

1 "Profits are like breathing. You need it to live, but it's not what you live *for*."

Discuss this statement by Andy Law, Chair and Cofounder of Britain's St. Luke's advertising agency.[43] Do you see hard evidence in the business world that this is more than just a wish or whim? What business people do you know who can say this with a straight face?

2 Do you agree with the notion that the digital divide is not so much a question of access but of education? If it is true as Esther Dyson observes that "You can put computers in community centres, but only the literate people are likely to go use them," what do you think of *The Economist*'s survey suggestion to make the most convenient way of obtaining welfare benefits be online? Would this be incentive enough to get those on the "wrong side of the digital divide" to use the Web.[44]

3 Jane Smiley, in her novel *Horse Heaven* (2000), summarizes the "division of labor" in many marriages of the wealthy as follows: "He earned all day every day and she spent all day every day."[45]

Have you known people like this? How many people dream of such a life? What kind of a life is this? What would Jesus say to such people?

4 Imagine what it must have been like when Proctor & Gamble's marketing department included Steve Case, Steve Ballmer, Intuit's Scott Cook, ebay CEO Meg Whitman, and ebay COO Brian Swette (pronounced "Sweetie").

What are you doing to bring together "Dream Teams" in your business and your church?

5 Play the song called "The Lost Chord" by Adelaide A. Procter. What would "The Lost Church" sound like? What would it look like? Would it be a church of good intentions, a roster of programs well planned, but at the end of the day, at the end of the year, there is little to show for its efforts?

In what way does this true story about one of the great battles of the Civil War find its parallel in the church?

> One of the turning points in the American Civil War was the battle of Vicksburg, the last major Confederate stronghold on the Mississippi River. The two commanding generals were Grant for the north and Pemberton for the South. In *The Lost Cause*, Pollard, the Southern historian, tells how Grant laid siege to the heavily fortified city. He kept mounting assault after assault until finally the defenses were broken. What was Pemberton doing all this time? He was, Pollard tells us, "immersed in official trifles, laboriously engaged in doing nothing."[46]

 6 What exactly is church historian Dale T. Irvin suggesting here?

> Most global-minded Christians today are properly cautious about uncritically extolling the civilizing values of Christian mission apart from a more self-critical appraisal. Many of us who celebrate the value of "contextualizing the faith" in other parts of the world are uneasy about aspects of the contextualizations going on at home. The cultural accommodation of many Western churches looks to some of us to be nothing short of a sign of their bankruptcy.[47]

What would a "contextualized" faith look like in the context of USAmerican culture? Would it have one "look"?
Is there one single future, or many futures?

7 HungryMinds.com had a "Multihat Award" that went to the employee who has had the most job descriptions. The record was five in less than a year.

Who would get the "Multihat Award" in your church/organization?

Check out Helping.org with its links to 620,000 nonprofits where you can donate funds or time.

The very forces providing the momentum behind the new economy are also producing cultural violence (Battle for Seattle), environmental destruction, and social disease. GCT stands for global chaos theory. GCT says that increasing globalization will lead to eruptions of guerilla warfare, terrorism, and protest. Yet Ferdinand Mount wonders whether "What we need . . . is less global chaos theory and more local chaos theory," since what seems to be going on is less a "clash of civilizations *between* the advanced West and the emerging cultures" and more "fratricide *within* those emerging cultures, of ethnic conflicts and civil wars, in which the West is mostly a puzzled observer."[48]

What do you think about this thesis?

 The medical center of the future will be a reinvented spa. Do you think this is an accurate statement?

Rent the movie *American Pie* (1999, R rated—I am assuming your group is over 21), and track three of the stars in particular: Thomas Ian Nicholas, Seann Scott, and Chris Klein.

When the movie is over, tell your group that these three "stars" are devout Christians who witness boldly about their faith to nonbelievers.[49] Let the discussion begin.

In their study of the church's interface with corporate life, researchers Laura Nash and Scotty McLennan reveal the degree to which churches do not care about the personal spirituality of business professionals.[50] Do you see this in your own church?

 Here is one CEO's opinion of clergy:

Theological training is important, not that I know much about it. . . . My pastor's training in the biblical area is terrific. Get him going on a Bible passage and he knows incredible things. But as soon as you get him on real issues, he's hopeless. He just doesn't understand how the world works, and worse, he thinks he has to be an authority on everything. I just cringe.[51]

Do you agree with this assessment?

Vietnam combat vet James Kimsey, founder and retired chair of America Online, the man who hired Steve Case to run the company back in 1983, established a fund at the Kennedy Center for the Performing

Arts so that any fifth grader in Washington, D.C. who wants to go to any event there can go free of charge.

What similar things could you or your church do to bridge the gaps?

15 As an exercise in probing the "digital divide," compare these two websites. One for Palo Alto, California, *(www.city.palo-alto.ca.us)* and the other for East Palo Alto, California *(www.pe.net/~rksnow/cacounty eastpaloalto.htm)*.

The former is the heart of Silicon Valley and home to dot com millionaires where the average house sells for nearly $700,000, the highest in North America.

The latter is on the other side of Highway 101 and boasts North America's highest murder rate.

Palo Alto's website has 251 sections and is a model of e-government. Among many other things, it allows users to send forms to the planning department and search the city's library catalogue. During storms, it even provides live video footage of flood-prone San Francisquito Creek.

How many pages does East Palo Alto's site contain?

Naturalization Class **7**

From Sharp to Fuzzy

They want somebody to tell 'em they have a
chance at the i-n-g of life and not just the e-d.

▶ Wiggs in Tom Robbins's *Jitterbug Perfume*[1]

Immigrants inhabited an Either/Or world. "Fuzzy" was negative. Natives inhabit an And/Also world. "Fuzzy" is positive.

To an immigrant academic, one of the worst put-downs is to be accused of "woolly reasoning" or "flaky thoughts" or "fuzzy thinking." In this native world, the highest logic is fuzzy logic. The best computers are fuzzy computers.

Without "sponge terms" — words with multiple and sometimes opposite meanings — natives cannot describe the world around them, filled with blurred genres, messy categories, multiple identities, no pure constructs, or ideal types. In fact, some moderns even admit that "fuzzy" could be more than just an add-smoke-and-mirrors strategy. Wasn't it Edmund Burke's maxim that a clear idea is a little idea?

Sociologists refer to identities as either vertical or horizontal. Vertical identities include social class, educational achievement, geographic location. Horizontal identities, however, are multiple and can cut close to the heart of who we are (a member of a cat club, an antique collector, NRA supporter, etc.). In the words of one fuzz theorist, "Fuzz gives up simple claims to certainty. Fuzz does not make us choose between the claims that the sky is blue or that it is not blue. Fuzz lets us say that the sky is both blue and not blue to some degree."[2] Fuzzy categories let us inhabit both vertical and horizontal identities.

FUZZY WUZZY

Metal must have two opposite poles to become magnets. Natives are not magnetized without the bringing together of opposites into a magnetic center. Paradox can create paralysis among immigrants. However, paradox is the second nature of natives. They find the ends with more contradictions than completions. In fact, natives have a near-fatal attraction for paradox—a fuzzy both/and-ness that is woven into the tapestry of the universe, a world in which matter is both particle and wave, a world comprised of both matter and antimatter.

REVERSE CURRENTS

The most dangerous, turbulent waters are those in which ocean currents mix with wind patterns to create reverse currents below the surface. The waves go in one direction, but the waters beneath go in another. The water on the surface is still and easy to read, but under the surface the waters are dangerously spinning.

In postmodern culture, reverse currents cannot be avoided. Natives cannot escape dealing with stillness and spinning, convergence and divergence at the same time. According to the "super" component of superstring theory, every particle has a partner particle. Is it convergence or divergence when Internet access appears on PCs, digital TV, microwaves, mobile phones, etc? It is both everything coming together and going apart at the same time.

> **It is good to hold on to the one thing and not lose hold of the other; for someone who fears God will succeed both ways.**
> ▶ Ecclesiastes 7:18 REB

Opposites are now umbilically bound to each other. Watts Wacker, who has explored what I call the "double ring" phenomenon more fully than anyone, warns leaders that "Every condition, every news story, every new human event comes slamming into town or onto the television screen or into the newspaper with its opposite firmly in tow, and the only choices we have are to go mad, die laughing, or try to live inside the contradictions."[3] Wacker explains our future where anything can happen and everything happens at once in terms of the exponential pace of change:

The acceleration in the rate of change coupled with the acceleration and massification of input has created a state of seemingly permanent paradox. A condition and its negation, a set of data and its apparent contradiction, a course of action and its own anticourse, no longer arrive incrementally or

sequentially; they arrive instanta-
neously and simultaneously, and
because they do, there is no time to
resolve the difference between them
by traditional methods. The space
between seeming opposites — physical space, psychological space,
space in time and emotion and
logic — has shrunk so dramatically
in the last decade that every condition, every course of action, every possibility has come to be permanently juxtaposed between its own polarities.[4]

> **The less you have on the inside, the more you need on the inside.**
> ► Clarence Jordan, founder of Koinonia Farm

Here is a baker's dozen of the reverse currents natives are riding:

(1) Drug commercials advertise the healing properties of certain pharmaceuticals . . . while simultaneous subtexts warn of devastating
potential side effects ("bowel disfunction," "impotence," etc.).
(2) Why is North America becoming addicted to wrestling, now the
most popular sport among natives? Because the WWF is an "hon-
est fake." Vince McMahon transitioned WWF from a "sport" to
"sport entertainment." WWF is the native version of a soap
opera.
(3) USAmerica is the world's biggest headache . . . and the world's
biggest hope.
     For the first time in the history of civilization, more people are
living in freedom and democracy than in tyranny, terror, and dic-
tatorship.
     Yet images of unfeeling fortune fly in the face of guileless
poverty. The ranks of US millionaires are swelling at the rate of
16% per year. In 1999, 7.2 million people topped the seven-fig-
ure mark in liquid assets, up from 3.4 million five years before.
Those worth over $5 million are increasing at a 46% annual clip.[5]
     On 25 May 1961, President John F. Kennedy spoke these
words:

> I believe that this nation should commit itself to achieving the
> goal, before this decade is out, of landing a man on the moon
> and returning him safely to Earth.[6]

Thus the Apollo Project was born. It culminated on 19 July
1969 with the first landing of men on the moon in Apollo 11.
Between these four years, July 1969 (Apollo 11) and December
1972 (Apollo 17), there were six landings of men on the moon.
     No one has been there since.

How was this done? The mobilization of the entire nation and the expenditure of huge sums of money: 2% of the US national income. The private sector started making things never before imagined.

Once people are presented with a dream that engages the heart as well as the mind, they do it!

What if the dream were a global dream that connected the best to the least?

(4) Christianity is declining in the West . . . and burgeoning around the world.

The numbers of atheists, agnostics, or nonreligious have gone from 0.2% of the planet Earth population in 1900 to 18.3% of the global population in 2000. In the UK, church-going Anglicans (4%) are outnumbered by those who used to be called "infidels."[7] USAmerica has more atheists and agnostics than it does Mormons, Jews, or Muslims.[8]

At the same time, there is massive growth of Christianity in Russia, Latin America, West Africa, and China. What some are calling "the greatest revival in history" is taking place today in China — one of the most atheistic and Christ-hating of regimes in history.[9]

There are 523 million charismatics/Pentecostals in the world today. It is impossible any longer to ignore this "Third Force" or "Third Stream" of Christendom. Some are calling it "a new expression and form of Christian faith and life."[10] Others call Pentecostals "populist mystics" (Harvey Cox) or "Catholics without priests" (historian Jean-Pierre Bastian). Harvard theologian Cox, who understands this movement better than most, notes that

> In Brazil on any given Sunday, more people are worshiping in Pentecostal churches than in Catholic churches. It is becoming evident . . . that the venerable old term "Christendom" has become obsolete. The majority of Christians are now black, brown, or yellow and live outside the Western world.[11]

(5) Our ethics are becoming more prudish . . . and more permissive.

Allan Bloom became the darling of conservatives because he took on intellectual, social, and sexual permissiveness and moral ugliness.[12] Bloom's best friend, novelist Saul Bellow, has written a thinly veiled novelistic biography of Bloom's life as a closeted gay who died of AIDS.[13] Bellow himself is 84 and fathered his fourth child at 83.[14]

(6) The more we lionize our heroes . . . the more we demonize them.

It has recently been uncovered that Thomas Jefferson, the author of the Declaration of Independence and a chief architect of the United States of America, had two families, enabling his living descendants to claim as ancestors both a president and a slave. Jefferson enjoyed a secret 20-year relationship with his slave Sally Hemmings, who bore him six (not one, but six) children.[15]

Tyler Cowen asks "What Price Fame?" His answer:

> The modern image of a leader is not Theodore Roosevelt charging up a hill, but rather Jimmy Carter fighting off a rabbit with a canoe paddle, Gerald Ford stumbling and bumping his head, or George Bush vomiting in the lap of the Japanese prime minister. Bill Clinton will be defined forever by his handling of the Monica Lewinsky affair. These images demystify power and produce a culture of disillusionment with politics and moral *leadership.*[16]

(7) The people of planet Earth are getting fatter . . . while the people of planet Earth are starving to death.

In 2000, half the world's population are struggling with obesity, while 1.3 billion people live on less than a dollar a day. Half the world's population (more than 3 billion people) are without telephone service, and one third of the people of the world have never even placed a phone call.[17] The combined assets of the world's three richest men (Bill Gates, Warren Buffett, Paul Allen) exceed by almost $20 billion the total GNP of the 43 poorest nations, which have a population of 600 million.[18]

By the way, the poorest people in USAmerica?

Elderly widows.

The richest people in USAmerica?

Elderly widows. The average person who receives a social security check, I suspect, has more assets than the average person who pays social security taxes.

(8) The greater the material fullness . . . the greater the spiritual emptiness.

Federal Reserve Board Chairman Alan Greenspan told Harvard University graduates in 1999 that they were embarking on "a material existence that neither my generation nor any that preceded it could have even remotely imagined."[19] "The average American today," George Gilder observes, "lives better than the millionaires of the 1800s."[20]

> **What does it profit . . . if you gain the whole world but lose your soul?**
> ► Jesus (paraphrase of Matthew 16:26)

The more material wealth, the greater the sense of spiritual poverty. Material overconsumption and spiritual malnourishment seem to go together. That is why this new gilded age can be a gospel age.

What are the greatest needs of the world? What are its deepest hungers?

It is for things of the spirit.

(9) The more we punch the accelerator . . . the more we need to slam on the brakes.

The Fast Lane requires Curb Service.

Leaders of the "back-to-basics" and simplicity movements are often not neo-Luddites, but high-tech pioneers. Some schedule "gadget-free gatherings" for staff; others flee to rural life and start farms. Still others, some the most wired and influential web-heads in Silicon Valley, go off the grid when they are at home. "You have to be able to tune the Silicon Valley stuff out or you forget what's going on in the rest of the world," explains one CEO who does not even have electricity in his five-room home overlooking Palo Alto and Mountain View.[21] After living with high-tech gadgets most of the day, some natives want their home life to be radically different. "I don't need more stimulation at home. I already get plenty of that at work," says one CEO.[22]

> **Seat belts should be connected at all times, even when the seat belt light is off.**
> ▶ official American Airlines policy

Business guru Tom Peters puts the need for down time like this: "The more convergence converges on me, the more I need LOTSA space To Think. To Exist. To make a difference."[23]

But beware: The more "free time" we have, the more time pressure we feel.

(10) Business culture is moving towards higher and higher centralization . . . and deeper and deeper decentralization. "Concentrated deconcentration" (the Dutch phrase) means that you centralize the communications and decentralize the operations. As the world becomes more globalized and localized at the same time, some areas need more, not less integration — for example, global standards in banking, accounting, law, etc. Even those opposing globalized structures (IMF, WTO, WB) in favor of localization cannot escape these reverse currents. Here is the closing sentence of Naomi Klein's *No Logo* (2000), her call-to-arms for "a citizen-centered alternative to the international rule of the brands":

That demand, still sometimes in some areas of the world whispered for fear of a jinx, is to build a resistance — both high-tech and grassroots, but focused and fragmented — that is as global, and as capable of coordinated action, as the multinational corporations it seeks to subvert.[24]

But at the same time, the more highly centralized one's operation, the more truly decentralized one needs to be. The chief executive of the most global brand in the world, Coca-Cola, has a new motto. Douglas Daft says that if Coca-Cola is to become a truly global player, it must "think local, act local."[25]

(11) The world is becoming more urbanized . . . and ruralized.

Almost half the world now is urbanized. By 2005, for the first time in human history, more people will live in cities than in the country.

Yet in more developed areas ruralization is taking place at a higher rate than urbanization. The romance of rurality is stronger than ever. The world's affluent are able to do both urbanization and ruralization at the same time — with a home in the city and periodic headings for the hills. Empty-nester immigrants and natives (especially single professionals) are rushing to the cities, giving them a "face-lift," upping property values and forcing new arrivals in the US to head to the suburbs.[26]

Distance may be dead, but place has never been more important.[27]

(12) The greater the complexity of the system . . . the greater the need for simplicity.

In *The Visionary's Handbook* (2000), Watts Wacker and Jim Taylor attempt to explain the emergence of a global syrup (Coke) and a global sandwich (Big Mac) in a choice culture:

What do we do with all that information, all those choices, all that connectivity? We choose our own reality and we simplify. From among the tens of thousands of possible soft drinks we could choose, we choose the one that requires the least thinking: Coke.

> **Neither more, nor more onerous, causes are to be assumed than are necessary to account for the phenomena.**
> ▶ Ockham's Razor[28]

From among the thousands of fast-food franchises we could stop at, we stop at the one that delivers the most predictable promise:

McDonald's. It's not connectivity that creates global branding. It's the fact that brands penetrate information spaces and edit for us. They allow us to disconnect from connectivity, and that's what makes them transcendent across reality barriers.[29]

The MIT media lab built software agents that were so complex that people did not trust them and thus did not use them. Keep software simple, says MIT scientists.

Ockham's Razor instructs us to get rid of the extraneous, get back to the basics. The more complex the world, the more simple the rules.

The irony bulks large: The integrated circuit, the most complex thing humans have created, is made up of the most plentiful and simple things in nature — sand, oxygen, water, and fire.

It is the same with the life of faith. The more a status quo is replaced by a fluxus quo, the more our values need to stay the same. In a world where everything changes, our center cannot change. In a world where the edges are getting softer, our core needs to be harder than ever.

So what is our core value? Jesus the Christ is our Core, our All-in-All Center.

(13) The more life is lived on screen and in cyberspace . . . the more life is spent "LIVE."

Far from replacing face-to-face encounters, electronic culture requires more face time and more reality. If there is one thing we have learned from the Age of Television, it is that screen time does not diminish the hunger for face time. Rather, the opposite holds true. The more you are online, the more demand there will be for your physical presence. How do you like it when an automated teller prints out "thank you." You know the ATM machine is not grateful. In fact, it makes you yearn all the more for a human "thank you."[30] The more you get to know someone electronically, the more you find ways to meet them in person. Cyber-living enhances the need for "the feel of friction" or what Esther Dyson calls "texture." Hence the time natives spend on the edge of thrill seeking and risk taking: BASE jumping,[32] snow-boarding, ice climbing, skateboarding, para-gliding.

> We have to learn to live in a world in which multiple realities are both true and reliable. And yet as sentient creatures, we also need to have a single sense of reality to operate from, to call home base.
> ► futurist/author Watts Wacker[31]

The surprise film of the 1990s, the *Blair Witch Project* and the Dogma brand of filmmaking are two kindred expressions of this reverse current. Dogma films began in 1995 with four Danish directors who were fed up with the big-production, Hollywood style of filmmaking. Dogma filmmakers subscribe to a "vow of chastity": (1) shooting done on location; (2) sound never produced separately from images; (3) film shot with a handheld camera; (4) shooting takes place where film takes space; (5) no "superficial action" (i.e., no violence); (6) 35mm format; (7) no flashbacks, no props, no makeup; (8) director never credited. The first Dogma film, Thomas Vinterberg's "Festen" (*The Celebration*, 1998), was soon followed by Lars von Trier's "Idioterne" (*The Idiots*, 1998). Even Stephen Spielberg is considering making a dogma film and testing his raw filmmaking skills.

EVERYTHING PERSONAL

Nikolai Bukharin had been a friend and comrade of Joseph Stalin. After a fake confession, a trumped-up trial, and death sentence, and just before putting a bullet through his head, Stalin said to his former friend, "Nothing against you personally."

Hitler said something similar about the Jews. Before having 6 million of them exterminated, he said "Nothing personal."

Foreign policy scholar George Walden suggests that "nothing personal" could "double as the twentieth-century's motto, and its bitterest joke."[33] "Everything personal" could serve as the motto of this first half of a century branded by self-portraiture as the artistry of our time. Here are two of the biggest words of the immediate future: "Live" and "Personal."

In an episode of the TV series *Buffy the Vampire Slayer*, Buffy's boyfriend shows up with another girl at a dance. Buffy goes up to him and demands, "What's the deal?"

"Didn't you get my message?"

"What, you broke up with my answering machine?"

In many ways, the churches need to invest more in LIVE epical relationships than in high-tech "fixes."[34] Electronic culture brings back, of all things, "the human touch." The ten fastest growing occupations from 1998 to 1999 were either "high tech" or "high touch": computer operators, paralegals, personal care and home health aides, social and human service assistants, physician's assistants.[35] According to John Naisbitt, the "high touch" is what "detoxifies" our relationship with technology.[36]

Once Jesus becomes our "Personal Lord and Savior," he also becomes our Social Lord and Savior. Once one is an apprentice of Jesus, a whole new relationship emerges between what is spiritual and what is material, between what is real and what is virtual, between who is enemy and who is friend, between who is an insider and who is an outsider.

One of the biggest questions in the Bible is this: Who is your neighbor? The parable of the Good Samaritan (Luke 10:29ff) gives an answer. Your "neighbor" (ton plesion or "the person near to you") is any person you intersect with in your journey who is in need. The poet Les Murray knighted this as the saintliness of Mother Theresa: "The day after the burial/of Mother Theresa, whose real grace/lay in knowing how little to generalise."[37] You can't make everyone your neighbor. But when you come across someone in need, can you make them your neighbor?

THE CRUCIFORM LIFE

The native language of Christianity is and/also: God is One and God is Three. Overemphasize one or the other, and it is heresy—modalism overemphasizes God's oneness and subordinationism overemphasizes God's three-ness. Jesus is wholly divine, and Jesus is fully human. God is immanent, and God is transcendent. We are both saint and sinner. Worship is the primal activity by which the church becomes itself through its holy mission in the world. Who peoples the church? Those born anew of water and fire.

There is one big Either/Or:

Choose this day whom you will serve (Josh. 24:15).
No one can serve two masters (Matt. 6:24).
Choose life or choose death (Deut. 30:19).
Choose one tree: The Tree of Life or the Tree of the Knowledge of Good and Evil (Gen. 2:9).

> **Hence I observe how needful it is for me to enter into darkness, and to admit the coincidence of opposites beyond all grasp of reason and there to seek truth.**
> ▶ Nicholas of Cusa (15th century)

But after the one big Either/Or, it is and/also living. The saving reverse current, Jesus' double command of love—love vertical and love horizontal, love God and love neighbor—has been sweeping us to heaven for 2,000 years. It is time to ride the waves.

Jesus was the master of both/and thinking.

My yoke is easy;
   my burden is light (Matt. 11:30).
Be as innocent as a dove,
   wise as a serpent (Matt. 10:16).
Do not worry about tomorrow —
   but sufficient unto the day is the evil thereof (Matt. 6:34).
Those who are not against us are for us (Mark 9:38–41);
   those who are not for us are against us (Matt. 12:30).
The Prince of Peace came,
   not to bring peace, but a sword (Matt. 10:34).
Love your neighbor as you love yourself (Matt. 22:39);
   unless you are willing to deny yourself, you cannot follow me
   (Matt. 16:24).
Exalt yourself and you will be humbled,
   humble yourself and you will be exalted (Matt. 23:12).
Come follow me, and I will give you rest (Matt. 11:29);
   come follow me, and I will give you a mission (Matt.16:24).
Be still and know that I am God (Ps. 46:10);
   feed the hungry and know that I am God (Matt. 25:34).
Come and live (John 10:10);
   come and die ("take up your cross" Mark 8:34).
Then the king will say to those at his right hand, "Come, O blessed
   of my Father, inherit the kingdom prepared for you from the foundation of the world; for I was hungry and you gave me food, I
   was thirsty and you gave me drink, I was a stranger and you wel-
   comed me" (Matt. 25:34–35 RSV).
The kingdom of God is not meat and drink; but righteousness, and
   peace, and joy in the Holy Ghost" (Rom. 14:17 RSV).

The life of faith is the life of wholeness. But wholeness is not oneness. Wholeness is harmony. Wholeness is singing with multiple voices that are in harmony with one another. A piece of music with only one part would hardly be "musical." Multiple parts that commingle in harmony is what makes music "musical."

God has multiple voices. Sometimes God speaks to us like to Elijah — in a soft, murmuring sound. Sometimes God speaks to us like to Moses on Sinai — in a consuming fire. A faith that "sings" is one that lives out of two realities:

Joy is the serious business of Heaven.
▶ C. S. Lewis, *Letters to Malcolm*[38]

We are created a little lower than the angels "For you are dust, and to dust you shall return," God says to Adam (Gen.3:19).

Lord, I believe. Help thou my unbelief.

Our citizenship is in two places: We are sojourners on this planet, and we are stewards of planet Earth.

The moment you come to life, you begin to die.

God dances with us in the certainties and mysteries of life. God leads us through the valley of the shadow.

We will never have peace in the Mideast until we learn Jesus' both/and thinking. Not the either/or strategy of war (win/lose), but the both/and strategy of web (collaboration, participation, affiliation).

> **Frail children of dust,**
> **and feeble as frail,**
> **in thee do we trust,**
> **nor find thee to fail.**
> ▶ "O Worship the King"[39]

Three religions claim the same space as their birthplace. Arabs call it Al-Quds. Jews call it Yerushalayim. Christians call it Jerusalem.

Why shouldn't Jerusalem become the first World City? The true City of God? Neither Jewish nor Palestinian, but the capital of both?[40]

Jesus' love is agape love. Agape love is made up of two dimensions: love of God and love of neighbor. The horizontal and the vertical go hand in hand. How do you show love of God? Love of neighbor.

The Spirit of God forms in us cross-shaped minds, bodies, and spirits. Christians live a Cruciform Life. And a Cruciform Life is a well-connected life that brings the ends together—the ebb and flow of love and hate, belief and unbelief, joy and suffering, trust and uncertainty, the disconsolate and the jubilant. The Cross is what bridges the banks, binds the ends, and marries the extremes of being.

Work fast, eat slow.

Jog paths, smell roses.

Be ahead of and behind the times.

CLASS #7 INTERACTIVES

1. Read and review Watts Wacker and Jim Taylor with Howard Means, *The Visionary's Handbook: Nine Paradoxes That Will Shape the Future of Your Business* (New York: HarperBusiness, 2000). Discuss their main thesis: "We live today inside a continuous collision of opposites" and relate it to the "reverse currents" outlined above.[41]

English theologian John Saward introduces five principles of biblical interpretation.[42]

1. Scripture is read in the church, not outside her. An ecclesial reading means a hermeneutic of participation.
2. Scripture is read in the light of the tradition — ancient fathers, medieval doctors, modern exegetes.
3. Scripture is read in the light of its historicity — historical truth is related to theological truth.
4. Scripture is read in the context of the Bible as a whole — not ideological selectivity.
5. Scripture is read with a Christocentric focus.

Discuss this Quintet of Exegesis and how normative it is in your own reading of the Scriptures.

 Ethicist Arthur Caplan predicts that the trafficking in gametes or genomes and genetic engineering will become so widespread in Millennium Three that "making babies sexually will be rare."[43]

Can you imagine such a world? How close are we to it? What are we doing today (both good and bad) that our ancestors could not imagine?

 Tom Sine suggests that the postmodern church may be "less a place to go *to* than a place to go *from* — a home for the people of Jesus Christ in a rapidly changing global future."[44]

Do you see any evidence of this? Have someone do some research on the co-housing movement that began in Denmark and is starting to spread in the USAmerica.

 How do "mind" and "consciousness" relate? Are they the same thing, or are they different? For example, can you "lose your mind" and still be conscious? Or, can you be "unconscious" and still be in your right mind?

Where does the "soul" fit into one's "mind" and "consciousness?"

 Sociologist Barry Glassner, author of *The Culture of Fear: Why Americans Are Afraid of the Wrong Things* (New York: Basic Books, 1999), contends that "We're living in about the safest times in human history, yet people seem to be more afraid than ever before."

Does this thesis ring true from your own experience? Why do you think we are so afraid?

 Timothy Koogle, CEO of Yahoo!, made $4.7 million a day in 1999, while the median household income that year was $110 a day.

Does "a rising tide lift all boats" (as President John F. Kennedy argued), or does "a rising tide lift only the yachts"?

How can we connect Yahoo! millionaires with the Yazoo Delta of Mississippi, one of the most destitute portions of our country?

 8 Discuss the outreach ministries of your church. Are you better at building walls or building bridges?

9 Read and review the book *Is America Breaking Apart?* by John A. Hall and Charles Lindholm (Princeton: Princeton Univ. Press, 1999). How much inequality can a democracy handle and still be a democracy? Or is that even the right question?

10 Machiavelli observed that in the Bible the armed prophets succeeded while the unarmed ones failed.

With what should we "arm" ourselves today in order to succeed? Is it true that to enjoy peace you must prepare for war?

 11 Check out The Amazing Real Fridge Cam at *www.electrolux.com/ node230.asp*. What is the appeal of this fridge in Västerhaninge, Sweden (just outside of Stockholm)? Why do so many people check out this fridge as much as their own?

Why do you think the Essens family agreed to this? What would you and your family say if asked?

12 Historian and former Librarian of Congress Daniel Boorstin has made the observation that USAmericans shop not to get what they want but to discover what they want. Discuss his thesis. Does it ring true? What does this say about us?

13 Compare these websites selling Christian gear:

> *www.livingepistles.com*
> *www.kerusso.com*
> *www.spiritualwear.com*
> *www.christillustrated.com*
> *www.ichthuscreations.com*
> *www.fishwear.com*
> *www.247christ.com/map.htm*
> *www.feargod.com*[45]

To these websites selling counter-Christian gear:

> *www.rof.com*
> *www.evolvefish.com*[46]

14 Go through hymnals and songbooks and find examples of some reverse currents: For example, "This world is not my home/I'm just a-passing through"; and "I've got a mansion/just over the hilltop/in that fair land where we'll never grow old"; yet at the same time "How Great Thou Art."

15 When asked what marketing is, WPP-head Martin Sorrell responds, "It's about getting people to kiss and punch at the same time."
The kiss is the creativity. The punch is the discipline.
Discuss this combination of creativity and discipline. Can you have one without the other? Is innovation possible without consolidation? What does child-rearing teach us?

16 Have someone do an exegesis of Leviticus 8:23–24, where the bodily extremities (right thumb, right big toe, right ear lobe) were touched with oil/blood upon entering into the priesthood. What might this mean? What was the theological significance of this ritual?

From Outer Space to Inner Space

What could change the direction of today's civilization? It is my deep conviction that the only option is a change in the sphere of the spirit, in the sphere of human conscience. It's not enough to invent new machines, new regulations, new institutions. We must develop a new understanding of the true purpose of our existence on earth. Only by making such a fundamental shift will we be able to create new models of behavior and a new set of values for the planet. In short, it appears to me that it would be better to start from the head rather than the tail.

▶ Vaclav Havel, president of the Czech Republic[1]

EDISON'S BREATH

In the same issue Albert Einstein was named the person of the 20th century, *Time* magazine named Thomas Edison the person of the 19th century.[2]

Thomas Edison's (1847–1931) best friend was Henry Ford (1863–1947). Their friendship was symbolized in 40 years of wintering next door to each other in Fort Myers, Florida.

Since Ford was much younger, scholars have speculated widely about what lay behind this extraordinary friendship. I suspect it was because each recognized himself in the other. Both were entrepreneurs who embraced failure. Ford defined failure as "the opportunity to begin again, more intelligently." Edison is famous for his "I didn't fail; I just learned a thousand ways NOT to make a light bulb." Both were curious about life in an almost childlike fashion. Once Edison was signing a guest book and came to the Interested In column. Edison wrote: "Everything."

Edison's wife Mina was a devout Methodist whose father was Lewis Miller, the Akron industrialist who helped found Chautauqua, where Thomas and Mina also kept a summer home.[3] Ford tried to help his older friend in every way he could. Ford gave Edison the first car off each Ford assembly line—the first Model T, the first Model A, the first V-8, the first Lincoln.[4] When Edison became so deaf the only way he could communicate was to tap messages in Morse code to his wife (which is how he proposed to her), or to have people cup their hands against his cheekbone where he could feel the vibrations, Ford brought his friend the three best hearing aids on the market, plopped them down on the table, and said: "Pick one."

Edison smiled and said, "No thanks."

"Why?" Ford asked.

"Well, if one of them worked, I'd have to listen to what you folks are saying, instead of getting along with my reading."

After everyone laughed and begged for the real reason, Edison said, "If one of them worked, Mina would make me go to church with her every Sunday."[5]

Appealing to his friendship with the Edisons, Ford asked their son Charles for a special favor. Charles, who would later became governor of New Jersey and secretary of the Navy, agreed to Ford's request. Charles sat by his dying father's bedside with a beaker, and collected his last exhaled breath on 18 October 1931. He then presented it to Ford.[6]

After Ford's wife Clara's died in 1950, this sealed vial was discovered next to Henry Ford's undisturbed hat and shoes. Today you can see the sealed beaker with Edison's last breath in the Henry Ford Museum (Dearborn, Michigan), a twelve-acre collection of some of the greatest inventions in history, which was originally called the Thomas Edison Institute and established by Ford to honor his hero and friend.

> **When you see everything that happens in the world of science and in the working of the universe, you cannot deny that there is a "Captain on the bridge."**
> ▶ Thomas Edison[7]

After Ford's death they renamed the museum after its benefactor, not the benefactor's best friend.

Why was Ford so obsessed with Edison's last breath? Why did he keep his friend's last breath next to his bed alongside his slippers and bathrobe? In capturing Edison's last breath, Ford believed he had in some way preserved Edison's spirit — and connected with that spirit daily as a rite of continuing inspiration and imagination.

Henry Ford was ahead of his time. Natives are capturing sparks of the soul in jars like immigrants captured fireflies.

THE INSCAPE LANDSCAPE

Immigrants search for truth "out there." Natives search for truth both "in here" and "out there" — outside the confines of normal space and time. Natives explore inner space as much as they do outer space. Innernauts are as common as astronauts are rare (fewer than 500 people have ever been in space).

Natives have shifted from "What are we doing today" to "How are we doing today?"

People of all faiths, and people of no faith, are on a spiritual quest. In spite of modernity's attempt to atheize the intellectuals and scientists, we now find ourselves in a world that is deeply spiritual. Even modernity's best religious minds never saw it coming (e.g., Peter Berger, Harvey Cox), though a few predicted the transforming power of religious experience. In 1977, long before "postmodern" took much form as an idea much less an idiom, E. F. Schumacher wrote these words:

> It may conceivably be possible to live without churches; but it is not possible to live without religion, . . . *The modern experiment to live without religion has failed*, and once we have understood this, we know what our "post-modern" tasks really are.[8]

Unlike Schumacher and a few others, the modern cultural elite has been taken aback by the human inability to live without transcendent content. Comedian/sage Jonathan Miller admits, "Although I am not a Christian, the idea of a God that incarnated itself into its own creation, in order to suffer the experience of being its own creation, is a fantastically productive metaphor."[9] The current spiritual awakening is nothing more than "the latest fashion in irrationality," an embarrassed Wendy Kaminer writes in the *Atlantic Monthly*.[10] On the last page of *God's Funeral,* the ex-Christian essayist and novelist A. N. Wilson shakes his head:

> One of the most extraordinary things about the twentieth century has been the palpable and visible strength of the Christian thing, the Christian idea. Just as Nietzsche's generation were declaring the death of

God and Thomas Hardy was witnessing His burial, religious thinkers as varied as Simone Weil, Dietrich Bonhoeffer, Nicholas Berdayev and Teilard de Chardin were waiting in the wings.[11]

The world is budding forth with fresh religious questions and quests. Media critic Jon Katz, who writes for Slashdot (slashdot.org), declares that next to sex and e-trading, nothing keeps a search engine humming longer than typing in the words "spirituality" or "religion."[12] By 2000, there were over 9,000 current titles under the subject heading "Spirituality and Religion" carried by Amazon.com. By 2000, there were 145,000 websites on spirituality and religion.

Even immigrants are getting bitten by the spiritual bug. Novelist Norman Mailer told Dick Staub, a radio talk show host and Internet entrepreneur, "Dick, I wish I would have known you were a seminary graduate; I would have gone out drinking with you. I used to go out drinking and talking about sex. Now I drink and talk about God. I'm obsessed with God."[13]

The spiritual is coming to the fore like never before. Notice I did not say "Christian" is coming to the fore. I said "spiritual." *The Sounder,* the local San Juan Islands neighborhood rag, does a regular feature called "Street Talk" in which passersby are asked a question. Only in the Pacific Northwest, or in the Desert Southwest, would you find this question being asked of the person on the street: "Do you celebrate Solstice, and if so, how?"

The responses say a lot about the post-Christian culture we are living in. One native responded, "I celebrate every day." Another native replied, "Yes. We do ceremonies in the evening." Another native said, "Yes. I just remember it's a wonderful day and a good time to party." The two immigrants asked the questions responded "No. It's just not on my radar, but I celebrate all the other pagan rituals" and "I change the filter on the furnace, and I also go to the parade." The only native who said "No" gave this reason why he didn't observe Solstice: "I celebrate my wedding anniversary on the same day."

One prediction rings the loudest from futurists: "Spirituality will be the holy grail of the third millennium." So what if we can live to 250 years? So what if I can take a drug that will double my IQ? So what if I can be a millionaire?[14]

SPIRITUALITY, YES! RELIGION, NO!

A woman was hired to conduct a phone survey. As she neared the end of a full day of reading questions, she grew weary. It was her last interviewee, and she came to a section that included the question: "What is your religious affiliation?" But in her weariness, she asked, "What is your religious affliction?"

▼ ▼ ▼

USAmerica is in the midst of one of the greatest spiritual quests in its history. George Gallup says that USAmericans are more "spiritual" now than at any time in the past 50 years.[15] Just look at the best-seller lists. A high proportion of the nonfiction list consists of the literature of soul and spirituality.

Natives are godaholics.

Unfortunately, Christianity in general and the church in particular are largely disconnected from the spiritual hungers of natives and are increasingly wary of engaging postmodern culture in biblically faithful but incarnational ways. In its "Millennium Special Edition," *The Economist* begins its treatment of the last thousand years with the observation: "Already Christianity, the faith once almost synonymous with Europe, is decaying in its homelands — as its rival, Islam, is not."[16] The Christian church is faring no better in North America.

According to the most recent research (World Values Study), the church has pews that are emptying out but the culture is becoming a spiritual parking lot.[17] The number of USAmericans who attend services at least once a month has dropped 5% from 1981 to 1998 (down 15% in Austria, 15% in Spain, 10% in West Germany, 9% in the Netherlands).[18] Only 12% of the 31 million young people in the US go to church, and 88% of that 12% drop out of church after leaving school. We are becoming less religious but more spiritual.

"Who wants to go with me to church this morning?"

That question gets fewer willing takers with every passing year. Natives are being raised en masse without benefit of church, must less clergy.

Natives are not rebellious against the church because rebellion presupposes intimacy with what one is rebelling against. Natives have not been deeply steeped and steepled in the traditions of the church as immigrants have. With almost zero familiarity with conventional religion, natives do not have their backs up or act up so much as start-up. In the words of futurist Cassidy Dale about Gen-Xers, "They are and will likely continue to be self starters. They just aren't as interested in rebelling as they are in getting something accomplished. Boomers are the professional rebels. Xers leave them to it."[20]

> **Spirituality is more about whether or not we can sleep at night than about whether or not we go to church.**
> ► Canadian theologian Ronald Rolheiser[19]

Natives are not going to patronize church for the reasons immigrants did. Thomas Jefferson confessed he went to church because it was the socially responsible thing to do. A skeptic and deist, Jefferson attended church not because he got anything out of it, but because he wanted to give organized religion "the sanction of my example."[21] Author Nancy Mairs makes a case for nonbelievers going to church and benefitting from going "through the motions" because these "motions" might not be "performing empty gestures but preparing a place into which belief could flood."[22]

Some are calling natives to do the same, but it simply will not happen. Natives do not think much of our solemn assemblies. A reporter asked a United Methodist youth representative what he thought of the 2000 General Conference meeting at Cleveland, Ohio: "Speaking as a youth and after being here for two weeks . . . I would not wish this on any of my friends."[23]

Here is what natives hear when the words "come to church" come to mind (a parody of an old hymn, "Take My Life"):

> Take our budget and let it be
> Faithfully paid for by thee
> Take all people at our door
> Make them sit here for evermore.[24]

> **We are looking to brands for poetry and for spirituality, because we're not getting those things from our communities or from each other. When Nike says, "Just do it," that's a message of empowerment. Why aren't the rest of us speaking to young people in a voice of inspiration?**
> ▶ Naomi Klein, author of *No Logo*[26]

For natives, the sound of "Come to Christ" inhabits a universe of meaning different from the words "Come to Church."

MIDAS TOUCH

This was modernity: You are nothing unless you have everything.[25] This is postmodernity: You can have everything and still have nothing.

Modernity's Midas touch changed human beings into things, and things into human desires. But a commonwealth of things turned out to be a ravaged spiritual empire. A carnival of consumption turned out to be a carousel of rage. So what if I can go wherever I want to go if I have no spiritual direction. So what if I can boast an aristocratic ancestry if I have no spiritual history.

For immigrants, science was the hope of the future. For natives, spirit is the hope of the future. Natives are looking for answers, not outward toward science and technology, but inward toward the spirit.

Henry Ford once complained, "How come when I want a pair of hands, I get a human being as well?" An executive in today's new economy might put it another way: "How come when I want a mind, I get a soul as well?"[27] Ask any one of the 31,000 corporate "consultants" hawking their wares about the importance of soul in today's workplace.

This historical movement from matter to spirit should not surprise us. Paul predicted it based on the Jesus story:

> Thus it is written: "The first [human] Adam, became a living being"; the last Adam became a life-giving spirit. . . . The first [human] was from the earth, a [human] of dust: the second [human] is from heaven. As was the [human] of dust, so are those who are of the dust; and as is the [human] of heaven, so are those who are of heaven. Just as we have borne the image of the [human] of dust, we will also bear the image of the [human] of heaven (1 Cor. 15:45, 47–49).

POPULAR CULTURE

Wherever one cuts natives, with however small a stick or prick, they spurt fountains of soul-clotted, soul-ful blood. Their blood is on every doorpost.

Every doorpost, that is, except the church. Natives' spiritual search is being conducted through popular culture and business culture more than through church culture. To the church, "popular culture" and "business culture" are things confined to quotation marks or approached only when outfitted in contamination suits.

One study of over thirty years of resolutions and public statements by church bodies on economic issues could find only three places where corporations were presented in a positive light. Whenever the church's "conviction politics" passed a resolution regarding business, it was mostly with clenched teeth railing against the demonology of the economic world.[28]

Immigrants feel superior to popular culture. Immigrant churches are proud that they make no concessions to popular culture. Just the name "pop culture" elicits a sneer. The church has an appetite for culture, as long as it is high: Bach and not Fatboy Slim, I'Mondevecchio and not McDonald's. It is as if Jesus Christ has something to fear from Mickey Mouse, Elvis Presley, or Celine Dion.

What the church does not understand, however, is that popular culture is becoming everyone's global culture. Main sources of identities still come from tribal sources. But everyone shares a common set of symbols, stories, songs, and characters. Postmodern culture has come full circle: Digital culture is returning us to the preindustrial world where elite culture and popular culture were mingled into one. Not to use popular culture in the communication of the gospel is not to reach natives. And even some immigrants.

Anne Graham Lotz was converted to Christ after watching the early Cecil B. DeMille movie "King of Kings." Ruth Graham saw how deeply affected her daughter was by the screen version of Jesus' life, and asked her if she wanted to confess her sins and ask Jesus into her life. So she did. It was not her father's preaching that brought Anne Graham Lotz to Christ. Popular culture brought her to her knees, in this case a popular culture that originated in Hollywood.

To make matters even more problematic for the church, popular culture like that in Cecil B. DeMille's day used to kowtow to church culture. Today it mostly mocks it. W. C. Fields found himself in hot water over a line in the 1939 film with Mae West, *My Little Chickadee*: "I know what I'll do; I'll go to India and become a missionary. I know there's good money in it, too." The motion picture censorship board, through its official Joseph Breen, challenged the line because the Hays Production Code ruled out anything "suggestive of an unfavorable, or derogatory, or comedy, reflection on the gentlemen of the cloth."[29] Nowadays that about describes the church's treatment by popular culture — "unfavorable," "derogatory," "comedic."

The family that prays together stays together.
▶ slogan coined in 1947 by Al Scapone, commercial ad writer

Natives have a passion for popular culture not because "pop" is a form of entertainment, but because it is a means of identity. The more "choice" the culture, the more natives identify with pop brands precisely because they do not have to make choices. The more the information, the more the chaos, the more natives need some things that are stable — a hamburger that is always the same; an acceptable "look" that you can purchase and not fret over; an experience that will always be the same no matter how homesick you are.

Media journalist Bill Moyers puts the story of popular culture somewhat mildly: "The most interesting story of our time . . . is emerging in the intersection between the secular and the spiritual."[30] The sacred's activity in the secular is more than an "interesting story." It is *the* prime story of our time.

Pop music is careening wildly down spiritual paths. Some of it can seem destructive. Tori Amos and Sarah McLachlan are mad at God most of the time. But they constantly refer to God and converse with God. Hip-hop rapper Mystikal (aka Mike Tyler) combines hard-core sex, dope, and smoking with thanking God for being "the head of my life" and for "keeping Your protective and comforting arms around my family and myself." Santana's 1999 *Supernatural* ventures into registers of the spirit where few theologians have gone. Musicians like Santana prove that only sound survives change.

Just take a look at some 1999 movies: *Being John Malkovich, Magnolia, Matrix, Fight Club, The Sixth Sense, The Blair Witch Project,* etc.[31] Perhaps the best commentary ever composed on a verse of Scripture (2 Cor. 4:18) is the movie *Matrix.*

According to *Business Week,* "A spiritual revival is sweeping across Corporate America as executives of all stripes are mixing mysticism into their management, importing into office corridors the lessons usually doled out in churches, temples, and mosques."[32] Companies like Taco Bell, Pizza Hut, and Wal-mart are hiring chaplains to visit employees in hospitals and employees with emotional problems. Over 10,000 Bible and prayer groups meet regularly in workplaces, which are now more hospitable to spirituality than public spaces (schools, courtrooms).[33]

The purposeful construction of our spiritual as well as somatic (physical) environment is changing both our living and play space. In this elusive, complex world, our homes are becoming more emotionally and spiritually charged than ever. And we are making them bigger to accommodate our expectations. In 1998, the average new house was 50% larger than in 1973.

Home is now a lofty and haloed place — a place of business, a place of healing (health spa), a place of retreat, a place of exercise, a place of spirituality, a place of memory-making. No wonder ceilings are going through the roof, and lofts are replacing living rooms. In our homes we are building spiritual hideaways — shady nooks, basking places — whether attached to bedrooms, bathrooms, gardens, even roofs (sky gardens that allow star-viewing perches). Our gardens gesture upwards through trees, obelisks, pergolas, arbors, gazebos, statues, relating earth and sky. Still pools bring sky and water together in ways that allow the spirit to move spirally. Behind it all is a desire for quiet, private, soulful space that functions in the same way that Dante conceived the cloister: "a grand staircase between heaven and earth."[34]

In our recreational lives we are searching for our souls. M. Scott Peck has staked out a specialty in the spirituality of golf, and Scotland's Findhorn community promotes itself as a way to bring the two together.[35] Or as their recent press release puts it, "Golf can be a tool for self-discovery, growth, and an exploration into spirit and your own inner potential and power."[36]

Academic bastions, usually the last to be invaded by anything having to do with faith, are now letting down

> **The intelligent man who is proud of his intelligence is like the condemned man who is proud of his large cell.**
> ▶ Simone Weil

some drawbridges. The Chancellor of the University of Massachusetts at Amherst, David K. Scott, wants to infuse spirituality into every arena of academic life. Scott foresees "a new integrative University" where "spirituality will be a natural ally rather than an enemy in the education of engaged citizens for an enlightened democracy." He calls for "a new unity of scientific, ethical, aesthetic, and religious institutions."[37]

MYSTERY-LOVING

The modern project sought to unravel every mystery. Its revolutionary duty was to set thinking straight. Moderns issued challenges against all comers. Even God.

Not for want of trying, anti-magic modernity proved unable to pluck out the heart of the mystery of life. In a transformed self's relation to the universe, virtually all of life turns out to be a mystery. Everything is unexplainable. Natives enjoy practicing mystery and performing mystical awareness. They do not feel a need to have answers to every question. Or as one native puts it, "I don't have to attend every argument I'm invited to." Natives do not think every crime against veracity is worth a crusade, every case a cause.

> A good question is never answered. It is not a bolt to be tightened into place but a seed to be planted and to bear more seed toward the hope of greening the landscape of ideas.
>
> ▶ dramatist/actor/poet John Ciardi[38]

For immigrants, when we disagree, one of us is mistaken. For natives, when we disagree, most likely both of us are mistaken. "We are all ignorant," said Will Rogers, "just on different subjects." Or as Paul put it, "For our knowledge is imperfect and our prophecy is imperfect, but when the perfect [God who is Love] comes, the imperfect will pass away" (paraphrase of 1 Cor. 13:9–10).

Bruce Sterling calls the science fiction writers job "teaching old dogmas new tricks."[39] The church's old dogmas need new tricks, but natives are disinclined toward doctrinal disputations. Not that they cannot delight in delicate doctrinal distinctions like the difference between *non posse pecare* vs. *posse non pecare* ("Jesus was not able to sin" vs. "Jesus was able not to sin"). But they feel no compulsion to take a stand on every doctrinal debate. They can hold in their minds a multiplicity of interpretations, and resist being trapped by the symbiotic antagonisms of the past. Natives keep ironic distances, cultivate idiosyncrasy, and value fair-mindedness over consistency. Natives think and feel by faith and intuition more than by formula and proof.

Mystery-loving natives do not want answers so much as they want help with the questions, help in choosing what questions their lives should be asking and answering. It is not what you know that is who you are, according to Sam Keen. Rather, "what you ask is who you are."[41] Those who help natives ask good questions are the mentors. Those who give answers are the tormentors. David Hopkins, College Class of 2000, starts his "The ABCs of Ministry in the 21st Century" with "A is for 'Authority'":

> **You cannot think or fight your way out of hell. You must feel your way out.**
> ▶ Nancy Venable Raine[40]

My advice to pastors and other leaders is this: do not sling your power around too much. Authority is viewed with skepticism and approached with caution, if at all. You are not the authority. Say that with me: "I am not the authority." Don't you feel better? You are just a perspective. If you fail to get this, then "A" will also stand for "Arrogant." This will be how many of the new era will view you. But do not forget, you are still a leader.[42]

Immigrant hierarchical models are being replaced by distributed decision making and mentoring. Immigrants preferred their mentors dead and buried. Natives prefer live mentors, but mentoring natives means:

(1) being a role model
(2) sharing experiences with them
(3) caring about them and joining them in asking deep questions about life
(4) pushing them to be better than they think they are
(5) introducing them to others
(6) esteeming their opinions and learning from them
(7) opening doors for new experiences and opportunities to prove themselves

"THE THINGS OF THE SPIRIT COME FIRST"

Take out an empty computer disc and weigh it.

Now imagine that you downloaded on that disc the codes to our nation's nuclear arsenal. Now you hold in your hand a disc that could send people to their death, empty out bank vaults, and start wars.

Weigh it.

Can you feel the difference? Can you see the difference?

Natives find the spiritual their native habitat partly because they do not insist something be proved to them before they believe it. It is not so much that seeing is believing as that believing is seeing.

Have you ever seen an atom?

No one has. Yet you know that it exists, and you build your life on your faith in its existence.

Have you ever seen an angel?

For natives it is much the same question. The presence and power of the invisible is commonplace. Natives know there is more to the universe than meets the eye. Astrophysicists call the matter you cannot see "dark matter." One kind of dark matter they call MACHOS (Massive Compact Halo Objects) is the size of large planets. But totally invisible.

Bernard Haisch is staff physicist at the Lockheed Martin Solar and Astrophysics Laboratory in Palo Alto, California. He is also scientific editor of *The Astrophysical Journal* and editor-in-chief of the *Journal of Scientific Exploration*. In a recent article on "Light, Matter and the Zero-Point Field," Haisch spilled some beans out of a particularly tight-laced bag. The biblical statement "And God said, 'Let there be light,' and there was light" is more than poetry, he disclosed. It is in truth a cosmological reality. In his words, "the solid, stable world of matter appears to be sustained at every instant by an underlying sea of quantum light."[43] Thanks to the yoking of information theory and physics, which says that information carried by light is forever, eternal life is now a scientific theorem.[44]

> ## If I hadn't believed it, I wouldn't have seen it.
> ▶ philosopher Yogi Berra

Soul Is Fundamental

Like energy, matter, and gravity, soul cannot be explained in terms of its constituent parts or manifestations.

Soul Is Indivisible[45]

Spirit overrides matter. The invisible presides and prevails over the visible. One of my favorite presidents was Calvin Coolidge. In a 5 July 1926 address in Philadelphia celebrating the 150th anniversary of the signing of the Declaration of Independence, "Silent Cal" waxed eloquent in this 4,500 word address. It is one of the great unadvertised speeches in the history of the US presidency. The founders of this nation, he asserted, "were a people who came under the influence of a great spiritual development and acquired a great moral power."

No other theory is adequate to explain or comprehend the Declaration of Independence. It is the product of the spiritual insight of a people. We live in an age of science and of abounding accumulation of material things. These did not create our declaration. Our Declaration created them. The things of the spirit come first. Unless we cling to that, all our material prosperity, overwhelming though it may appear, will turn to a barren scepter in our grasp.[46]

Who has seen the wind?
Neither I nor you:
But when the leaves hang trembling
The wind is passing thru.
Who has seen the wind?
Neither you nor I:
But when the trees bow down their heads,
The wind is passing by.

► Christina Rossetti[47]

The church has tried everything except the one thing that is needed. It has tried to be an inclusive church. It has tried to be a confessional church. It has tried to be a program-driven church. It has tried to be a purpose-driven church. It has tried to be a seeker-sensitive church.

What if it tried to be a spiritual church?

One of the reason so many natives can still be attracted to "old-fashioned evangelists" is that they address everyday problems from a spiritual perspective. In 1999 evangelist Kenneth Copeland devoted an entire sermon to the question "Why should you not be overweight?" All of the usual arguments were missing. His one point driven home many ways was this: You aren't a chipmunk that must hoard food. Trust and serve God. God doesn't want us to store extra resources in barns, and God doesn't want us to store extra weight on our bodies. Obesity is a spiritual inefficiency in trusting and serving a loving, providing God.[48]

GOING NON-LOCO

Moderns went loco. Postmoderns are nonloco.

Nonlocalism is one of the "greatest discoveries" in the history of modern science.[49] Thanks to a 1982 experiment by Alain Aspect at the University of Paris, it is now a "scientific fact" that there are more things to heaven and earth than you can see out your window. There is more to life, and more to relationships, than what you can see with your eyes, or hear with your ears, or touch with your hands, or smell with your nose, or taste with your tongue. What happens in one location reverberates throughout the universe.[50]

Theologian Paul Tillich once told the Dean of Duke Divinity School that his best audiences were theoretical physicists.[51] Perhaps it is time for theologians and spiritual leaders to be good audiences for theoretical physicists.

When the principle of nonlocality is brought together with superstring theory, the mysteriousness of the universe glows in neon. Once again, what is unseen is much more plentiful and real than what is seen. Once one moves into nonlocalism, one shifts into a spiritual realm of vibration and higher level of consciousness. At the most subatomic and galactic levels, it is all spiritual.

What is superstring theory? Ask ten different physicists how quantum theory works, and you get ten different answers. Even more so for superstring theory. But crudely, superstring is the only theory which ties together all the pillars of 20th-century physics — quantum mechanics and general relativity, the very small and the really huge.

Superstring theory states that the building blocks of the universe are basically "strings" which are also known as vibrating "loops." The theory posits, however, that the universe is more than four-dimensional (three of space, one of time). In fact, string theory requires the universe to be 10-dimensional or even 11-dimensional. Each string is a vibration made from these 10 or 11 dimensions. The only issue is whether the loop is open or closed.

In other words, superstring theories require the existence of multiple parallel universes. Superstring physicists are now pondering why only three of the space dimensions get big, and the other seven or eight curled-up space dimensions stay small.[52] Some superstring physicists are arguing that there are not just extra space dimensions, but extra time dimensions as well. But all superstring physicists are deeply humble about the ability of our gray matter to understand all in its entirety. Can a slug understand Einstein? Could the human brain, imprisoned in four dimensions, ever understand an 11-dimensional universe? Could we humans understand how the universe is composed and created?

One more thing with which most superstring physicists are in agreement: The world is put together with such coherence, such order, such simplicity, such beauty, that it suggests a sublime consciousness, a driving force, that put it all together.

Did the laws of physics create this elegance? Some end up here.[53]

Did a higher consciousness or God create this elegance?[54] I begin here.

Each of us decides where to end and begin.

CLASS #8 INTERACTIVES

 Compare the features offered by these spirituality websites:

www.beliefnet.com
www.explorefaith.org
www.christianity.com

What are the differences? The similarities?

2 The German philosopher Oswald Spengler predicted that a rise in spirituality would be a part of the "last gasp" of a dying Western civilization "that in cultural wintertime springs from tortured consciences and spiritual hunger."

As we seed a new postmodern civilization, what are your predictions about the future — both good and bad?

3 Try Bruce Cook's suggestion of a youth retreat weekend on the Trinity that would feature the 1999 movies *The Matrix* (Jesus), *The Sixth Sense* (Holy Spirit), and *The Red Violin* (Father).

Check out these and/or other web pages on *The Matrix:*

"*The Matrix* as Messiah Movie: The Real Message Encoded Within *The Matrix,*" awesomehouse.com/matrix (accessed 9 June 2001).
"The Spiritual Matrix: Why is *The Matrix* a Popular Movie?" www.heaven.net.nz/writings/matrix (accessed 9 June 2001).

Try to find similar pages for *The Sixth Sense* and *The Red Violin.*

 Musician David Wilcox has written that

Each generation has to reinvent the wheel when it comes to understanding Jesus and the whole nature of his message. It doesn't come from an institution, and it doesn't come pre-packaged. It has to be a daring leap of faith that is something you have to do because you can't not do it. You don't know where it's taking you, it always feels as if it's never been done before, and it always has to grow fresh and come out of nowhere.[55]

What do you think? Would you put it differently? If so, are you more immigrant or native?

5 Molecular cell biologist Ursula Goodenough, former president of the Institute on Religion in an Age of Science and author of *The Sacred Depths of Nature* (1998) says this about herself:

I regard myself as a religious non-theist, meaning that God questions are not central to my quest and, indeed, get in the way of it. But I am deeply informed and moved by the texts and the art of traditional and indigenous religions, and I believe they offer us much guidance and wisdom as we chart our paths.[56]

What does this one quote tell us about postmodern culture?

 6 Discuss these words of Tom Bandy. Are they too harsh? Are they right on target?

The end of the millennium has seen the publication of a growing number of "bio-planning" books written by leaders of large churches. These books offer principles and plans for church growth in the larger context of the autobiography of the church leader. The birth of a visionary leaders is a compelling story, and many of these books offer tremendous insights into church growth in a chaos of cultures. In the pursuit of that vision, however, these leaders too often appear as falsely self-deprecating, inflexible over seeming trivialities, and all ready with ultimatums.

The spiritually hungry, institutionally alienated Christian reader is left with a lingering worry. Has the coach surrendered to a vision or elevated a personal perspective? Has the coach crossed the boundary between vision and arrogance? Is the eccentric behavior, passionate irascibility, "in your face" methodology, and confident risk-taking a sign that Moses is once again leading the Israelites to the Promised Land . . . or a sign that Moses is having a temper tantrum with the tablets of God?

The "bio-planning" books of successful post-modern apostles — and tragic cult leaders — are beginning to look uncomfortably alike. Too often they reveal a subtle shift from the conviction that God has revealed a vision, to the conviction that God has revealed a strategic plan. This is the transition from authenticity to arrogance. It is an escape from moral responsibility. It is the transition from an authentic belief that "It's not me, but God working through me!". . . to the inauthentic arrogance that tacitly communicates "I am God!"[57]

7 Futurist Cassidy Dale believes that churches should be swapping members all the time in the name of missions. In this scenario, an established church would send out "missionaries" (also known as "loaners") to help another church (whether church plant or mission project or building plan). Discuss whether or not the concept of "loaners" should be extended to church members?

8 There are more than 360 references to the Holy Spirit in New Testament. Check them out at random and see what insights you discover into the ways of the Spirit.

9 Postmoderns are prone to argue that religion is a private matter and thus beyond commentary any more than any other choice of how to live—whether it is the choice of a spouse, the choice of a dress, or the choice of a neighborhood.

Is there anything wrong with this line of reasoning?

10 Some theologians have conjectured that the world is becoming more spiritual partly because spirit matters. In other words, the spiritual which was always present in the material world is emerging more and more into consciousness. What do you think of this thesis? Is it biblical? How does it compare with the doctrine of the Incarnation where the Logos becomes Logo?

11 Visit some monastic websites:

www.christdesert.org
www.aspen.com/stbenedicts
www.sja.osb.org
www.monks.org
www.osb.org

12 Nobel-Prize winning economist and University of Chicago professor Robert Fogel has focused his scholarly attention on this *Fourth Great Awakening* (2000), as he calls it. Foget argues that there are 15 spiritual resources or "immaterial commodities" necessary to cope with the challenge of modern life:

a sense of purpose . . . a vision of opportunity . . . a sense of the mainstream of work and life . . . a strong family ethic . . . a sense of community . . . a capacity to engage with diverse groups . . . an ethic of benevolence . . . a work ethic . . . a sense of discipline . . . the capacity to focus and concentrate one's efforts . . . a capacity to resist the lure of hedonism . . . a capacity for self education . . . a thirst for knowledge . . . an appreciation for quality; self-esteem.[58]

Would your list be the same? How do we get these resources, these immaterial assets? How are they developed? What religious and civic organizations are helping to nurture them?

From Clockwork Orange to Web Green

*If you look at a grain of wheat very closely, you
will be overwhelmed by the glory of God.*

▶ Martin Luther

The Newtonian coloration of the modern world as Clockwork Orange
is being replaced with a Web Green view of the universe marked by
interweaving, intricacy, collaboration, and self-organization.[1]

The move from Clockwork Orange to Web Green is the move from
mechanism to organism; from reductionist science to holistic, integral science; from permanent and physical to dynamic and virtual; from atomic
isolation to embedded relationships; and from nature as something you
are glad to see to nature as something glad to see you.[2]

Immigrants are car-driving utilitarians who see red when the word
"environmentalist" pops up. Natives are "cell-phone naturalists" for whom
the idea of "environmental" is a green and moral vision.[3]

When a native is accused of being an "environmentalist," the person
being attacked wears the badge with pride. Both pro technology and pro
nature, natives believe that if humans cannot solve our environmental problems, the rest of our problems will not need to be worried about.[4] The future
is with the natives. By a margin of 70–23%, USAmericans would give
environmental protection a priority over economic growth.[5] Nine out of
ten of us say environmental concerns will influence our vote for president
of the US.[6]

The challenge of Christianity in a green light world is in helping natives find God in nature without making a god of nature.[7] This is where the light turns red. If we learned anything about nature in the Clockwork Orange world, it was if you push ecology too far, it becomes eugenics.

Natives are interested in everything supernatural. But when the super is natural, it is the ultimate in supernatural. When given a choice, natives choose what is natural over what is human made — natural fibers over synthetic fibers; solar energy over fossil fuels; a homegrown, garden-shed faith over a flower-shop, potted spirituality. It is the difference between waiting to see the stagey arrival of the swallows of Capistrano or the slapdash docking of the turkey vultures of Hinckley, Ohio.

Natives are hill-walkers, bird-watchers, mountain-climbers, flower-planters whose relationship with nature is a moral relationship. Those that awaken them to daily earth magic are their saints and seers. Natives will be willing to pay as much to hire a good gardener as a good dentist. They think organically, use organic metaphors to describe technology, and view all of life as an ecosystem in the same way a tree is an ecosystem.

A big oak or beech can weigh 30 tons, cover 2,000 square yards, include 10 miles of twigs and branches, and in the course of a year pump several tons of water as high as 100 feet, produce a new crop of 100,000 leaves, and cover half an acre of trunks and branches with a new pelt of bark. For natives the rainforest is not just out there somewhere; the rainforest is inside us, too.

The "background" rate of extinction is from one to ten species per year. The forefront rate of extinction today is from 70 to 700 species per year, or up to two species per day.[8] In the words of University of Leiden biologist Kees Bare, "There came a sad moment when I realized that most of these species are extinct. It gave me the feeling that dissecting these fish is like cutting up a Rembrandt to learn what paints he used."[9]

An Amazonian rain forest canopy alone boasts up to 30 million insect species new to science. How fast we are losing these unnamed, unknown life forms is a native battle cry.

You do not "go back to nature." You go inside to nature. We are a part of nature. Just look at our DNA. All of nature is a part of us in that genetic endowment. The fruit fly *(Drosophilia melanogaster)* shares about 50% of its DNA with humans. In other words, flies are 50% of the way to being human. Chimpanzees share about 97% of their DNA with humans. So do ferns — they are 97% human. The human body is one of the natural wonders of the world. Literally.

But at the same time — and this is where the deep ecologists are wrong and immigrants right — what a difference that 3% makes. Humans are not just another part of nature. Homo sapiens are called to a special, sapiential relationship *within* creation. We have the ability to change and transform nature. This PC I am working on is "natural," but it is a transformed nature that enables me to do this. The question is whether our transformations of nature will be wise (sapiential) or foolish (farcical). We can learn more and more, but understand less and less.

"The trends are clear," notes the *Christian Science Monitor*. "Companies are going environmental."[10] Ray Anderson, "the king of carpet tile," is an immigrant with more than a visa. Founder, Chair, and CEO of Interface, the $1 billion a year leader in the floor

> *Expandit in cruce manus, ut comprehenderet orbis fines.*
> **God stretched out his arms upon the Cross to embrace the furthest bounds of Earth.**
> ▶ St. Cyril of Jerusalem[11]

covering industry, Anderson had a true-to-his-Baptist-roots conversion experience a few years ago. "I had a revelation about what industry is doing to our planet," he testified to an audience of CEOs. When he realized that 23,000 pounds of raw material are consumed for each USAmerican per year, "I stood convicted as a plunderer of the earth." The technologies of the modern era, he thundered, were "voracious" and "a form of collective suicide. . . . In the future, people like me will go to jail."

> Interface of Atlanta, my company, is changing course to become sustainable — to grow without damaging the earth and manufacture without pollution, waste, or fossil fuels. If we get it right, our company and our supply chain will never have to take another drop of oil.

Pointing a finger at Chris Fay, then CEO of the British unit of Royal-Dutch/Shell, he admonished, "We want to put you out of business."[12] Interface plants one tree in the rain forest for each 4,000 mile air trip taken by one of its 7,600 plus employees.

That pointy-fingered poking at a friend is a foretaste of the barbs and jabs natives will thrust at those who fail to repent of their unnatural ways. In the native way of doing business, profits are no longer the sole criteria of success. Being green is now part of being in the black. In the last couple of years, Shell and BP have embraced the concept of the triple bottom line: economic, social, and environmental impact.

Natives can tell when the air they are breathing is air God never designed them to breathe. Their kids have 500 chemicals in their fatty tissues that do not belong there. The blackened air and sinking immune system are manifested in the astounding percentage of USAmericans who take prescription or nonprescription allergy medication: 51%.[13] They live in cities with more black tar than green spaces. Houston's asphalt equates to 30 parking spaces per resident.[14]

One can already begin to hear native rumblings and grumblings. They want "the death of birth" to end.[15]

St. Augustine singled out an amphibian, the salamander, to reveal the miraculous omnipotence of God.

Natives want to know how the North American wood frog survives being frozen solid. No other vertebrate can do this.

Natives want to know how the gastric brooding frog, now extinct, nurtured its infants *amid* its stomach acids. No other animals can do this.

Natives want to know how many drugs can be derived from the skin toxins produced by amphibians. We do not even know how many amphibians there are before they are gone—disappearing and deforming in front of our eyes.

> **The land, virtually powerless before political and commercial entities, finds itself finally with no defenders ... the rivers dammed and shrunken, the soil washed away ... acidic lakes, skies empty of birds, fouled beaches, the poisonous slags of industry, the sun burning like a molten coin in ruined air.**
>
> ▶ Barry Lopez[16]

The problem of waste, extinction, and pollution is not just a recent one. Rather it is an accumulating and accelerating one that has reached exponential levels of alarm. Londoners in the 1820s complained of discovering "leeches" in their water, small jumping animals which resembled shrimps. At other times they complained of an "oily cream" and a "fetid black deposit." No wonder. One water company, the Grand Junction Company, was drawing its water from the Thames at a point opposite one of the largest sewer outlets.

The first Paris water company was founded in 1778 by the Perrier brothers. They were careful where they drew their water. They still are to this day. Clean water, the oil of the future, will be even more of a privately owned, traded commodity in the 21st century. In airports already a container of pure water costs more than a gallon of gas. Water that springs from one of the most pristine places on Earth, or water that boasts regulated laboratory bottling conditions, will cost twice the price of Evian or Perrier today. With one-fifth of the world's fresh water supply, Canada owns the future.

CHAIN OF BEING

But perhaps the greatest divide separating native and immigrant is in their respective views on creation and particularly interspecies connections. Natives prize both physical and spiritual relations with animals.[17] Animals are now given moral consideration. Animal welfare is no longer voluntary. How you treat your animals is no longer up to you.

Cambridge biochemist Rupert Sheldrake asks, "Why does the cat always disappear when you plan to take her to the vet?"[18] The question is explored more fully on his website, which boasts a TV clip of a dog that knows when his owner decides to come home, which proves dogs are smarter than humans since we never do know when the dog will decide to come home.

> **Environmentalists changed their terminology to "rain forests" and "wetlands" because no one would give them money to save jungles and swamps.**
> ► comedian George Carlin

Billionaire Oprah Winfrey calls her many dogs (jarringly to immigrant ears) "People with fur." Martha Stewart feels similarly about her chows. Natives treat pets as part of the family. Virtually every benefit (legal, health insurance, life insurance, etc.) that accrues to humans will soon accrue to pets. Pets are now more welcome than kids at many upscale hotels.[19] When a ferry's brakes failed and the dock was destroyed, rendering Orcas Island inaccessible to ferry service, the first "food run" at the island's only grocery store was pet food. Natives need at least one plant and/or pet whose life depends on them.

The summer of 1998 witnessed a history-making ad campaign for Whiskas Homestyle Favorites. The ad messages were pitched directly to the cats. Yes, you read that correctly: The ads appealed not to the human owners of the cats, but to the cats themselves. Through rustling leaves, mouse talk, and purring allusions, cats were lured to the product pitch. A feline focus group tested its success.

To immigrant ears, hearing all this is the sound of words not working together. Much like our embarrassed ancestors reacted angrily to the news that humans might be an evolutionary

> **People tell me the animals would be better off in the wild, and I say, "What wild?"**
> ► Werner Heuschele, director of the Center for Reproduction of Endangered Species (CRES), also known as the Frozen Zoo, of the San Diego Zoological Society

upgrade on chimps and apes. The story is told of the wife of a Victorian bishop, who, on learning that Charles Darwin had suggested people were descended from apes, "hoped that it was not true—but that if it is, then that it does not become widely known." Immigrants view animal coddling as a put-down of the Great Chain of Being that places humans above every other species. But for natives, as for Jesus himself in his relationship with the animal kingdom, the "chain of being" is a true "chain," a "circle of life" that links all life together in a bond that is only as strong as its weakest link.[20] Growing numbers of natives are disaffected with evolutionary theory, but not because it links humans to animals.[21]

Ann Griffiths (1776–1805) was an 18th-century Welsh poet and Calvinist Methodist who lived her short life at a little thatched house at Dolwar Fach in the Welsh parish of Llanfihangel-yng-Ngwynfa. When the Griffiths family could not go to church on Sundays, for whatever reason, the dog went in their stead.[22]

Growing numbers of corporations are offering pet day care. Companies are allowing employees to bring their pets to work for all or part of the day.

Why not churches?

AND BACK TO RED

The journey from red to green must come back to red again. The greatest deficiency in the green mentality is its lack of a sense of sin, or what Pope John Paul II has called our "offense against God."

> **We have some bad habits that only God can cure!**
> ▶ Los Angeles gang member to a church group[23]

All this talk about the "inner child" is vapid and insipid nonsense without a prior realization of the "inner brat." Rodgers and Hammerstein, who wrote the song from *South Pacific* that goes "you've got to be carefully taught to hate," must have never had children or brothers and sisters. The truth is children have to be taught to be kind and loving. *Not* doing unto others as they do unto you comes naturally.

Cruelty is hardwired into the human DNA. We are born with a congenital heart defect. It is called original sin. Name the problems of the world: pick one, any one. From the 500,000 murderers, convicted and undetected, living in USAmerican society, to the whirling weather dervish unleashed by global warming.[24] The many problems of the world have really only one name. For all the problems of the world are actually only one problem: the three graces and four cardinal virtues vs.

the seven deadly sins. Sin is the one enduring sociological and psychological category.

Former slave trader John Newton, who saw crimson when he wrote the hymn "Amazing Grace," had a devotional exercise that he used almost as a mantra: "I may, I must, I do remember . . . I have sinned, but Christ has died."

We may, we must, we do remember . . . we have sinned . . . and we will sin.

But Christ has died.

Christ has risen.

Christ will come again.

Maranatha.

CLASS #9 INTERACTIVES

1 Ask every member of your group to draw a picture of nature. Do not give them any more direction than that.

How many drew a picture of a person? How many drew a lake or a tree? Mountains, sea, desert? Why don't we think of ourselves as "natural"? If God became "flesh," didn't God make "flesh" something natural and loving?[25]

2 Study these key environmental texts:

Genesis 1
Genesis 2:15
Nehemiah 9:6
Psalm 24:1
Matthew 6:25–34
Colossians 1:19–20

3 Writers Ursula Le Guin and poet Carol Ann Duffy suggest the exercise of looking in an animal's eyes. In *The Other Country*, Duffy asks you to tear off the calendar photo of a jungle ape and look at it:

His eyes hold your eyes
as you crumple a forest in your fist.[26]

Ursula Le Guin invites us to stare directly into any animal's eyes:

What are you seeing? What are they seeing? Rilke [in "Eighth Duino Elegy"] says that what the animal sees is pure being, the truth. The animal doesn't know its own death, it looks through it:

> What is outside, we know from the face
> of the animal only; for we turn even the
> youngest child
> around and force it to see all forms
> backwards, not the openness
> so deep in the beast's gaze. Free from death.
> Only we see that. The free animal
> has its dying always behind it
> and God in front of it, and its way
> is the eternal way, as the spring flowing.

Again, this is profoundly mystical, and it sounds sort of silly to talk about it outside of poetry. But I think Rilke is right. That's why contact with animals is a sacred thing — because they know something we don't. We know a lot, but we had to give up something in order to know what we know. That's why we must not lose contact with the animals, and why I'm spooked by people who have.[27]

4 With what parts of this declaration do you agree or disagree:

For millennia we have presumed on nature's good nature. We've expected her to provide for us, to forgive us, to indulge us our ill-considered and hurtful ways. But now culture has absorbed nature and we are the larger entity. It is time for us to reciprocate, to exhibit a generosity commensurate with our station. No more longing for babyish innocence, for the moral high ground of the powerless! We are not now that impotent, and the wish to be so is unseemly. It is time for us, as a species, to put away childish things and to accept our roles as part and partner of nature.[28]

5 Some environmentalists have gone BANANAs — Build Absolutely Nothing Anywhere Near Anybody. Some anti-environmentalists have gone imbecilic, or in their words IMBY — In My Back Yard.
What is the biblical and ethical response?

6 Go back as far as you can into your childhood and pull out of your memories the first person who introduced you to the wonders of nature. Relay it to someone in your group.

7 Go back in time to when our ancestors discovered that the human voice could be taken out of the natural body and put into a machine, where it could be magnified and manufactured even to say things it never said. How startling did this appear to them then? How startling is it today? What are some "startlements" natives might anticipate, and not just in the realm of sound and image?

8 Read and discuss the article by United Methodist layman and Sunday school teacher Bill McKibben, "Climate Change and the Unraveling of Creation," *Christian Century* (8 December 1999), 1196–99.

What would it mean if Christians were to show themselves "good stewards" of creation? What would it mean if the church were to lead the fight to protect and conserve planet Earth?

9 According to Romans 13:1–7, what is the function of civil government? Does the suppression of evil include violations against the environment?

10 Would you recognize the "desecration of life" if you saw it? How? Is such "desecration" the same as "decreation" — reversing what God started?

11 For a five-minute devotional on creation, see *www.theartmill.com/creation.htm.*

12 Eight percent of electricity consumption in USAmerica is said to be due to Internet-connected computers, many of which are increasingly left on all the time. Do you see any ethical issues in this?

13 As a disciple of Jesus, what is your favorite word?

Endtroduction

When Jesus said, "I am the **Way**, the **Truth**, and the **Life,**" he was giving us the three progressive steps of a dusk to dawn gospel.[1] Christianity is based on an image: Jesus the Christ. Jesus, the very **I**mage of God, invites us to **P**articipate in a pilgrim **Way** (step one is "Follow Me") that leads us into richer and deeper **E**xperiences of **Truth.** From step two, one can then build the only **Life** ("Feed My Sheep") in which the circuits are completed that **C**onnect with God, others, and creation.

At the dawn of Millennium Three, Christianity faces the most **EPIC** intellectual and spiritual advance in the history of civilization. Internet technology is amplifying the worldwide flow of new kinds of experiences, interactions, images, and connections.

For some WWW is World War III.

For others WWW is another wave of change for the church to ride and drive.

Is it dusk or dawn?

On 17 September 1787, while the US Constitution was being signed by the last members of the convention, Benjamin Franklin turned to some of his colleagues seated around him and asked them to look towards the president's chair. He pointed out a sunburst that seemed to frame the back of the seat, and observed that one of the most difficult of tasks for a painter was to distinguish a rising from a setting sun.

> I have often and often, in the course of the session, and the vicissitudes of my hopes and fears as to its issue, looked at that behind the President, without being able to tell whether it was rising or setting; but now at length, I have the happiness to know, that it is a rising, and not a setting sun.[2]

What will the church see out the door in the first decade of Millennium Three? Enthusiasm is a choice. Passion is a choice. Will the church greet the future with open arms? Or will the church keep refusing to take the hand of the future?

Will you take the future into your hands?

The natives are restless. The natives are hungry.

Will we trust God with God's own gospel and go native?

Will our theme song be "A Mighty Fortress Is Our God"? Or will our song be "A Mighty Fortress Is Our Church"?

ENDTRODUCTION INTERACTIVES

 Margaret Wheatley refers to the necessity of re-founding movements in this fashion:

> The institutions that we have do not work. They will never work again. They are the wrong form for this age. Institutions are prisons for the spirit. Don't waste your time trying to fix them. This is a great moment for re-founding, for re-creation.[3]

Return to the time and spirit of the founding of your church or organization. What were the original energies that created you? How can you live out of them? Go back to the Why (why are we doing this?) and Who (who called us?).

 Theologian David Lowes Watson has suggested that every church, every committee ask itself every week: "Is it really worth the life of our Lord, what we're doing?"
Try it.
Is it?

Ask each other this question posed by Herbert O'Driscoll: "Do you want to be a mourner, lamenting the passing of the church as you knew it, or do you want to be a midwife, helping to birth a new Christianity?"[4]

Why do you think we are afraid to trust God with the gospel?

Discuss this quote from the poet and Nobel Laureate Joseph Brodsky in a commencement speech to the University of Michigan at Ann Arbor, 1991:

> The world you are about to enter and exist in doesn't have a good reputation. It's been better geographically than historically; it's still far more attractive visually than socially. It's not a nice place, as you are soon to find out, and I rather doubt that it will get much nicer by the time you leave it. Still, it's the only world available: No alternative exists, and if one did, there is no guarantee that it would be much better than this one. It is a jungle out there, as well as a desert, a slippery slope, a swamp, etc. — literally — but what's worse, metaphorically, too. Yet, as Robert Frost has said, "The best way out is always through." He also said, in a different poem, though, that "to be social is to be forgiving."[5]

Notes

INTRODUCTION 1: WHAT IT IS

1. Douglas S. Robertson, *The New Renaissance: Computers and the Next Level of Civilization* (New York: Oxford Univ. Press, 1998), 187.

2. "The Patch MS Forgot to Apply," *Wired News* (6 November 2000). See www.securitybeat.com/cgi-bin/link.cgi?url=http://www.wired.com/news/culture/0,1284,39984,00.html (accessed 26 June 2000).

3. Before becoming a consultant at Microsoft in February 2000, Furdyk began and continues to run a second company, Buy Buddy.com. J. Martinez, "Microsoft Figures the Best Way to Predict the Future Is Ask It," 26 February 2000. See www.seattletimes.nwsource.com/news/business/html98/altnet_20000226.html (accessed 13 December 2000).

4. Clive Thompson, "Meet the New Boss," *Shift* (September 2000): 53–58.

5. See www.linux.org/ (accessed 13 December 2000).

6. Jeff A. Taylor, "Balance Sheet," *Reason* 32 (November 2000): 8. See www.reason.com/ (accessed 9 December 2000).

7. In early 2000, Norwegian police raided the house of one startled teenager who naively decoded the software protecting films.

8. G. Pascal Zachary and Robert Frank, "High-Tech Hopes: Countries Are Pinning Their Economic Dreams These Days on a New Truism: Innovation Can — and Does — Happen Anywhere," *Wall Street Journal*, 25 September 2000, R4.

9. See, for example, James Adams, *The Next World War: Computers Are the Weapons and the Front Line Is Everywhere* (New York: Simon & Schuster, 1998).

10. For the role of adults in guiding children's ability to evaluate and interpret computer information, see Henry Jenkins, "Empowering Children in the Digital Age: Towards a Radical Media," *Radical Teacher* 50 (1997): 30–35.

11. Mark L. Alch, "Get Ready for the Net Generation," *USA Today: The Magazine of the American Scene* (July 2000): 26–27. See also Ambassador Philip Lader's Address to the London Business School (2 May 2000) called "Emerging Technologies," *Vital Speeches of the Day* 66 (1 September 2000): 697: "If the businesses founded by graduates and faculty of the Massachusetts Institute of Technology formed an independent nation, the companies' revenues would make that nation the world's 24th largest economy, somewhat smaller than South Africa's and greater than Thailand's. These 4,000 MIT-related enterprises employ 1.1 million people and have annual worldwide sales of $232 billion."

12. Watts Wacker and Jim Taylor with Howard Means, *The Visionary's Handbook: Nine Paradoxes That Will Shape the Future of Your Business* (New York: HarperBusiness, 2000), 21.

13. Why 1962? According to the study known as "The Digital Citizen 2000," the median age of the "very wired" is 38 years old; the "somewhat wired" is 44; the "not wired" is 56. "The chasm between the information haves and have-nots is first and foremost a function of age." Karen Breslau, "One Nation, Interconnected," *Wired* (May 2000): 136–54. See *www.wired.com/wired/archive/8.05/poll.html* (accessed 24 April 2001). Every page of Rick Lawrence's *TrendWatch* (Loveland, Colo.: Group Publishing, 2000) is further proof of this fact.

14. For more on the normativity of wiredness, see Breslau, "One Nation, Interconnected," 136–54.

15. Quoted by Diana Bagnall in "Born to Be Wired," *The Bulletin* [GPO Box 5245, Sydney, NSW, Australia 2001] (15 August 2000): 25.

16. REM (Musical Group), "It's the End of the World As We Know It," in their CD titled *Document* (Universal City, Calif.: I.R.S., 1987). For the complete lyrics see *www.geocities.com/mmeyer_hermann/EndOfTheWorld.html* (accessed 26 June 2001).

17. Elizabeth Weil, "The Future Is Younger than You Think," *Fast Company* (April 1997), 93. See *www.fastcompany.com/online/08/kids.html* (accessed 13 December 2000).

18. With thanks to Brad Henderson for this Latin phrase.

19. Bruce Feller, op-ed piece for the *New York Times* (23 November 1998), as referenced in Wacker and Taylor, *Visionary's Handbook*, 84.

20. Wacker and Taylor, *Visionary's Handbook*, 86–87.

21. Wacker and Taylor, *Visionary's Handbook*, 83.

22. As quoted in George Anders, "Voyage to the New Economy," *Fast Company* (July 2000): 152. See *www.fastcompany.com/online/36/migration2.html* (accessed 24 April 2001).

23. For figures on post-1900 immigrants and their descendants, see *Immigration and Ethnicity: The Integration of America's Newest Arrivals*, ed. Barry Edmonston and Jeffrey S. Passel (Washington, D.C.: Urban Institute, 1994), 61.

24. Immigrants today comprise about 33% of net population growth. By the time 2025 rolls around, they will comprise 100% of net population growth. See historian John Harmon McElroy's *American Beliefs: What Keeps a Big Country and a Diverse People United* (Chicago: Ivan R. Dee, 1999), 60.

25. For the International Theological Commission Study, "Memory and Reconciliation: The Church and the Faults of the Past" (December 1999), see *www.cin.org/docs/memrecon.html* (accessed 21 April 2000). For Pope John Paul II's "Homily of Holy Father Asking Pardon" (12 April 2000), see *www.cin.org/jp2/jp000312b.html* (accessed 21 April 2000).

26. For more on this AncientFuture faith, see my *FaithQuakes* (Nashville: Abingdon, 1994) and *Post-modern Pilgrims: First Century Passion for the 21st Century World* (Nashville: Broadman & Holman, 2000). For an excellent elaboration of a European perspective on AncientFuture faith, see Gerard Kelly, *RetroFuture:*

Rediscovering Our Roots, Recharting Our Routes (Downer's Grove, Ill.: Inter Varsity Press, 2000); published also as *Get a Grip on the Future* (London: Monarch, 1999).

27. Bella Bathurst, *The Lighthouse Stevensons: The Extraordinary Story of the Building of the Scottish Lighthouses by the Ancestors of Robert Louis Stevenson* (New York: HarperCollins, 1999), 10.

28. In 2000 the chances of survival were 98%.

29. As referenced by Pamela Wells, "Medea or Madonna?" *TLS: Times Literary Supplement* (17 March 2000): 3.

30. This was first mentioned by Edward Lane, as referenced by Robert Carver, "Foreigners Cannot Come Here," *TLS: Times Literary Supplement* (28 April 2000): 35.

31. For more on these last five illustrations see David Hillman and David Gibbs, *Century Makers: One Hundred Clever Things We Take for Granted Which Have Changed Our Lives Over the Last One Hundred Years* (New York: Welcome Rain, 1999), 62, 68, 103. See also Rosemary Hill, "The Best Thing Until Sliced Bread," *TLS: Times Literary Supplement* (4 June 1999): 36.

32. For a dissenting view see Charles Jonscher's *The Evolution of Wired Life: From the Alphabet to the Soul Catcher Chip—How Information Technologies Change Our Worlds* (New York: John Wiley, 1999), 1–7, where he argues that the changes that took place in 1900–1960 (telephone, electricity grid, cars and superhighways, television, jet transport, nuclear weapons) are far more dramatic than those changes of the last 40 years.

33. As cited in Elizabeth Weil, "Time to Slow Down," *Fast Company* (May 2000): 393. See *www.fastcompany.com/online/34/ifaqs.html* (accessed 24 April 2001).

34. Stanford Symposium: Will Spiritual Robots Replace Humanity by 2100, "Spiritual Robots: Hans Moravec Presentation," see *www.technetcast.com/tnc_play_stream.html?stream_id=259* (accessed 28 December 2000).

35. See *www.casio.com/watches/product.cfm?section=16&market=0&product=3682/* (accessed 24 April 2001).

36. Thanks to Earl Bakken, cofounder of Medtronics and engineer of the first battery powered pacemaker. See "The History of Medtronics," *www.medtronic.com/corporate/history.html* (accessed 24 April 2001).

37. "By all material dimensions, today's poor—the bottom fifth—live a lot better than the upper-middle class of 1950." See Kevin Kelly, "Wealth Is the Right Thing to Do," *Wired 7* (September 1999): 156. See *www.wired.com/wired/archive/7.09/prophets.html* (accessed 24 April 2001).

38. As quoted in Peter Bishop, "The Waves of Creative Destruction: Technology Past, Present and Future," *Waves of Creative Destruction, real-futures.com/wavesdestruction.htm* (accessed 21 February 2000).

39. Bill Gates with Nathan Myhrvold and Peter Rinearson, *The Road Ahead* (New York: Viking, 1995), 373.

40. Ibid., 11.

41. Francis Fukuyama, *The End of History and the Last Man* (New York: Free Press, 1992), xi–xii.

42. Quoted by psychiatrist/philosopher Roger Walsh in "Essential Spirituality," *Pathways* 9 (January–March 2000): 13.

43. As quoted by Waylon B. Moore, "Mentoring Your Pastor," *Mentoring Newsletter* 19 (May 2000): 1–2. See *www.mentoring–disciples.org/Pastor.html* (accessed 8 December 2000). The pastor-parishioner relationship will be altered even more fundamentally than the physician-patient relationship is being altered by cyber-medicine.

44. Daniel Klaidman and Matt Reed, "The New Defectors: An Increasing Number of Ultra-Orthodox Jews Leave the Fold," *Newsweek* (13 December 1999): 52, 54; quote on 54.

45. "Demming" refers to reducing someone to a demographic profile.

46. The language of "immigrant" and "native" I have borrowed from a couple of sources: John Perry Barlow's first use of it in reference to cyberspace, "an immigrant's fear of a strange new land into which he will be forcibly moved and in which his own child is a native." See his "Crime and Puzzlement: In Advance of the Law on the Electronic Frontier," *Whole Earth Review* 68 (Fall 1990): 54; from London Business School professor John W. Hunt's use of it to refer to those "forced into wealth creation through circumstance" in "Many Faces of Wealth Creators," *Financial Times* (26 January 2000): 12. The "immigrant" metaphor was the subject of a cover treatment and theme issue of *Fast Company* (July 2000). See *www.fastcompany.com/online/36/index.html* (accessed 24 April 2001).

47. Isaiah 11:6 and Matthew 19:14 paraphrased.

48. T. S. Eliot, "Little Gidding," in his *Four Quartets,* (New York: Harcourt, Brace, 1943), 35.

49. Ian Shapiro, *Democratic Justice* (New Haven, Conn.: Yale Univ. Press, 1999).

50. Raymond Carver, "Steering by the Stars" in *No Heroics, Please: Uncollected Writings* (New York: Vintage Books, 1991), 132.

INTRODUCTION 2: WHAT IT MEANS

1. Tom Sine, "Getting Ready for a One-World Future," *Current Thoughts & Trends* 16 (February 2000): 27.

2. Randall Balmer, "The Kinkade Crusade," *Christianity Today* (4 December 2000): 48–55. See *www.christianitytoday.com/ct/2000/014/6.48.html* (accessed 31 December 2000).

3. Psychoanalysis has a word for this phenomenon: "scotomization" is when you deny something that is too painful to face. David Korten advocates a dual hospice/midwife role for leaders in his books. See *When Corporations Rule the World* (San Francisco: Berritt-Koehler, 1995) and *The Post-Corporate World: Life After Capitalism* (San Francisco: Berritt-Koehler, 1999).

4. Through vignettes from 1901 to 1969, Lukacs portrays the death of Western civilization. "What I have in mind is the erosion of beliefs and of institutions and of manners and morals and habits that can no longer be restored. The pen-

dulum never swings back. History is not a mechanical clock. . . . The Romans near their end, the mediaeval people near their end, knew something was happening to them, but they did not know where they were — at the end of an entire age in history." In this accent on "ending" Lukacs is more right than Barzun. See Lukacs, *A Thread of Years* (New Haven, Conn.: Yale Univ. Press, 2000).

5. Jacques Barzun, *From Dawn to Decadence: 500 Years of Cultural Life: 1500 to the Present* (New York: HarperCollins, 2000), 796.

6. Former president of the Southern Baptist Convention Jimmy Allen, who has lost a daughter-in-law and a grandson to AIDS, and who has another grandson who is HIV-positive. Allen also has a gay son with AIDS. See "Judgmentalism Is Deadly to Human Relationships," *Record: Newsletter of Evangelicals Concerned* (Summer 1994): 1, as quoted in Martin E. Marty's *Context* (15 November 1994): 6.

7. Thanks to philosopher Dallas Willard for this metaphor.

8. In typical double-ring fashion, 82% say things are also getting worse (the postmodernist always rings twice). See Yankelovich Partners survey, as accessed in Watts Wacker and Jim Taylor with Howard Means, *The Visionary's Handbook: Nine Paradoxes That Will Shape the Future of Your Business* (New York: HarperBusiness, 2000), 6. For more on the double ring, see my postmodern trilogy, *SoulTsunami: Sink or Swim in New Millennium Culture* (Grand Rapids: Zondervan, 1999), *AquaChurch: Essential Leadership Arts for Piloting Your Church in Today's Fluid Culture* (Loveland, Colo.: Group, 1999), and *SoulSalsa: 17 Surprising Steps for Godly Living in the 21st Century* (Grand Rapids: Zondervan, 2000).

9. Only one in eight believes that our children's lives will be like ours. From a worldwide survey conducted by *Fast Company* and Roper Starch, "It's Your Choice," *Fast Company* (January/February 2000): 212. See *www.fastcompany.com/online/31/choice.html* (accessed 25 April 2001).

10. The quotes are from a 1902 essay by the prophetic H. G. Wells on the future-directed self, as quoted by Stephen Kern in *The Culture of Time and Space, 1880–1918* (Cambridge, Mass.: Harvard Univ. Press, 1983), 94.

11. E. L. Doctorow, *City of God* (New York: Random House, 2000).

12. Karen Breslau, "One Nation, Interconnected," *Wired* (May 2000): 136–54, 138. See *www.wired.com/wired/archive/8.05/poll.html* (accessed 25 April 2001).

13. I first heard the phrase "If God so loved the world, why can't the church?" at the home of Betty and Elmer O'Brien from pastor/professor John Baker-Batsel.

14. The inspiration for insight comes from Dennis Peacocke, who tells of jogging one day in 1997 and hearing the Holy Spirit judge his other-worldliness and fixation on the "end times" rather than the "ends of the earth": "'Dennis, you and I are going in opposite directions. I'm moving more and more to get *on* the Earth, and you're waiting to get off it.'" Dennis Peacocke, *Doing Business God's Way: Almighty & Sons* (Santa Rosa, Calif.: Rebuild, 1995), 5–6.

15. Brian Medway is senior pastor of Grace Christian Fellowship in Canberra and a leader in renewal conferences. See *www.pastornet.net.au/grace/index.html* (accessed 19 December 2000).

16. Ellen Glasgow, "Spirit-Loneliness," as quoted in Susan Goodman, *Ellen*

Glasgow: A Biography (Baltimore: Johns Hopkins Univ. Press, 1998), 55. Written in 1905, it is quoted from the Ellen Glasgow Papers, accession number 5060 (University of Virginia Library, Charlottesville).

17. "The Pauline Group's strong and intimate sense of belonging, their special beliefs and norms, their perception of their own discreteness from 'the world' did not lead them to withdraw into the desert, like the Essenes of Qumran. They remained in the cities, and their members continued to go about their ordinary lives in the streets and neighborhoods, the shops and agora. Paul and the other leaders did not merely permit this continued interaction as something inevitable; in several instances they positively encouraged it (1 Cor. 5:9–13)." See Wayne A. Meeks, *The First Urban Christians: The Social World of the Apostle Paul* (New Haven: Yale Univ. Press, 1983), 105.

18. Tom Bandy, "Focus on a Fresh Start," *Net Results* (August 2000): 16–18. See *netresults.org/index.html* (accessed 25 April 2001).

19. Adrian Hastings, "Mission," *Encyclopedia of Theology, The Concise Sacramentum Mundi*, ed. Karl Rahner (New York: Seabury, 1975), 968.

20. William M. Easum, "It's Time to Tell the Truth About Christians and Our Churches," *Net Results* (21 February 2000): 22.

21. The first person I heard say this was Harold Lewis, Senior Pastor of Lincoln Park United Methodist Church in Washington, D.C.

22. "Discerning the Times," *Next* 6 (Winter 2000): 2. See *leadnetinfo.org/NEXTs/next_4q/NEXTv6WinterA.pdf* (accessed 25 April 2001).

23. An abbreviated and earlier version of this book first appeared as an ebook on Amazon.com in November 2000 under the title *The Dawn Mistaken for Dusk: If God So Loved the World, Why Can't We?* (Grand Rapids: Zondervan, 2000).

24. Tom Peters as quoted in Regina Fazio Maruca, "State of the New Economy: Voices," *Fast Company* (September 2000): 106. See *www.fastcompany.com/online/38/one.html* (accessed 2 December 2000).

25. Wacker and Taylor, *Visionary's Handbook*, 16.

26. G. K. Chesterton, "The Ballad of the White Horse," in *The Collected Poems of G. K. Chesterton* (New York: Dodd, Mead, 1980), 210, "And Alfred, hiding in deep grass,/Hardened his heart with hope."

27. Douglas John Hall, *Thinking the Faith: Christian Theology in a North American Context* (Minneapolis: Augsburg, 1989), 84.

28. Quoted by zoologist Frans de Waal in Chris Floyd, "Virtuous Species: The Biological Origins of Human Morality: An Interview with Frans de Waal," *Science & Spirit* 11 (April/May 2000): 14–15. See *science-spirit.com/articles/Article detail.cfm?article_ID=184* (accessed 25 April 2001).

29. Graham T. T. Molitor, "Millennial Perspectives on Employee Benefit Changes," *Vital Speeches of the Day* 66 (15 May 2000): 470.

30. Gerard Kelly, *RetroFuture: Rediscovering Our Roots, Recharting Our Routes* (Downers Grove, Ill.: InterVarsity, 2000), 38.

31. Salman Rushdie, "Crashes That Brought Us Back to Earth — Instantly," *The Sydney [NSW, Australia] Morning Herald* (10 August 2000): 12.

32. Midas Dekkers, *The Way of All Flesh: The Romance of Ruins* (New York: Farrar, Straus, and Giroux, 2000), 260.

INTRODUCTION 3: IT'S A WWW WORLD

1. As quoted in Aidan Nichols, *Christendom Awake: On Re-Energising the Church in Culture* (Grand Rapids: Eerdmans, 1999), 229.

2. Leonard Sweet, *SoulTsunami: Sink or Swim in New Millennium Culture* (Grand Rapids: Zondervan, 1999).

3. Douglas S. Robertson, *The New Renaissance: Computers and the Next Level of Civilization* (New York: Oxford Univ. Press, 1998), 180.

4. Peter Brimelow, "Why They Call It Harvard College," *Forbes* (9 March 1998): 50–51.

5. Karen Breslau, "One Nation, Interconnected," *Wired* (May 2000): 136–54.

6. Luciano Floridi, *Philosophy and Computing: An Introduction* (London: Routledge, 1999). For more on Floridi's thesis, check out Luciano Floridi's website, *www.wolfson.ox.ac.uk/~floridi/* (accessed 25 April 2001).

7. "Bioterials" is a word coined by Richard W. Oliver in *The Coming Biotech Age: The Business of Bio-Materials* (New York: McGraw Hill, 1999), 13–14, to describe the coming together of organic and inorganic materials (gene engineering, redesign of the atomic structure of paints, ceramics, plastics, etc) into a new substance.

8. Robertson, *New Renaissance*, 57.

9. Vivian Pospisil, "Who Invented the Computer," *Industry Week* (5 July 1999): 14.

10. As quoted in Abraham Pais, *The Genius of Science: A Portrait Gallery of 20th Century Physicists* (New York: Oxford Univ. Press, 2000), 198.

11. For more on what I call this EPIC essence to native culture, see my *Postmodern Pilgrims: First Century Passion for the 21st Century World* (Nashville: Broadman & Holman, 2000). Also see Derrick de Kerchove's *Connected Intelligence: The Arrival of the Web* (Toronto: Somerville House, 1997).

12. Anne Hird, *Learning from Cyber-Savvy Students: How Internet Age Kids Impact Classroom Teaching* (Sterling, Va.: Stylus, 2000), 4.

13. For internet usage see Cisco Systems Government Affairs Facts and Stats, "Internet Usage." See *www.cisco.com/warp/public/779/govtaffs/factsNStats/Internet_Usage.html* (accessed 25 April 2001).

14. Ed Zander, "Ahoy, Internet Companies — Huge Iceberg Ahead," *USA Today* (7 June 2000): 15A.

15. For Latin American examples, see the novels of Gabriel García Márquez (i.e., *Strange Pilgrims: Twelve Stories* [New York: Knopf, 1993] or *Of Love and Other Demons* [New York: Knopf, 1995]) and Oscar Hijuelos (i.e., *Empress of the Splendid Season* [New York: HarperFlamingo, 1999] or *Mr. Ives' Christmas* [New York: HarperCollins, 1995]).

16. Finland, Sweden, and Norway have 30 Internet users per 100 adults, the highest per-capita Web-surfing population in the world. US has 28 users per 100 adults. "E-Commerce, the Global Currency," *Trend Letter* 18 (30 September 1999): 4.

17. For example of what is going on in Brazil, see Robin Eveleigh, "Very PC," *Geographical Magazine* 72 (July 2000): 64–67.

18. World Economic Forum ranked Singapore the most competitive economy in 1999 (US came in second, Hong Kong third, Taiwan fourth, and Canada fifth). In 2000 the US ranked first, followed by Singapore, Luxembourg (up from seventh in 1999), Netherlands (up from nineth), and Ireland (up from tenth). Canada had dropped to seventh, Hong Kong to eighth, and Taiwan had dropped to eleventh. See "The Global Competitiveness Report: 2000: Table 1. Growth Competitive Ranking," www.weforum.org/reports_pub.nsf/ (accessed 1 December 2000).

19. AnnaLee Saxenian, as quoted by Berkeley sociologist Michael Lewis, The New New Thing: A Silicon Valley Story (New York: Norton, 2000), 116. As of 2000, there were 11 software development centers and over 75,000 programmers in five Indian states.

20. The bandwidth speeds are from 2.5 to 40 gigabits per second. See "India to Pave On-Ramp to Information Superhighway," Science 287 (4 February 2000): 763.

21. By the end of 2001, people along the Alaska and Klondike highways will have more bandwidth and higher-speed access than most affluent homes in America. "Bringing the Internet to the Four Corners of the Globe," Trend Letter 19 (7 September 2000): 1.

22. British alternative worship leader Andii Bowsher asks us to do a "thought experiment of imagining how to disciple Christians in a context without readily available scriptures and without the presupposition of functional reading ability — how well does much evangelical piety survive such conditions?" See Bowsher, "New Age Evangelical: Biblical Christianity for an Emerging Post-Secular Culture." See home.onet.co.uk/~andii/newagevangelical.html (accessed 25 April 2001).

23. In Canada, self-employment, the free-agency norm of the future, accounts for 80% of Canada's 6.5% net job growth from 1989 to 1997. This compares to self-employment accounting for 12% of 10.4% job growth in USAmerica over the same period. See Trend Letter 19 (3 February 2000): 8.

24. Some are saying five years from now or even less. The Gartner Group predicts this by 2003.

25. Jim Daniell, CEO at OrderTrust, Lowell, Massachusetts, estimates that one-third of the total US economy is already being "reassigned" because of the Internet. See David Dorsey, "The People Behind the People Behind E-Commerce," Fast Company (June 1999): 186. See www.fastcompany.com/online/25/ecommerce.html (accessed 25 April 2001).

26. Libraries vied with each other to purchase his collection (including the Library of Congress). But the elitist, anti-Ralph Kramden sniff of libraries turned Rumsey off as much as it did Steve Wynn, who invested over $300 million in Renoirs, Picassos, Van Goghs, etc., to display at the 1.6 billion Bellagio in the gangster-founded, fastest growing city in North America (Wynn believes in spending casino revenues on things, as he puts it, "good for the soul" (as quoted in Paul Mendelson, "Las Vegas Visionary Who Bet on a Winner," Financial Times [21–22 August 1999]: 3). Rumsey is working with Luna Imaging to put his entire collection online. Of course, in classic both/and fashion, this still begs the question of where his collection will ultimately end up.

27. With thanks to Steve Horswill-Johnston, Associate General Secretary of United Methodist Communications (Nashville, Tenn.) for this insight.

28. "Patent Wars," *The Economist* (6 April 2000): 75–78. Available for view and purchase online at *www.economist.com/displayStory.cfm?Story_ID=332256* (accessed 25 April 2001). Even here, however, the digital divide becomes apparent: "There are 48 countries with more than a million people (in 1995), and with at least half of these living in tropical areas: with a total population of 750m, they took out just 47 of the 51,000 American patents issued to foreign inventors in 1997." See Jeffrey Sachs, "A New Map of the World," *The Economist* (22 June 2000): 81–83. See *www.economist.com/displayStory.cfm?Story_ID=80730* (accessed 25 April 2001).

29. Michael Schrage, "The Debriefing: John Seely Brown," *Wired* (August 2000), 206. See *www.wired.com/wired/archive/8.08/brown.html?pg=2&topic=&topic_set=* (accessed 1 December 2000).

30. What the Web can do to connect a group that heretofore has been isolated and without much connection to each other is manifested at PlanetOut!, a vortal for gaylebt of 825,000 registered members where the content is driven by the people themselves. PlanetOut! emails 500,000 people every weekend. Half of the site is generated by people talking to one another.

31. First coined by economists at Wartburg Dillon Read, an investment bank.

32. Cecile M. Jagodzinski, *Privacy and Print: Reading and Writing in Seventeenth-Century England* (Charlottesville: Univ. Press of Virginia, 1999).

33. John Perry Barlow, "On Being Human in a Digital Age," unpublished keynote address at Pop!Tech 2000, Cambridge, Maine (27 October 2000). For more information visit their web page using keyword "Pop!Tech 2000."

34. Paul K. Feyerabend, "Explanation, Reduction, and Empericism," in *Scientific Explanation, Space, and Time*, ed. Herbert Feigl and Grovr Maxwell, vol. 3 of *Minnesota Studies in the Philosophy of Science* (Minneapolis: University of Minnesota Press, 1962), 58–59.

35. Clayton Christensen, *The Innovator's Dilemma: When New Technologies Cause Great Firms to Fail* (Boston, Mass.: Harvard Business School Press, 1997).

36. Janet Frame, "The Park," in *The Lagoon and Other Stories* (London: Bloomsbury, 1951), 161.

37. So argues John Seely Brown and Paul Duguid, *The Social Life of Information* (Boston: Harvard Business School, 2000), 5.

38. "Death of the Salesmen," *The Economist* (20 April 2000): 59. Available for viewing or purchase online at *www.economist.com/displayStory.cfm?Story_ID=304054* (accessed 25 April 2001).

39. UPS handles more than 55% of all goods ordered via the Internet. Even so, over the past five years First-Class mail volume grew by 7.5 billion pieces, an average growth rate of nearly 2% a year. Paul Carlin, "Can the US Postal Service Survive?" *Vital Speeches of the Day* 66 (1 December 1999): 111–12.

40. So argues the Boston Consulting Group (*www.bcg.com*). The global market for paper stood at 80 million metric tons at the beginning of the 1980s. At the end of the 1990s it almost doubled to reach about 140 million metric tons.

41. Devin Gordon, Seth Stevenson, and Marc Peyser. "Main Street's e-Recovery," *Newsweek* (3 April 2000): 8.

42. "Internet Economics: A Thinkers' Guide," *The Economist* (30 March 2000): 64. Available for viewing or purchase on the Web through *www.economist.com/displayStory.cfm?Story_ID=298218* (accessed 25 April 2001).

43. J. L. Austin, as quoted in Scott Campbell, "Defending Common Sense," *Partisan Review* 67 (Summer 2000): 501–2. See *web.bu.edu/partisan review/archive/2000/3/campbell.html* (accessed 20 December 2000).

44. See Tim Berners-Lee with Mark Fischetti, *Weaving the Web: The Original Design and Ultimate Destiny of the World Wide Web by Its Inventor* (San Francisco: HarperSanFrancisco, 1999), and "Lost in Cyberspace," *The Economist* (16 December 1999): 78–80. Available for viewing or purchase online through *www.economist.com/displayStory.cfm?Story_ID=327520* (accessed 25 April 2001). Some names you may not have heard of: Dave Walder, Craig Partridge, Ray Tomlinson (three Cambridge, Mass. engineers who created ARPANET), Mark McCahill (programmer who led the team that developed Gopher), Joseph Hardin, Chris Locke, Gordon Cook, Tim Berners-Lee.

45. Lyrics of "Put Your Lights On" available online at *www.santana.com/supernatural/put.asp* (accessed 25 April 2001).

46. David Wallis, "Act 2.0," *Wired* (May 2000): 194. See *www.wired.com/wired/archive/8.05/act2.html* (accessed 25 April 2001).

47. As quoted in Frank Rose, "Rupert Discovers the Internet," *Wired* (March 2000): 252. See *www.wired.com/wired/archive/8.03/rupert.html* (accessed 25 April 2001).

48. C. S. Lewis, "Answers to Questions on Christianity," in his *God in the Dock: Essays on Theology and Ethics* (Grand Rapids: Eerdmans, 1970), 58.

49. Gerard Baker, "King of the Economy," *Financial Times* (8/9 January 2000): 7. Under the caption "Can America's new economy be steered with an old-economy compass?" the British journal *The Economist* states that "Alan Greenspan may be the god of global finance, but his efforts to steer America's economy are proving rather like navigating outer space with a compass." See "To Boldly Go . . . ," *The Economist* (25 March 2000): 29. Available on the Web for purchase only at *www.economist.com/displayStory.cfm?Story_ID=295742* (accessed 25 April 2001).

50. Stewart Alsop, "The E-volution of Big Business: E or Be Eaten," *Fortune* (8 November 1999): 86.

51. See David Henry, "Buffett Still Wary of Tech Stocks," *USA Today* (1 May 2000): B2. Available for purchase on the Web through *usatoday.pqarchiver.com* (accessed 27 April 2001).

52. Bob Dylan, "The Times They Are A-Changin'." See *members.tripod.com/~Raincloud771/poetry/dylan/times.htm* (accessed 27 April 2001).

53. Dylan, "Things Have Changed," as quoted in "Expecting Rain." See *www.expectingrain.com/dok/cd/2000/thingshavechanged.html* (accessed 27 April 2001).

54. Tom Wolfe, "What Do a Jesuit Priest, a Canadian Communications Theorist, and Darwin II All Have in Common: Digibabble, Fairy Dust, and the Human Anthill," *Forbes ASAP* (4 October 1999): 218. See *www.forbes.com/asap/99/1004/212.htm* (accessed 27 April 2001).

55. Peter F. Drucker, "Management's New Paradigms," *Forbes* (5 October 1998): 152. See *www.forbes.com/global/1998/1005/0113052a.html* (accessed 27 April 2001).

56. Quoted in Thomas Hohstadt, *Dying to Live: The 21ˢᵗ Century Church* (Odessa, Tex.: Damah Media, 1999), 4. Even though in June of 2000, Smith-Corona filed for bankruptcy, one will still be able to get typewriter parts well into the future. In spite of the introduction of cars, you can still find blacksmiths and horse-and-buggy makers.

57. See *www.slashdot.org* or, */.* for short, where people submit on average 400 news items per day which are then edited by the participants themselves (accessed 27 April 2001). To learn more go to *www.gnu.org* and click the "licenses" button (accessed 27 April 2001).

58. The study was conducted by Norman Nie of Stanford and Lutz Erbring of the Free University of Berlin. Stanford Institute for the Quantitative Study of Society (SIQSS), "Study of Social Consequences of the Internet." See *www.stanford.edu/group/siqss/Press_Release/internetStudy.html* (accessed 27 April 2001).

59. For the best critique of Nie and Erbring's work, see Elizabeth Weise, "A Circle Unbroken by Surveys," *USA Today* (22 February 2000): 3D. Available for purchase on the Web through *usatoday.pqarchiver.com* (accessed 27 April 2001).

60. Thanks to David Stambaugh.

61. Robert Schutz (a.k.a. Brother Roger or Frère Roger), *This Day Belongs to God* (Baltimore: Helicon, 1961), 29.

62. One version can be found in *The Circular of Janus* 18:5 (1 May 1998). See this joke page on the Web for the poem: *www.stream.redlink.com/fun/ago.htm* (accessed 27 April 2001).

63. See "Saint Isidore of Seville (c560–636) Proposed Patron of Internet Users," *www.catholic.org/isidore/* (accessed 20 December 2000).

64. Karin Laub, "Blind Pair Accused in Cyberscam," *DenverRocky Mountain News* (29 October 1999): 54A. See also Associated Press, "Brothers in Cybercrime"; ABCNews.com: Blind Men Accused of Elaborate Hacker Schemes. See *abcnews.go.com/sections/tech/DailyNews/israel_cybercrime991028.html* (accessed 27 April 2001).

NATURALIZATION CLASS 1: FROM MANUAL TO DIGITAL

1. See Matthew 10:14.

2. Douglas Rushkoff defines *screenager* as "a child born into a culture mediated by the television and computer." See his *Playing for the Future: How Kid's*

Culture Can Teach Us to Thrive in an Age of Chaos (New York: HarperCollins, 1996), 3. For an early use and discussion of screenagers, see Iain Woolward, "The Care and Feeding of Screenageers for Fun and Profit," *Red Herring Magazine* (December 1994). See *www.herring.com/mag/issue16/care.html* (accessed 28 December 2000).

3. J. Leslie Houlden, "The Stranger from Heaven," *TLS: Times Literary Supplement* (21 April 2000): 3.

4. The study called "Kids and Media @ the New Millennium" was released the fall of 1999 by the Kaiser Family Foundation. See *www.kff.org/content/1999/1535/pressreleasefinal.doc.html* (accessed 27 April 2001). According to the Kaiser study, the only kinds of media that fewer than half of children have access to are premium cable channel subscriptions (about 44%) and the Internet (45%). For more see Joan Raymond, "Kids Just Wanna Have Fun," *American Demographics* (February 2000): 60. Available for purchase on the Web at this address: *www.contentville.com/product/product.asp?ProdID={036ED10F-DFFD-4EF6-9D93-89EEA885ED47}* (accessed 27 April 2001).

5. Michael R. Bonsignore, "Global Connectivity: For Every Action There Is a Chain Reaction," *Vital Speeches* 66 (15 July 2000): 605.

6. Kaiser Family Foundation survey of 3,000 children between the ages of two and eighteen. All media were lumped together.

7. Congressman J. C. Watts Jr., "Teaching Individual Self-Restraint: Taking Responsibility for Your Children's Actions," *Vital Speeches of the Day* 66 (15 June 2000): 521.

8. Bruce Sterling, ed., *Mirrorshades: The Cyberpunk Anthology* (New York: Arbor House, 1986), xi.

9. This does not even factor into the equation artificial life. For the implications of this, see N. Katherine Hayles, *How We Became Post-Human: Virtual Bodies in Cybernetics, Literature, and Informatics* (Chicago: Univ. of Chicago Press, 1999), 234.

10. Raymond Kurzweil, *The Age of Spiritual Machines: When Computers Exceed Human Intelligence* (New York: Viking, 1999). See the quote from Kurzweil by Otis Port in "Artificial Intelligence: Machines Will Be Smarter Than We Are," *Business Week* (23–30 August 1999): 120.

11. Hans Moravec, *Robot: Mere Machine to Transcendent Mind* (New York: Oxford Univ. Press, 1999).

12. Port, "Artificial Intelligence," 120.

13. The quote appeared originally on the Web in Douglas Hofstadter's description of the symposium "Will Spiritual Robots Replace Humanity by 2100?" held at Stanford University (1 April 1999) as verified in an email letter from the author, 10 January 2001.

14. Theoretical physicist Paul Davies, "Quantum Computers: The Quest for the Dream Machine," available in Metaviews archives. See *www.meta-list.org* (search under Paul Davies) (accessed 27 April 2001). Also published as "Quantum Computing: A Key to Unlocking the Ultimate Reality?" *Science & Spirit* 11

(May/June 2000): 41. See *www.science-spirit.org/articles/articledetail.cfm? article_id=199* (accessed 27 April 2001).

15. Davies, "Quantum Computers."

16. For more on the Stanford Symposium: "Will Spiritual Robots Replace Humanity by 2100?" see *www.technetcast.com/tnc_program.html?program_id=82* (accessed 28 December 2000).

17. Quoted in Christian Tyler and Danny Hills, "Why the Future May Be Getting Out of Control," *Financial Times* (27/28 November 1999): X.

18. For the story of "Fairchild's Mule," see Fiammetta Rocco's review, "Of a Practical Nature," *The Economist* (13 May 2000): 86. Available for purchase only from *www.economist.com* (accessed 27 April 2001) or the full account in Michael Leapman, *The Ingenious Mr. Fairchild: The Forgotten Father of the Flower Garden* (London: Headline, 2000).

19. That is why Christians have a history of changing their names. Roman Catholics still add a name at confirmation. Popes take new names on their election (as do nuns and monks when they enter the religious life). I would not be surprised if natives started celebrating their new identity as Jesus' disciples by taking on new names at their conversion and baptism.

20. This is found in the John Templeton Foundation Statement by Freeman J. Dyson at the Templeton Prize News Conference, 22 March 2000. See *www. templeton.org/prize/fd_statement.asp* (accessed 27 April 2001).

21. The full quote is as follows: "I have the seven notes of the scale and its chromatic intervals at my disposal . . . strong and weak accents are within my reach, and . . . in all these I possess solid and concrete elements which offer me a field of experience just as vast as the upsetting and dizzy infinitude that had just frightened me. . . . What delivers me from the anguish into which an unrestricted freedom plunges me is the fact that I am always able to turn immediately to the concrete things that are here in question. Whatever diminishes constraint diminishes strength." As quoted in Jeremy Begbie, *Voicing Creation's Praise: Towards a Theology of the Arts* (Edinburgh: T&T Clark, 1991), 211. The quote is from Igor Stravinsky, *Poetics and Music in the Form of Six Lessons,* trans. Arthur Knodel and Ingolf Dahl (Cambridge, Mass.: Harvard Univ. Press, 1970), 85, 87.

22. Karen Breslau, "One Nation, Interconnected," *Wired* (May 2000): 138. See *www.wired.com/wired/archive/8.05/poll.html* (accessed 27 April 2001).

23. Len Wilson, *The Wired Church: Making Media Ministry* (Nashville: Abingdon, 1999), 39–40.

24. Graham T. T. Molitor, "The Next 100 Years: 'The Big Five' Engines of Economic Growth," *Vital Speeches of the Day* 65 (1 September 1999): 677.

25. Mark Gerson, "Dress for Success? Casual Bucks Trend," *USA Today* (8 March 2000) 29A. Available for purchase on the Web through *usatoday. pqarchiver.com* (accessed 27 April 2001).

26. Thanks to Bruce Cook for this reference.

27. Breslau, "One Nation, Interconnected," 150–51. According to Breslau, "Business, not government, should continue leading the way." See *www.wired.com/ wired/archive/8.05/poll.html* (accessed 27 April 2001).

28. Douglas S. Robertson, *The New Renaissance: Computers and the Next Level of Civilization* (New York: Oxford Univ. Press, 1998), 148.

29. Ibid., 147.

30. Soul guest Oprah Winfrey, "Inner Revolution," January 2000, Gary Zukav Home Page, *www.zukav.com/index.htm* (accessed 27 April 2001).

31. Mary Lacombe, "Pushing the Process: Science, Religion and Society: An Interview with Ann Pederson," *Science & Spirit* 11 (May/June 2000): 48. See *science-spirit.com/articles/Articledetail.cfm?article_ID=206* (accessed 27 April 2001).

NATURALIZATION CLASS 2: FROM LINEAR TO LOOP

1. M. Scott Peck, *Golf and the Spirit: Lessons for the Journey* (New York: Three Rivers Press, 1999), 3.

2. This has been established by a team of English and Italian neuroscientists using positron emission tomography which scans blood-flow changes as patients read certain words. See Bruce Bower, "Readers' Brains Go Native," *Science News* (22 January 2000): 58.

3. This research was conducted by E. A. Maguire, D. G. Gadian, I. S. Johnsrude, and others, "Navigation-related Structural Change in the Hippocampi of Taxi Drivers," *Proceedings of the National Academy of Sciences, USA* 97 (2000): 4398–403. Available online at *www.pnas.org/cgi/content/full/97/8/4398? maxtoshow=&HITS=40&hits=40&RESULTFORMAT=&titleabstract=Navigation-Related+Structural+Change+in+the+Hippocampi+of+Taxi+Drivers&searchid=QID_NOT_SET&stored_search=&FIRSTINDEX=&fdate=1/1/1996* (accessed 27 April 2001).

4. Jocelyn Penny Small, *Wax Tablets of the Mind: Cognitive Studies of Memory and Literacy in Classical Antiquity* (London: Routledge, 1997), xiii, 151 (for papyrus reference). See especially "Tools of the Trade," 141–59; "Research Techniques," 160–76.

5. Quoted by Bruce Bower in "Cultures of Reason: Thinking Styles May Take Eastern and Western Routes," *Science News* (22 January 2000): 56.

6. Marshall McLuhan believed that our five senses have a biological need to be in equilibrium with each other. For more on the need for sensory balance, see *Counterblast* (New York: Harcourt, Brace & World, 1969) and *Understanding Media: The Extensions of Man* (New York: McGraw-Hill, 1964), especially the chapter entitled "Media," 308–37. McLuhan argued significantly that television was not a visual but an "aural and tactile" medium.

7. As quoted in John Tolva, "Changing Media," *Changing Behavior,* (10 February 1996). See *www.mindspring.com/~jntolva/hp/change.html* (accessed 29 December 2000).

8. Kaiping Peng and Richard E. Nisbett, "Culture, Dialectics, and Reasoning About Contradiction," *American Psychologist,* (September 1999): 741–54. See also Incheol Choi, Nisbett, and Ara Norenzayan, "Causal Attribution Across Cultures: Variation and Universality," *Psychological Bulletin* 125 (1999): 47–63;

"Eastern and Western Perceptions of Causality for Social Behavior: Lay Theories about Personalities and Social Situations," in *Cultural Divides: Understanding and Overcoming Group Conflict* (New York: Russell Sage Foundation, 1999), 239–72. Some other important names in research into emotion, cognition, and the human brain that I have not yet had the chance to canvass are the writings of Antonio Damasio, University of Iowa; John Allman, California Institute of Technology; Eric Kandel, Columbia University; and Patricia Kuhl, University of Washington.

9. As quoted by Scott Bukatman, "Gibson's Typewriter," *South Atlantic Quarterly* 92 (Fall 1993): 627.

10. For a full account see A. R. Luria, *The Making of Mind: A Personal Account of Soviet Psychology*, ed. Michael Cole and Sheila Cole (Cambridge, Mass.: Harvard Univ. Press, 1979), 58–80; for the white bear story see 77–78.

11. This argument, initially stated by Marshall McLuhan, was developed more fully by physicist Robert K. Logan, *The Alphabet Effect: The Impact of the Phonetic Alphabet on the Development of Western Civilization* (New York: William Morrow: 1986).

12. "For the illusion of information-space to work, you had to be able to get your hands dirty, move things around, make things happen. That's where direct manipulation came in. Instead of typing in obscure commands, the user could simply point at something and expand its contents, or drag it across the screen. Instead of telling the computer to execute a particular task — 'open this file' — users appeared to do it themselves. There was a strangely paradoxical quality to direct manipulation: in reality, the graphic interface had added another layer separating the user from his or her information. But the tactile immediacy of the illusion made it seem as though the information was now closer at hand, rather than farther away. You felt as though you were doing something directly with your data, rather than telling the computer to do it for you." See Steven Johnson, *Interface Culture: How Technology Transforms the Way We Create and Communicate* (San Francisco: HarperEdge, 1997), 21.

13. Johnson, *Interface Culture*, 14–15, 17.

14. As quoted in "Lost in Cyberspace," *The Economist* (18 December 1999): 78. Available for viewing or purchase from *www.economist.com* (accessed 27 April 2001).

15. Rick Lawrence, *TrendWatch* (Loveland, Colorado: Group Publishing, 2000), ch. 3, p. 63 in galleys.

16. Aristotle, *Nicomachean Ethics*, trans. W. D. Ross (Oxford: Charendon, 1908; Institute for Learning Technologies, 1995). See *www.ilt.columbia.edu/academic/digitexts/aristotle/nicomachean ethics/book02.html* (accessed 10 January 2001).

17. For this reason some web theorists are arguing against the use of the word "user." They contend that whenever the word "user" is used it be replaced by "player."

18. *The Republic of Plato*, rev. ed., trans. B. Jowett (New York: Wiley, 1901), 234, as quoted in Douglas S. Robertson, *The New Renaissance: Computers and the Next Level of Civilization* (New York: Oxford Univ. Press, 1998), 96.

19. Students now do twice as poorly as in 1960, with declining scores since 1960.

20. Virginia Site for Educators: Standards of Learning, "History and Social Science, Grade Ten," *www.knowledge.state.va.us/main/sol/solview.cfm?curriculum_abb=HSS&category_abb=10* (accessed 27 April 2001).

21. Gerald W. Bracey, "We Crush Children Under Unrealistic Standardized Tests," *USA Today* (2 September 1999): 17A. Available for purchase through *usatoday.pqarchiver.com* (accessed 27 April 2001). See also Educational Standards, "South Dakota Social Studies Standards: Sixth Grade," *www.state.sd.us/deca/ContentStandards/Social/68stand.htm* (accessed 27 April 2001).

22. Small, *Wax Tablets of the Mind*. For the rationalization of memorization see "The Historical Development of Ancient Memory Techniques," 81–137; and "Indirect Applications of the Art of Memory," 224–39. For the rationality of knowing where to find things, see "The Organization of Collections of Words," 41–52; "Retrieval: Documents and Texts," 53–71; and "Research Techniques," 160–76.

23. This is a 700% increase since 1990. In the year 2000, 10% of elementary school-aged boys were taking Ritalin.

24. This is the thesis of Sydney Walker III, *The Hyperactivity Hoax: How to Stop Drugging Your Child and Find Real Medical Help* (New York: St. Martin's Press, 2000).

25. Anne Hird, *Learning from Cyber-Savvy Students: How Internet Age Kids Impact Classroom Teaching* (Sterling, Va.: Stylus, 2000).

26. Jeffrey Lent, *In the Fall* (New York: Atlantic Monthly, 1999), 268.

27. With thanks to Jim Zazzera, Pastor of Cordova Presbyterian Church, Rancho Cordova, Calif., for this insight. Email Jimzaz@aol.com (22 February 2000).

28. Craig Sullivan, "Artist Breaks Out of Graphic Limit," *Albuquerque Journal: Journal North* (29 September 2000): 6.

29. Quoted by Nicholas Hammond, "Reading Between the Cracks: The Deliberate Disorder of Pascal's Pensées," *TLS: Times Literary Supplement* (19 May 2000): 7.

30. See the research at Harvard Business School on those who write negative versus positive book reviews: Teresa M. Amabile, "Brilliant but Cruel: Perceptions of Negative Evaluators," *Journal of Experimental Social Psychology* 19 (1983): 146–56, and earlier Teresa M. Amabile and Ann H. Glazebrook, "A Negativity Bias in Interpersonal Evaluation," *Journal of Experimental Social Psychology* 18 (1982): 1–22.

31. John H. Holland, *Emergence: From Chaos to Order* (Reading, Mass.: Addison-Wesley, 1998), 1.

32. "America's Education Choice," *The Economist* (1 April 2000): 17. Available for viewing or purchase at *www.economist.com/displayStory.cfm?Story_ID=297396* (accessed 27 April 2001).

33. Phone: 800-242-2460. Thanks to Marcia Sprinkle of First Baptist Church, Washington, D.C., for alerting me to this organization.

34. Quoted in John Sutherland, "Last of the Nomads" [review of Laurence Lerner, *Wandering Professor* (London: Caliban, 1999)], *TLS: Times Literary Supplement* (12 November 1999): 12.

35. Douglas S. Robertson, *The New Renaissance: Computers and the Next Level of Civilization* (New York: Oxford Univ. Press, 1998), 156–57.

36. Hird, *Learning from Cyber-Savvy Students,* 25. She further warns that "until teachers become fluent online learners alongside their students, schools run the risk of becoming increasingly irrelevant to students growing up in the Internet Age" (12).

NATURALIZATION CLASS 3: FROM WORD TO IMAGE

1. As quoted in "Alienated Troubadour of Reconciliation: An Interview with John Michael Talbot," *Re: Generation Quarterly* 5 (Winter 1999/2000): 26.

2. George E. Sweazey, *Preaching the Good News* (Englewood Cliffs, N.J.: Prentice-Hall, 1976), 244.

3. See Francis Schüssler Fiorenza and Gordon D. Kaufman, "God," in *Critical Terms for Religious Studies,* ed. Mark C. Taylor (Chicago: Univ. of Chicago Press, 1998), 136–59.

4. Douglas Raybeck and Stephanie Dorenbosch, Michael Sarapata and Douglas Herrmann, "SWF ISO LTR: The Quest for Love and Meaning in the Personals," Paper presented at the 98th Annual Meeting of the American Anthropological Association, Chicago, Ill., 24–28 November 1996. See *www.hamilton.edu/media/personals.html* (accessed 19 July 2000).

5. Thanks to columnist/essayist Arianna Stassinopoulos-Huffington for this information.

6. I am relying heavily here on the findings of Stanford University economics professor Thomas MaCurdy. For more of his work see *search.atomz.com/search/?sp-q=Thomas+MaCurdy&sp-a=000515be-sp00000000* (accessed 30 April 2001).

7. As quoted in Brian R. Clack, *Wittgenstein, Frazer and Religion* (New York: St. Martin's Press, 1999), 30.

8. Mark Turner, *The Literary Mind* (New York: Oxford Univ. Press, 1996), 12. Turner defines parable thus: "Parable is the projection of story," 7.

9. Ibid., 5.

10. Ibid., 168.

11. Frederic Golden, "Albert Einstein: Person of the Century;" Stephen Hawking, "A Brief History of Relativity"; J. Madeleine Nash, "Einstein's Unfinished Symphony"; and Roger Rosenblatt, "The Age of Einstein," *Time* (31 December 1999): 62–95. See *www.pathfinder.com/time/time100/poc/magazine/albert_einstein5a.html* (accessed 30 April 2001).

12. Michael D. Lemonick, "Was Einstein's Brain Built for Brilliance?" *Time* (28 June 1999): 54. See *www.pathfinder.com/time/magazine/articles/0,3266,27180,00.html* (accessed 30 April 2001).

13. Michael Paterniti, *Driving Mr. Albert: A Trip Across America with Einstein's Brain* (New York: Dial, 2000).

14. Robert Bellah, "Between Religion and Social Science," in his *Beyond Belief: Essays on Religion in a Post-Traditional World* (New York: Harper & Row, 1970), 246.

15. Sandra F. Witelson, Debra L. Kigar, Thomas Harvey, "The Exceptional Brain of Albert Einstein," *The Lancet* 353 (19 June 1999): 2149–53, quote on 2152.

16. Lemonick, "Was Einstein's Brain Built for Brilliance?" 54.

17. For more on this see chapter 3 of my *Post-modern Pilgrims: First Century Passion for the 21st Century World* (Nashville: Broadman & Holman, 2000), 85–108.

18. Antonio Damasio, *The Feeling of What Happens: Body, Emotion in the Making of Consciousness* (New York: Harcourt Brace, 1999), 30.

19. "The cooking process" comes from Patrick Bateson and Paul Martin, *Design for a Life: How Behavior and Personality Develop* (New York: Simon & Schuster, 2000), 16. "During pregnancy ten mothers regularly read aloud, as if to their unborn child, a story called 'To Think That I Saw It on Mulberry Street.' Later, after they had been born, these same babies were given the opportunity to suck, either more or less frequently than usual, in order to hear a recording of their mother reading 'To Think That I Saw It on Mulberry Street,' as opposed to another story. The newborn babies learned to alter their sucking behavior to hear not just their own mother's voice, but also the sound patterns of the particular story that had been repeatedly read to them before they were born." Bateson and Martin, *Design for a Life*, 26.

20. Turner, *Literary Mind*, 134–35.

21. Kalle Lasn, *Culture Jam: The Uncooling of America* (New York: Eagle Brook, 1999), 165–83.

22. John Naisbitt with Nana Naisbitt and Douglas Philips, *High Tech/High Touch: Technology and Our Search for Meaning* (New York: Broadway Books, 1999), 3.

23. An earlier version of this section appeared as a column in *Rev. Magazine* 3:5 (May/June 2000).

24. In his upcoming *Digital Discipleship,* successor book to *E-vangelism* (Lafayette, La.: Vital Issues, 1998), Andrew Careaga challenges clergy to visit some Christian teen chat sites and overhear what the kids in their pews are really talking about. See Careaga's excerpt "It's a Bod Mod Cyberworld," *NextWave* (January 2000), www.next-wave.org/jan00/Its_a_bod_mod_cyberworld.htm (accessed 30 April 2001).

25. Pastor Dave Hart of Sanctuary San Diego (www.webpulse.com/sanctuary), a church that ministers to San Diego's Goth culture, has written an excellent teaching on the subject, "Tattoo or Not Tattoo: That Is the Question." See www.webpulse.com/sanctuary/message/pastor_dave/tattoo_not_tattoo/tattoo_not_tattoo.html (accessed 30 April 2001).

26. I borrow this language of apprenticeship from Tom Nelson, founding pastor of Christ Community Church in Leawood, Kansas. Nelson talks about being an apprentice rather than disciple because he thinks the word *apprentice* is more accessible and less loaded with baggage than the word *disciple*.

27. Charles Hoffacker, "Praying with Icons," *Christianity and the Arts 7* (Spring 2000): 9.

28. Flannery O'Connor, "Parker's Back" in her *Collected Works* (New York: Library of America, 1988), 658–59, 662–70. Thanks to doctoral student Ned Buckner for this reference.

29. Michele Gold, "Gratitude is a Sanctuary" in Louise L. Hay and friends, ed. Jill Cramer, *Gratitude: A Way of Life* (Carlsbad, Calif.: Hay House, 1996), 90–91.

30. Len Wilson, *The Wired Church: Making Media Ministry* (Nashville: Abingdon Press, 1999), 41.

31. See, for example, "A Gardening Credo," in *The Gardener's Essential Gertrude Jekyll,* introd. Elizabeth Lawrence (Boston: David R. Godine, 1986), 23–50.

32. Cathy Olofson, "Just the (Meaningful) Facts: Report from the Futurist," *Fast Company* (December 1999): 80. See *www.fastcompany.com/online/30/futurist.html* (accessed 30 April 2001).

33. Plato, "Phaedrus," in his *Lysis or Friendship, The Symposium, Phaedrus,* trans. from the Greek by Benjamin Jowett (New York: Heritage Press, 1968), 202.

34. Ibid., 203.

NATURALIZATION CLASS 4: FROM VAST TO FAST

1. Christian Tyler, "Memo to the Future," *Financial Times: Weekend* (3–4 June 2000): 1.

2. Stewart Brand, "Taking the Long View," *Time,* special ed. (April/May 2000): 86. See *www.time.com/time/reports/earthday2000/longview01.html* (accessed 30 April 2001).

3. The phrase, first used by Susan Ferraro, *Remembrance of Things Fast* (New York: Dell, 1990); also an award winning film: *Remembrance of Things Fast* (1994), directed by John Maybury; and used later by Owen Edwards, "Remembrace of Things Fast," *Forbes ASAP* (2 December 1996). See *www.forbes.com/asap/120296/html/owen_edwards.htm* (accessed 1 July 2000).

4. Tom Peters, "A Brawl with No Rules," *Forbes ASAP* (21 February 2000): 155. See *www.forbes.com/asap/2000/0221/155.html* (accessed 30 April 2001).

5. *Places Rated Almanac,* Millennium ed., ed. David Savageau and Ralph D'Agostino (Foster City, Calif.: IDG Books, 2000), 3.

6. Douglas Hofstadter was the first to talk about *Time* magazine's "time capsule" to be opened at 3000. The editors of *Time* fully expected humans to be around to open it up. But Hofstadter wonders whether humans as we know them will be around in 3000. Will humans have so migrated and morphed into something else that they will be in unrecognizable form?

7. By 2029, some scientists are saying we will be able to scan the human brain without making much of a mess of things. How? By sending scanners through the bloodstream. By creating virtual reality from within.

8. As told in Douglas S. Robertson, *The New Renaissance: Computers and the Next Level of Civilization* (New York: Oxford Univ. Press, 1998), 172.

9. Les Murray, "One Kneeling, One Looking Down," *Conscious and Verbal* (Manchester, England: Carcanet, 1999), 11.

10. Hillvue Heights Church is located in Bowling Green, Kentucky (www.hillvue.com); Hillsongs Church is located in Sydney, Australia (www.hillsclc.org.au). (Both sites accessed 30 April 2001.)

11. Listen to Russell Fragar's song "Church on Fire" from the video by Hillsongs Australia, Touching Heaven Changing Earth (Mobile, Ala.: Hillsongs Music Australia, 1998). De-evangelism works with natives. The more Hillvue Heights Church tells people "You aren't ready yet to come to our church," the more people want to come. Note how the more the Dali Lama warns people to stick to their own religion, the more people become Buddhist.

12. Noah Hawley, "Do You Have the Courage to Be Legendary?" Shift (April 2000): 60. See www.shift.com/shiftstd/html/onlinetoc/2000/8.3/html/scient-ex.html (accessed 27 April 2000).

13. Tom Peters, "A Brawl with No Rules," p. 155.

14. As per Lester Thurow's calculation.

15. Richard Sennett contrasts "career" with the word "job" which in the English of the 14th century meant a "lump or piece of something which could be carted around." Richard Sennett, The Corrosion of Character: The Personal Consequences of Work in the New Capitalism (New York: Norton, 1998), 9.

16. Elliott Masie as quoted in Lucy McCauley, "Learning 101," Fast Company (October 2000): 110. See www.fastcompany.com/online/39/one.html (accessed 2 December 2000).

17. For an example from a low viscosity church see the story of worship leader Kim Miller and her skydive, as told in Michael Slaughter with Warren Bird, Real Followers: Beyond Virtual Christianity (Nashville: Abingdon, 1999), 123–34.

18. The image of hearing life's "recess bells" comes from Mary Furlong, founder of ThirdAge.com.

19. Director of the Royal Observatory, Greenwich, Kristen Lippincott, quoting a University of Sussex endocrinologist in Heath Row, "A (Really) Brief History of Time," Fast Company (June 2000): 60. See www.fastcompany.com/online/35/greenwich.html (accessed 30 April 2001).

20. See www.longnow.org (accessed 30 April 2001).

21. Graham T. T. Molitor, "Millennial Perspectives on Employee Benefit Changes," Vital Speeches of the Day 66 (15 May 2000): 457.

22. As quoted in Alan M. Webber, "Why Can't We Get Anything Done?" Fast Company (June 2000): 178. See www.fastcompany.com/online/35/pfeffer.html (accessed 30 April 2001).

23. David Shenk, Data Smog: Surviving the Information Glut (New York: HarperCollins, 1997), 29, 31.

24. Quoted in Clive Thompson, "Not Tonight, Dear. I'm Lazy," Shift (July/August 2000): 36. See www.shift.com (accessed 30 April 2001).

25. An exact quote from David Butcher, "Adidas Adopts Adept Stars for Interactive Training Site," Revolution 1 (May 2000): 78.

26. Samuel Johnson, Prologue to "The Tragedy of Irene," in The Works of Samuel Johnson in Nine Volumes, Oxford English Classics (Oxford: Printed for William Pickering, London, 1825), 1:29.

27. James Taylor, "Sun on the Moon," James Taylor Online-Lyrics, www. james-taylor.com/albums/sunonmoon.shtml (accessed 30 April 2001).

28. As quoted in Gerard Kelly, *RetroFuture: Rediscovering Our Roots, Recharting Our Routes* (Downers Grove, Ill.: InterVarsity, 2000), 51.

29. Watts Wacker and Jim Taylor with Howard Means, *The Visionary's Handbook: Nine Paradoxes That Will Shape the Future of Your Business* (New York: HarperBusiness, 2000), 7.

NATURALIZATION CLASS 5: FROM "MAKE SENSE" TO "MAKE SENSE"

1. Third stanza of Folliot S. Pierpoint, "For the Beauty of the Earth," (1864), *The United Methodist Hymnal: Book of United Methodist Worship* (Nashville: United Methodist Publishing House, 1989), 92.

2. Similarly, up until the 19th century "nervous" meant "strong, energetic, courageous" and only later came to mean exactly the reverses what it is today.

3. Dionysius of Halicarnassus, "Demosthenes," in his *The Critical Essays in Two Volumes,* trans. Stephen Usher, Loeb Classical Library (Cambridge, Mass.: Harvard Univ. Press, 1974), 1:323.

4. Edward M. Hallowell, *Connect* (New York: Pantheon, 1999), 202.

5. Ibid., 200–201.

6. Robert Wuthnow, "Questions and Answers: Spirituality in America Since the 1950s," *Sacred Journey* 51 (February 2000): 12. See also his *After Heaven: Spirituality in America Since the 1950s* (Berkeley: Univ. of California Press, 1998).

7. Jonathan Israel, "Driven to Greatness [Review of Simon Schama's *Rembrandt's Eyes*]," *TLS: Times Literary Supplement* (5 November 1999): 4.

8. As Karen Armstrong shows in her book *The Battle for God* (New York: Knopf, 2000) fundamentalisms (whether Christian, Jewish, Islam) are rationalist attempts at propounding truth (see especially her introduction, ix–xv). See also Richard Mouw, *The Smell of Sawdust* (Grand Rapids: Zondervan, 2000), 119: "There is an irony of sorts to be considered here. Fundamentalism is widely know for its anti-intellectualism — this is the pattern analyzed with such skill by Mark Noll in his *The Scandal of the Evangelical Mind*. But a proper understanding of fundamentalism requires clarity about the *sense* in which it is anti-intellectual: Fundamentalists oppose the kind of thinking that goes on in the academy; they are not given to careful, nuanced formulations of issues that are basic to the human condition; they often deal in cliches and proof texts. . . . But there is also an important sense in which fundamentalism is *highly* intellectual, in view of the fact that fundamentalists make much of the need for intellectual assent to specific doctrinal propositions. They aren't happy until they know that their candidates for conversion really believe the fundamentals."

9. Rolf Jensen, *The Dream Society: How the Coming Shift from Information to Imagination Will Transform Your Business* (New York: McGraw-Hill, 1999), 16, 183–84.

10. Sheldon Vanauken, *A Severe Mercy* (New York: Harper & Row, 1977), 85.

11. Cathy Olofson, "Dream Society: Report from the Futurist," *Fast Company* (October 1999): 84. See *www.fastcompany.com/online/28/futurist.html* (accessed 30 April 2001).

12. Alex R. Garcia-Rivera, *The Community of the Beautiful: A Theological Aesthetics* (Collegeville, Minn.: Liturgical, 1999), 46.

13. Andy Warhol, *The Philosophy of Andy Warhol: From A to B and Back Again* (New York: Harcourt Brace Jovanovich, 1975), 151.

14. George Hunter has a new book that describes this approach: *The Celtic Way of Evangelism: How Christianity Can Reach the West . . . Again* (Nashville: Abingdon, 2000).

15. For more, see *www.sanctuaryonline.org* (accessed 15 June 2001).

16. See, for example, Kris Newcomer, "Merchants Bear Witness in Style: Merchandise at Christian Booksellers Convention Ranges from High-fashion Ties to Coffee Mugs, Toys and Pencils," *Rocky Mountain News* (28 June 1994).

17. The $1.3 million dress obliterated the previous record of $222,500 paid for Princess Diana's gown sold in 1997.

18. Charles Simpkinson and Anne Adamcewicz Simpkinson, *Soul Work: A Field Guide for Spiritual Seekers* (New York: HarperCollins, 1998).

19. Miles Davis with Quincy Troupe, *Miles: The Autobiography* (New York: Macmillan, 1990), 381.

20. Tom Bandy, *Coaching Change: Breaking Down Resistance, Building Up Hope* (Nashville: Abingdon, 2000), 139 (in manuscript form).

21. SungHo Lee, SLee0202@aol.com.

22. Connie Cavanaugh, "*On Mission*'s Believe It or Not Churches!" *On Mission* 2 (September/October 1999): 11–15.

23. Watts Wacker and Jim Taylor with Howard Means, *The Visionary's Handbook: Nine Paradoxes That Will Shape the Future of Your Business* (New York: HarperBusiness, 2000), 199.

NATURALIZATION CLASS 6: FROM "WHO AM I?" TO "WHAT IS TO BE DONE?"

1. Douglas John Hall, *Why Christian? For Those on the Edge of Faith* (Minneapolis: Fortress, 1998), 35–36, 39, 40.

2. Down the list were "Will I have life after death?" (19%) and "Why do bad things happen?" (16%). See *Pastor's Weekly Briefing* (10 September 1999): 2.

3. Christopher Beem, *The Necessity of Politics: Reclaiming American Public Life* (Chicago: Univ. of Chicago Press, 1999), 256.

4. Roger Lewin and Birute Regine, *The Soul at Work: Listen, Respond, Let Go: Embracing Complexity Science for Business Success* (New York: Simon & Schuster, 2000), 324. "Business is and will be the most potent force for social transformation in the world."

5. "Campuses today are Athenian city-states," says Vartan Gregorian, formerly President of Brown University. As quoted in William Leach, *Country of Exiles: The Destruction of Place in American Life* (New York: Pantheon Books, 1999), 128.

6. William Leach, *Country of Exiles: The Destruction of Place in American Life* (New York: Pantheon Books, 1999), 130–32.

7. Laura Nash and Scotty McLennan, *Church on Sunday, Work on Monday: The Challenge of Fusing Christian Values with Business Life* (San Francisco: Jossey-Bass, 2001), ch. 6.

8. Robert H. Frank, *Luxury Fever: Why Money Fails to Satisfy in an Era of Excess* (New York: Free Press, 1999), 111.

9. "Notes From the Guest Register," *Inc.* (August 1998): 11.

10. For more on this see the chapter on play in my *SoulSalsa: 17 Surprising Steps for Godly Living in the 21st Century* (Grand Rapids: Zondervan, 2000), 155–62.

11. For evidence that businesses are accommodating natives, see the prevalence of flex hours, dress-down days, etc. One in six employers surveyed say they permit naps at work (16%). As cited in Mary Harvey, " Sleepless in America," *American Demographics* (July 2000): 10. Available for purchase online at *www.contentville.com/product/product.asp?ProdID={B4B90BBD-738D-4473-B120-29D76FB1CA0C}* (accessed 30 April 2001).

12. Sheenagh Pugh, "Tutorial," in his *Stonelight* (Bridgend, Wales: Seren, 1999), 58.

13. Christian Schumacher, Work Structuring Ltd. chair, *God in Work* (London: Lion, 1998).

14. AP report "Tree-sitter Branches Out on the Ground," *Gaston Gazette* (12 June 2000).

15. "Audiences for daytime soap opera have declined by 83% since 1991; the 11 shows that now run on the 3 old national networks each lost viewers over the past year." "Has the Bubble Burst for American Soap?" *The Economist* (5 February 2000), 76. Available online to subscribers at *economist.com*. See also Rebecca Gardyn, "Media Channels: 'Tis the Season," *American Demographics* (September 2000), 30. See *www.contentville.com/product/product.asp?ProdID={71154E45-0CC3-43E5-86F2-BBFEBE8456ED}* (accessed 6 June 2001).

16. According to former Harvard professor and current dean of the London Business School, John Quelch.

17. These figures come from the US Census Bureau. See *www.census.gov* (accessed 30 April 2001).

18. John Fetto, "Wide Open Spaces: Rural America Awaits a Surge of Retirees," *American Demographics* (October 1999): 44. See *www.contentville.com/product/product.asp?ProdID={9AD49A82-3F48-4C8D-B8E8-C8DBDCF6ED7B}* (accessed 30 April 2001). In 1999, 13% of home sales in the US were for second homes. In 1997, it was 8%. In 1999, 38% of second homes sales did not involve a mortgage; boomers paid cash.

19. According to a BBC poll in 1999. For words and music see John Lennon, "Imagine," Jan's Music Page, *www.geocities.com/Broadway/Alley/1210/Imagine.html* (accessed 30 April 2001).

20. Thomas G. Weiss and Jarat Chopra, "Sovereignty Under Siege: From Intervention to Humanitarian Space," in *Beyond Westphalia? State Sovereignty and International Intervention*, ed. Gene M. Lyons and Michael Mastanduno (Baltimore: Johns Hopkins Univ. Press, 1995), 114.

21. As quoted by William Van Dusen Wishard in "Globalization: Humanity's Great Experiment," *The Futurist* (October 1999): 60.

22. Pico Iyer, *The Global Soul: Jet Lag, Shopping Malls, and the Search for Home* (New York: Knopf, 2000), 19.

23. *World Social Science Report 1999*, ed. Ali Kazancigil and David Makinson (Paris: UNESCO, 1999), 84–154.

24. Countries that allow double citizenships as of 2000 include Canada, Ireland, France, Poland, and the Dominican Republic. The Welsh-born "knight" Sir Anthony Hopkins became a US citizen in April 2000. He will keep his citizenship in the UK.

25. See Synergetics on the Web, "Desovereignization," *www.teleport.com/ ~pdx4d/grunch.html* (accessed 30 April 2001). See also R. Buchminster Fuller, *Critical Path* (New York: St. Martin's Press, 1981), 202.

26. The worldwide pandemic of HIV-1 may be attributable to a single cross-species event between a human and a chimpanzee (whether the zoonosis was a polio vaccine or a sexual act). Hence the need to be careful in zenotransplantation (putting pig hearts in human hearts) and the cultivation of breeding pits for human animal parts, etc.

27. Wishard, "Globalization: Humanity's Great Experiment," 60.

28. Claritas, the Arlington, Virginia-based marketing company divides American society into 62 distinctive lifestyle types it calls "clusters" or "clustered worlds," up from 40 segments during the 1970s and 1980s. See Susan Mitchell, "Birds of a Feather," *American Demographics* (February 1995): 42. See *www.contentville. com/product/product.asp?ProdID={5CA856AC-EB47-45EC-B5F3-769F9FED05B1}* (accessed 30 April 2001).

29. Michael J. Weiss, *The Clustered World: How We Live, What We Buy, and What It Means About Who We Are* (Boston: Little, Brown, 2000), 166.

30. Conversation with Lon Chavez, Director, Missions Division, California, Southern Baptist Convention (22 November 2000).

31. Weiss, *The Clustered World*, 10.

32. As of 1999, 750 million speak English and 1 billion are learning it. There are these varieties of English in the 1999 Encarta World English Dictionary: British, American, Canadian, Caribbean, Scottish, Irish, Welsh, South African, South Asian, South East Asian, Australian, and New Zealand. Kathy Rooney, ed., *Encarta World English Dictionary*. See *dictionary.msn.com/ewedmedia/ 11k_IMA-ADPCM.AIF/A17/A1778100.aif* (accessed 30 April 2001).

33. Two Washington, D.C., think tanks independently released reports that show the income gap widening during the 1990s between the rich and the poor: the Economic Policy Institute *(www.epinet.org)* and the Center on Budget and Policy Priorities *(www.cbpp.org)*. (Both sites accessed 30 April 2001.)

34. As calculated by former US Treasury Secretary Robert E. Rudin in "The Global Economy: Opportunities and Risks," address delivered to the London School of Economics, London, England (2 February 2000). See *www.lse.ac.uk/events/ 02.02.rubin.htm* (accessed 13 July 2000).

35. As cited by Thomas W. Hazlett, "Passages: Eleven Years that Shook the World," *Reason* (June 2000): 18.

36. Sharif Abdullah, *Creating a World That Works for All* (San Francisco: Berrett-Koehler, 1999), xi.

37. Statement by Freeman J. Dyson at the Templeton Prize News Conference, 22 March 2000. See *www.templeton.org/prize/fd_statement.asp* (accessed 30 April 2001).

38. Abdullah, *Creating a World That Works for All*, 19–20.

39. Philanthropy News Network Online (*pnnonline.org*) is where you can connect with people who are giving away computers, lcd projectors, etc. You apply online and are accepted or rejected online (accessed 4 April 2001).

40. Joseph Epstein, "Move It On Down," *TLS: Times Literary Supplement* (23 July 1999): 27.

41. So argues Yale professors Bruce Ackerman and Anne Alstott, *The Stakeholder Society* (New Haven: Yale Univ. Press, 1999), 143.

42. David Parlett, *The Oxford History of Board Games* (New York: Oxford Univ. Press, 1999), 349–53.

43. Roger Lewin and Birute Regine, *The Soul at Work: Listen, Respond, Let Go: Embracing Complexity Science for Business Success* (New York: Simon & Schuster, 2000), 260.

44. Quoted in "Government and the Internet: The Next Revolution," *The Economist* (24 June 2000), insert: 27. Available for view and purchase at *www.economist.com* (accessed 16 July 2000).

45. Jane Smiley, *Horse Heaven* (New York: Knopf, 2000).

46. Paul Benjamin, *The Vision Splendid: Working (Book Four)* (Washington, D.C.: American Press, 1997), 53.

47. Dale T. Irvin, "The Gift of Mission," *Christianity Today* (6 December 1999): 59.

48. Ferdinand Mount, "All Coherence Not Quite Gone," *TLS: Times Literary Supplement* (14 January 2000): 28.

49. Walt Mueller, "Whose God Is it Anyway?" *YouthCulture@2000* (Winter 1999): 1.

50. Laura Nash and Scotty McLennan, *Church on Sunday, Work on Monday: The Challenge of Fusing Christian Values with Business Life* (San Francisco: Jossey-Bass, 2001).

51. Ibid., ch. 8.

NATURALIZATION CLASS 7: FROM SHARP TO FUZZY

1. Tom Robbins, *Jitterbug Perfume* (New York: Bantam Books, 1984), 263.

2. Bart Kosko, *The Fuzzy Future: From Society and Science to Heaven in a Chip* (New York: Harmony Books, 1999), 3.

3. Watts Wacker and Jim Taylor with Howard Means, *The Visionary's Handbook: Nine Paradoxes That Will Shape the Future of Your Business* (New York: HarperBusiness, 2000), 20.

4. Ibid., 17–18.

5. As quoted by Jeff A. Taylor, "Balance Sheet," in *Reason* 32 (December 2000): 10. See *www.reason.com/0012/balance.html* (accessed 9 December 2000).

6. John F. Kennedy, *To Turn the Tide: A Selection from President Kennedy's Public Statements from His Election Through the 1961 Adjournment of Congress,*

Setting Forth the Goals of His First Legislative Year, ed. John W. Gardner (New York: Harper, 1962), 74–75.

7. Max Wilkinson, "How to Follow 2000 Years of Sex, Violence and Brutality?" in "Financial Times Survey: The Millennium" *Financial Times* (6 December 1999): 2:23.

8. "Atheists and Agnostics Are Infiltrating Christian Churches," *Barna Report* (October/December 1999): 4–5. See also the 15 October 1999 press release, *www.barna.org/cgi-bin/PagePressRelease.asp?PressReleaseID=2* (accessed 30 April 2001).

9. The figures are quoted in *Current Thoughts and Trends* 16 (February 2000): 3.

10. Richard Shaull and Waldo Cesar, *Pentecostalism and the Future of the Christian Churches: Promises, Limitations, Challenges* (Grand Rapids: Eerdmans, 2000), xiii.

11. Harvey Cox, "Into the Age of Miracles: Culture, Religion, and the Market Revolution," *World Policy Journal* 14 (Spring 1997): 87–95.

12. Allan Bloom, *The Closing of the American Mind* (New York: Simon and Schuster, 1987).

13. Saul Bellow, *Ravelstein* (New York: Viking, 2000).

14. "Milestones," *Time* (24 January 2000): 23. See *www.time.com/time/magazine/article/0,9171,1101000124-37614,00.html* (accessed 30 April 2001).

15. Pat Wingert, "Jefferson's Other Family," *Newsweek* 7 (February 2000): 57. See *newsweek.com/nw-srv/printed/us/so/a2866-2000jan30.htm* (accessed 24 February 2000).

16. Tyler Cowen, *What Price Fame?* (Cambridge, Mass.: Harvard Univ. Press, 2000), 50–51.

17. Alain L. Sanders, "Six Billion People . . . and Counting," *Time Daily* (19 July 1999): *www.time.com/time/nation/article/0,8599,28310,00.html* (accessed 30 April 2001). Robert La Franco, "Mobile Telephony: The Sky's the Limit," *Forbes* (23 February 1998): 80. See *www.forbes.com/forbes/98/0223/6104080a.htm* (accessed 30 April 2001).

18. $156 billion (assets of three richest men) as compared to $136.2 billion (total GNP of the 43 least developed countries with a combined population of 600 million people.) See Alain L. Sanders, "Six Billion People . . . and Counting," *Time Daily* (19 July 1999). See *www.time.com/time/nation/article/0,8599,28310,00.html* (accessed 30 April 2001).

19. As quoted in Bruce Horovitz, "'90s Luxury Beyond Top of the Line," *USA Today* (6 July 1999): 1A. See *usatoday.pqarchiver.com* (accessed 23 June 2000).

20. Kevin Kelly, "Wealth Is the Right Thing to Do," [interview with George Gilder] *Wired* (September 1999): 156. See *www.wired.com/wired/archive/7.09/prophets.html* (accessed 30 April 2001).

21. Pui-Wing Tam, "Taking High Tech Home Is a Bit Much for an Internet Exec," *Wall Street Journal* (16 June 2000): A1.

22. Ibid., A8.

23. Tom Peters, "Please . . . I Just Need Some Quiet Time," *Forbes ASAP* (4 October 1999): 37. See *www.forbes.com/asap/1999/1004/037.html* (accessed 30 April 2001).

24. Naomi Klein, *No Logo: Taking Aim at the Brand Bullies* (New York: Picador, 2000), 446.

25. Richard Tomkins interview with Douglas Daft, "Global Chief Thinks Locally," in *Financial Times* (1 August 2000): 12.

26. For more of this see Annette Fuentes, "Won't You Be My Neighbor?" *American Demographics* (June 2000): 60–62. Available for purchase online at *www.contentville.com/product/product.asp?ProdID={D1C006D9-B290-481D-9B6C-0A691609953B}* (accessed 30 April 2001).

27. See Joel Kotkin, *The New Geography: How the Digital Revolution Is Reshaping the American Landscape* (New York: Random House, 2000), 6.

28. As quoted in Jan Sapp, *Evolution by Association: A History of Symbiosis* (New York: Oxford Univ. Press, 1994), 180. For a fuller explanation see Karl Pearson, *The Grammar of Science,* 2d ed. (London: Adam and Charles Black, 1900), 537.

29. Wacker and Taylor, *The Visionary's Handbook,* 18.

30. According to the President of Interactive Delivery Systems for Bank One, Bruce Leucke, "60 percent of bankone.com customers tell us they still want access to our physical banking centers and other channels." See his "Hang On for a Wild Ride," *Vital Speeches of the Day* 65 (1 September 1999): 684.

31. Ibid., 23.

32. BASE Jumping is parachute jumping from a fixed object (**b**uilding, **a**ntennae, **s**pan, or **e**arth) rather than from an airplane.

33. George Walden, "Thunder in the Air," *TLS: Times Literary Supplement* (24 March 2000): 6.

34. For more on these epical relationships, see my *Post-modern Pilgrims: First Century Passion for the 21ˢᵗ Century World* (Nashville: Broadman & Holman, 2000).

35. For more information see *stats.bls.gov:80/news.release/ecopro.t06.htm* (accessed 24 April 2000).

36. John Naisbitt with Nana Naisbitt and Douglas Philips, *High Tech/High Touch: Technology and Our Search for Meaning* (New York: Broadway Books, 1999), 3.

37. Les Murray, "Prime Numbers," *Conscious and Verbal* (Manchester, England: Carcanet, 1999), 39.

38. C. S. Lewis, *Letters to Malcolm: Chiefly on Prayer* (New York: Harcourt, Brace & World, 1964), 93.

39. Fifth verse of Robert Grant's, "O Worship the King," (1833) in *The United Methodist Hymnal: Book of Untied Methodist Worship* (Nashville: The United Methodist Publishing House, 1989), 73.

40. I am told this idea was first suggested by novelist Salman Rushdie. There are many examples of shared holy spaces in the early Islamic period. For example, Umayyad Caliph Hisham (724–43) did not destroy the shrine of the saint

Sergius, a Christian martyr of the early fourth century, when he made Rusafa his residence. Rather, he built a mosque in the courtyard of the church and offered both Muslims and Christians access to the site. For more examples in the early Islamic period, see Elizabeth Key Fowden, *The Barbarian Plain: Saint Sergius between Rome and Iran* (Berkeley: Univ. of California, 1999), 175–77. See also the example of Shivta in the Negev, where the small mosque nestles in the narthex of the Byzantine church.

41. Wacker and Taylor, *The Visionary's Handbook,* 1.

42. John Saward, "Regaining Paradise: Paul Claudel and the Renewal of Exegesis," *Downside Review,* 114 (1996): 79.

43. Quoted in *Science & Spirit* 10 (January/February 2000): 31.

44. Tom Sine, "Not Your Father's Commune," *Re: Generation Quarterly* 6 (July 2000): 22.

45. As compiled by Craig Bird, "Gearing Up," *FaithWorks* 3 (July/August 2000): 7. See *www.faithworks.com/articles/article%20archive/gearingup.htm* (accessed 30 April 2001).

46. Ibid.

NATURALIZATION CLASS 8: FROM OUTER SPACE TO INNER SPACE

1. Vaclav Havel, "Introductory Essay" in Sharif Abdullah, *Creating a World That Works for All* (San Francisco: Berrett-Koehler, 1999), viii.

2. Paul Gray, "Thomas Edison (1847–1931)," *Time* (31 December 1999): 184–86, 195. See *www.pathfinder.com/time/magazine/articles/0,3266,36752,00. html* (accessed 30 April 2001).

3. James D. Newton, *Uncommon Friends: Life with Thomas Edison, Henry Ford, Harvey Firestone, Alexis Carrel, & Charles Lindbergh* (New York: Harcourt Brace, 1987), 3.

4. Ibid., 10.

5. Ibid., 12.

6. Edison's death was one of the biggest blows in Ford's life. In fact, Ford and his wife Clara never returned to their Fort Myers home after Edison's death. They couldn't face the memories of Florida without Thomas and Mina.

7. As quoted in Newton, *Uncommon Friends,* 30.

8. E. F. Schumacher, *A Guide for the Perplexed* (London: Jonathan Cape, 1977), 153.

9. As quoted in P. J. Kavanagh, "Bywords," *TLS: Times Literary Supplement* (7 January 2000): 14.

10. Wendy Kamirer, "The Latest Fashion in Irrationality," *Atlantic Monthly* (July 1996): 103–106. See *www.theatlantic.com/issues/96jul/angels/angels.htm* (accessed 30 April 2001).

11. A. N. Wilson, *God's Funeral* (New York: Norton, 1999), 354.

12. As referenced in Andrew Careaga, "It's a Bod Mod Cyberworld," *Next-Wave* (January 2000). See *www.next-wave.org/jan00/Its_a_bod_mod_cyberworld. htm* (accessed 30 April 2001).

13. Personal correspondence, 1 December 1999.

14. For more predictions see David Kristof and Todd W. Nickerson, *Predictions for the Next Millennium: Thoughts on the 1000 Years Ahead* (Kansas City, Mo.: Andrews McMeel, 1999).

15. What evidence does Gallup cite to back this up? (1) a "bull-market spirituality," (2) a religion of "me and Thee," (3) a "hunger for experience," (4) search for "roots amid the relativism," (5) a "quest for community." George Gallup and Timothy Jones, *The Next American Spirituality: Finding God in the Twenty-first Century* (Colorado Springs: Victor, 2000), 43–64. See also "Gallup Poll Topics A–Z: Religion," *www.gallup.com/poll/idicators/indreligion.asp* (accessed 13 December 2000).

16. "The Millennium of the West," *The Economist* (31 December 1999): 9. Available for viewing or purchase from *www.economist.com* (accessed 30 April 2001).

17. See my *SoulTsunami: Sink or Swim in New Millennium Culture* (Grand Rapids: Zondervan, 1999), 165–235.

18. The research was conducted by the University of Michigan's Institute for Social Research (IRS). See Ronald Inglehart and Wayne Baker, "Modernization, Cultural Change, and the Persistence of Traditional Values," *American Sociological Review* 65 (February 2000): 46–48.

19. Ronald Rolheiser *The Holy Longing: The Search for a Christian Spirituality* (New York: Doubleday, 1999), 7.

20. 6 April 2000 email from *CassidyD21@aol.com*.

21. Gertrude Himmelfarb's immigrant mentality thinks this is still possible, even a good idea. See her *One Nation, Two Cultures* (New York: Knopf, 2000), 86.

22. Nancy Mairs, "Turning and Turning," in her *Ordinary Times: Cycles in Marriage, Faith, and Renewal* (Boston: Beacon Press, 1993), 68.

23. Lane Davis, Alabama-West Florida Conference, quoted in *Newscope* 28 (19 May 2000). See *www.umph.org/resources/publications/newscope_default. html* (accessed 30 April 2001). Thanks to Tom Hyde for this reference.

24. Christopher Levan, *Living in the Maybe: A Steward Confronts the Spirit of Fundamentalism* (Grand Rapids: Eerdmans, 1998), 67.

25. "Modernity was the shifting of the leverage point of capitalism from production to consumption, from necessity to wish. It was a difficult project: all desires had to be reduced to those that could be put on the market, and thus desires were reduced to needs and experienced as such." Greil Marcus, *Lipstick Traces: A Secret History of the 20th Century* (Cambridge, Mass.: Harvard Univ. Press, 1989), 129.

26. Naomi Klein, as quoted in Curtis Sittenfeld, "No-Brands-Land, *Fast Company* (September 2000): 244. See *www.fastcompany.com/online/38/nklein.html* (accessed 2 December 2000).

27. Roger Lewin and Birute Regine, *The Soul at Work: Listen, Respond, Let Go: Embracing Complexity Science for Business Success* (New York: Simon & Schuster, 2000), 22.

28. Mark Ellingsen, *The Cutting Edge: How Churches Speak on Social Issues* (Geneva, Switzerland, and Grand Rapids: Published for the Institute for Ecumenical Research, Strasbourg, France, by WCC Publications and Eerdmans, 1993), 26-40, 182–202.

29. Simon Louvish, *Man on the Flying Trapeze: The Life and Times of W. C. Fields* (New York: Norton, 1997), 439.

30. Convocation speech at Wake Forest University, as reported in Bob Allen, "America Looking for Inclusive Religious Vision, Moyers Says," *Biblical Recorder: Journal of the Baptist State Convention of North Carolina* (20 December 1997). See *www.biblicalrecorder.org/news/12_19_97/moyers12-19.shtml* (accessed 30 April 2001).

31. Unveiled references to Jesus occurred in many 1999 films, including *The Matrix, Star Wars Episode 1: The Phantom Menace, Dogma, The Greatest Story Ever Told,* and *End of Days.*

32. Michelle Conlin, "Religion in the Workplace: The Growing Presence of Spirituality in Corporate America," *Business Week* (1 November 1999): 151–57, quote on 152.

33. Ibid., 152.

34. This was the top trend at the 2000 National Association of Home Builders Convention at the Dallas Convention Center, according to Sue Doerfler, "Inner Renewal: Home Buyers Want Spiritual Hideaways, Cozier No-Hassle Homes," *Arizona Republic* (5 February 2000): AH1.

35. M. Scott Peck, *Golf and the Spirit: Lessons for the Journey* (New York: Harmony Books, 1999).

36. As quoted in "Compass," *Utne Reader* (March/April 1999): 20.

37. Eric Goldscheider, "Spiritual Rebirth: Chancellor Foresees Return of Religion," *Boston Globe* (3 October 1999).

38. John Ciardi as quoted in *Reader's Digest* (1 December 1980): 144.

39. Bruce Sterling, ed., *Mirrorshades: The Cyberpunk Anthology* (New York: Arbor House, 1986), xi.

40. Nancy Venable Raine, *After Silence: Rape and My Journey Back* (New York: Crown, 1998), 244.

41. Sam Keen, "What You Ask Is Who You Are," *Spirituality & Health* (Spring 2000), 30.

42. David Hopkins, "The ABCs of Ministry in the 21st Century," *Next Wave* (January 2000). See *www.next-wave.org/jan00/ABCs_of_Ministry.htm* (accessed 30 April 2001).

43. Bernard Haisch, "Brilliant Disguise: Light, Matter and the Zero-Point Field," *Science & Spirit* 10 (September/October 1999): 30–31. See *www.science-spirit.com/articles/articledetail.cfm?article_id=126* (accessed 30 April 2001). Haisch continues, "If it is the underlying realm of light that is the fundamental reality propping up our physical universe, let us ask ourselves how the universe of space and time would appear from the perspective of a beam of light. The laws of relativity are clear on this point. If you could ride a beam of light as an observer, all of space would shrink to a point, and all of time would collapse to an instant. In the reference frame of light, there is no space and time. If we look up at the Andromeda galaxy in the night sky, we see light that from our point of view took 2 million years to traverse that vast distance of space. But to a beam of light radiating from some star in the Andromeda galaxy, the transmission from its point of origin to our

eye was instantaneous. There must be a deeper meaning in these physical facts, a deeper truth about the simultaneous interconnection of all things."

44. See Gary E. R. Schwartz and Linda G. S. Russek, *The Living Energy Universe* (Charlottesville, Va.: Hampton Roads, 1999).

45. For the concept of fundamental laws and properties see David Chalmers, *The Conscious Mind: In Search of a Fundamental Theory* (New York: Oxford Univ. Press, 1996), esp. 126–29.

46. Calvin Coolidge, "The Inspiration of the Declaration: Speech at Philadelphia, Pennsylvania, on the One Hundred and Fiftieth Anniversary of the Declaration of Independence, July 5, 1926," *Founders Library: The 20th Century: Writings and Speeches of Political Figures.* See *www.founding.com/library/index.cfm?id=342&parent=20&searchTerms=coolidge&search=1* (accessed 30 April 2001).

47. Christina Rossetti, "Who Has Seen the Wind?" from *Sing-Song: A Nursery Rhyme Book* (1872) in *The Complete Poems of Christina Rossetti,* ed. R. W. Crump (Baton Rouge: Louisiana State Univ. Press, 1986), 2:42.

48. Elizabeth Lesser has compiled a helpful list of "dangers of the new spirituality," as she puts it. (*Spirituality & Health* [Spring 2000]: 51.) The dangers of the current spiritual renaissance include (1) Narcissism; (2) Superficiality; (3) The Never-Ending Process of Self-Improvement; (4) Instant Transformation; (5) Desire for Magic; (6) Grandiosity; (7) Romanticizing Indigenous Cultures; (8) The Inner-Child Tantrum; (9) Ripping Off the Traditions; (10) The Guru Trip. See also her *The New American Spirituality: A Seeker's Guide* (New York: Random House, 1999), 59–62, where she calls them the "top-ten list of the 'weeds' of the new American spirituality."

49. For an example from the field of medicine see "The Case for Nonlocality," ch. 3 of Larry Dossey's *Reinventing Medicine: Beyond Mind-Body to a New Era of Healing* (San Francisco: HarperSanFrancisco, 1999), 37–84.

50. For an explanation of Alain Aspect's "Bell Affect," see Ernest C. Lucas, "The 'New Science' and the Gospel," in Martyn Eden and David F. Wells, *The Gospel in the Modern World: A Tribute to John Stott* (Downers Grove, Ill.: InterVarsity, 1991), 129.

51. The dean was Thomas A. Langford, and the story can be found in "Blending the Academic with the Spiritual," *In Trust* 11 (Spring 2000): 24.

52. Brian Greene, *The Elegant Universe: Superstrings, Hidden Dimensions, and the Question for Ultimate Theory* (New York: Norton, 1999), 184–209.

53. See Jane Katra and Russell Targ, *The Heart of the Mind: How to Experience God Without Belief* (Novato, Calif.: New World Library, 1999), or Hawaii physicist Victor Stenger, who in *The Unconscious Quantum: Metaphysics in Modern Physics and Cosmology* (Amherst, N.Y.: Prometheus Books, 1995), contends that there is no design to the universe and a designer is irrelevant. To prove this, he has a web-based universe-creation game based on monkeys creating this universe. See *spot.colorado.edu/~vstenger/* (accessed 30 April 2001).

54. Many scientists are coming out of the closet and confessing to transcendent experiences. Charles Tart is collecting these stories for his online journal, *TASTE: The Archive of Scientists' Transcendent Experiences.* See *www.issc-taste.org/index.html* (accessed 30 April 2001).

55. As quoted in Steve Rabey, "David Wilcox's Wilderness Path," *Re: Generation Quarterly* 5 (Winter, 1999/2000): 28. See *www.regenerator.com/contents.html* (accessed 30 April 2001).

56. Mary Lacombe, "Emergent Wonder: The Sacred Depths of Nature: An Interview with Ursula Goodenough," *Science & Spirit* 11 (April/May 2000): vi. See *science-spirit.com/articles/Articledetail.cfm?article_ID=187* (accessed 30 April 2001).

57. Tom Bandy, *Coaching Change: Breaking Down Resistance, Building Up Hope* (Nashville: Abingdon, 2000), 179–80 (in manuscript form).

58. Robert William Fogel, *The Fourth Great Awakening & the Future of Egalitarianism* (Chicago: Univ. of Chicago Press, 2000), 205–7.

NATURALIZATION CLASS 9: FROM CLOCKWORK ORANGE TO WEB GREEN

1. See Sally J. Goerner, *After the Clockwork Universe: The Emerging Science and Culture of Integral Society* (Edinburgh: Floris Books, 1999).

2. "Life should be such that Nature is happy to see you" is the spiritual principle of Dadi Janki.

3. The phrase "cell-phone naturalists" is that of National Public Radio commentator Julia Redpath.

4. One of the fastest-growing directions in native thinking is towards free-market environmentalism, whose motto is "Wealth is Health."

5. Gallup Poll Surveys, CNN/USAToday/Gallup Poll (13–16 January 2000). See *www.gallup.com/poll/surveys/2000/Topline000113/q21.asp* (accessed 30 April 2001).

6. Michael deCourcy Hinds begins his Voter 2000 segment on "The Politics of Pollution" with this declaration: "Most Americans like to consider themselves environmentalists. They rank the environment among the top ten election year issues." *American Demographics* 22 (May 2000): 16. See *www.contentville.com/product/product.asp?ProdID={DF1BA000-C73F-4712-864D-419677E528BB}* (accessed 30 April 2001).

7. For an anthology of texts on finding God in the natural world, see Anne Rowthorn, *Earth and the Stars: Reconnecting with Nature Through Hymns, Stories, Poems, and Prayers from the World's Great Religions and Cultures* (Novato, Calif.: New World Library, 2000). Also see Tony Campolo, *Let Me Tell You a Story* (Nashville: Word, 2000).

8. Beverly Peterson Stearns and Stephen C. Stearns, *Watching, From the Edge of Extinction* (New Haven: Yale Univ. Press, 2000), ix–x.

9. As quoted in Stearns and Stearns, *Watching, From the Edge of Extinction*, 117, 135.

10. Quoted in "Environment-Friendly Operations to Boost Profit, Not Just Image," *Trend Letter* 19 (13 April 2000): 5.

11. Cyril of Jerusalem, *Catechesis* 13:28. *Cyrilli Hierosolymarum Archiepiscopi Opera Quae Supersunt Omnia*, ed. W. C. Reischl and J. Pupp (Hildesheim: Georg Olms Verlagsbuchhandlung, 1967), 2:87.

12. Gwen Kinkead, "In the Future People Like Me Will Go to Jail," *Fortune* (24 May 1999): 190.

13. Michael J. Weiss, "The Season for Sneezin'," *American Demographics* (April 1999): 13. See *www.contentville.com/product/product.asp?ProdID= {E5D0F835-19AF-4732-8865-7F4E7F95CA84}* (accessed 30 April 2001).

14. Jane Holtz Kay, *Asphalt Nation: How the Automobile Took Over America and How We Can Take It Back* (New York: Crown, 1997), 64.

15. Harvard biologist E. O. Wilson coined this phrase.

16. Barry Lopez, *About This Life: Journeys on the Threshold of Memory* (New York: Knopf, 1998), 137, 141.

17. Mary Lou Randour, *Animal Grace: Entering a Spiritual Relationship with Our Fellow Creatures* (Novato, Calif.: New World Library, 2000).

18. See Rupert Sheldrake, *Dogs That Know When Their Owners Are Coming Home and Other Unexplained Powers of Animals* (New York: Crown, 1999), 121. See also *www.sheldrake.org/dogs* (accessed 30 April 2001).

19. At the Lake Placid Lodge in upstate New York, for $50 extra a night your traveling animal companion can have his or her very own bed with turn-down service at bedtime and treats at tea time, but children under 12 are not allowed. See *www.lakeplacidlodge.com/z-home.htm* (accessed 30 April 2001).

20. For more on Jesus' relationships with animals, see my *The Jesus Prescription for a Healthy Life* (Nashville: Abingdon, 1998), 161–64.

21. Immigrants are by and large natural Darwinists. Natives are naturally Designists. G.O.D. is an acronym now circulating among some scientists for "Grand Organizing Design." Even scientists who are Darwininans have gone beyond "natural selection" to a more nuanced Darwinianism in which there is design inevitability: "There are certain 'fundamental' structures of organisms that are not at all determined by the arbitrary experimentation and weeding out that evolution is thought to involve. Instead, these structures have an inevitability about them, being driven by the basic physics and chemistry of growth. If life were started from scratch a thousand times over, it would every time alight on these fundamental structures eventually." See Philip Ball, *The Self-Made Tapestry: Pattern Formation in Nature* (New York: Oxford Univ. Press, 1999), 103.

22. Ann Griffiths, as quoted in A. M. Allchin, *Ann Griffiths: The Furnace and the Fountain* (Cardiff: Univ. of Wales Press, 1987), 7.

23. As quoted in Ronald Rolheiser, *The Holy Longing: The Search for a Christian Spirituality* (New York: Doubleday, 1999), 43.

24. Political scientist/criminologist John J. Dilulio Jr. as quoted in David Gelernter, "What Do Murderers Deserve?" *Utne Reader* (March/April 1999): 52. See *www.utne.com/bSociety.tmpl?command=search&db=dArticle.db&eqheadlinedata =What%20do%20Murderers%20Deserve%3F* (accessed 30 April 2001).

25. Thanks to David Stambaugh.

26. Carol Ann Duffy, "Ape," in her *The Other Country* (London: Anvil, 1990), 20.

27. As quoted in Jonathan White, ed., *Talking on the Water: Conversations About Nature and Creativity* (San Francisco: Sierra Club Book, 1994), 109.

28. Eric Zencey, *Virgin Forest: Meditations on History, Ecology, and Culture* (Athens: Univ. of Georgia Press, 1998), 164.

ENDTRODUCTION

1. John 14:6.

2. *Journal of the Federal Convention*, kept by James Madison, ed. E. H. Scott (Chicago: Albert, Scott, 1893), 763.

3. Margaret Wheatly, at a conference in Ottawa, Canada, in May 2000, as verified in an email from her office.

4. Herbert O'Driscoll, as quoted by Lori J. Rosenkvist in "Time Out—Time Away," *Clergy Journal* (February 2000): 5.

5. Joseph Brodsky, "Speech at the Stadium" in *On Grief and Reason: Essays* (New York: Farrar Straus Giroux, 1995), 145–46.

Wake up and dance!

SoulSalsa

17 Surprising Steps for Godly Living in the 21ˢᵗ Century

LEONARD SWEET

Leonard Sweet wants to show you the ins and outs of living an old-fashioned faith in the new-fangled times. In his engaging, wonderful, thought-bytes style, Sweet invites you to

- Mezuzah your universe
- Do dirt and do the dishes
- Cycle to church
- Give history a shove
- Cheer rivals from the bench
- Dance the salsa

SoulSalsa unpacks it all in ways that can change how you live if you let them. You can be a man or woman who walks the ancient path of a disciple in the world of the future. Because the future is now — and now is the time to practice the "17 Lifestyle Requirements for Membership in the Postmodern Body of Christ." Time to enter the dance of a culture that desperately needs to see your moves.

Check out the *SoulSalsa* song, playing on a Christian music station near you — or download the mp3 from *www.SoulSalsa.com* (or search for it on Napster!).

Softcover   ISBN 0-310-24280-0
Audio Pages®
   Abridged Cassettes   ISBN 0-310-23482-4
www.SoulSalsa.com

Pick up a copy today at your favorite bookstore!

ZONDERVAN™

GRAND RAPIDS, MICHIGAN 49530 USA
WWW.ZONDERVAN.COM

The best way to wake up to the dawn:
Take a swim!

SoulTsunami

Sink or Swim in New Millennium Culture

LEONARD SWEET

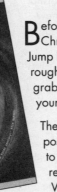

Before you go out and seize the new day for Christ, you'll need a little morning exercise. Jump into *SoulTsunami!* Sure, the water's cold and rough, but you'll know which way to swim if you grab the ten Life Rings Sweet provides to keep your head above water.

The Life Rings explore critical factors that define postmodern culture — from its spiritual longings, to its relationship with technology, to its global renaissance in art and invention, and more. With each come intellectual and spiritual exercises to prepare pastors, lay leaders, and other influential Christians for effective interaction with the new millennium world.

As your passionate and prophetic swimming coach, Sweet will make you remove your tunnel-vision goggles and feel the sting of the swelling postmodern flood. He will encourage and affirm you and the rest of God's lifeguard team — the church — helping you build the stamina required to rescue a world out to sea.

Softcover   **ISBN 0-310-24312-2**
Audio Pages®
   Abridged Cassettes   **ISBN 0-310-22712-7**
www.SoulTsunami.com

Pick up a copy today at your favorite bookstore!

ZONDERVAN™

GRAND RAPIDS, MICHIGAN 49530 USA
WWW.ZONDERVAN.COM

The Dawn Mistaken for Dusk

If God So Loved the World, Why Can't We?

LEONARD SWEET

In his first book conceived and acquired specifically to be delivered electronically, Leonard Sweet contends that the church is blind to the changes that are dragging us into the future. Therefore, it is losing its influence as an agent of change and grace in the world. "There are now some companies who absolutely want to change the world more than the church," writes Sweet. He sees the church at a crossroads. It will either see the future as a new dawn and therefore embrace it as opportunity. Or, it will see the future as dusk and therefore hide from the darkness of the world. Sweet believes that God will be in the future, with or without us, and that an "Acts 27" movement is afoot. This book serves as a "naturalization manual" to help Christians achieve full citizenship in the new, postmodern world. It will teach them how to go from being immigrants to natives. From foreigners in a strange land to people of God, confident and at home in a rapidly changing world.

ebook   **ISBN 0-310-23223-6**

Visit your favorite ebook provider to purchase your NIV eBible today!

ZONDERVAN™

GRAND RAPIDS, MICHIGAN 49530

www.zondervan.com

A Is for Abductive
The Language of the Emerging Church

LEONARD SWEET, BRIAN D. MCLAREN, AND JERRY HASELMAYER

*An Essential Guide for Understanding
the Language and Ideas
of the Twenty-first Century*

This witty but substantive primer explores the basic concepts and vernacular of postmodern ministry. This "postmodern ministry-for-dummies" will help "immigrants" learn to speak PSL (postmodern as a second language), so they can better live, minister, and make a difference in the emerging postmodern context.

Topics covered include:
- Abductive Method/Augmentation
- Branding/Blur/Body/Be-live
- Outside the Box Thinking/Open-Endedness/ Outward-focused/Organic
- PALS (Partnership/Alliance/Liaisons/ Strategic Collaborations)/Paradox

Softcover ISBN: 0-310-24356-4

Pick up a copy today at your favorite bookstore!

ZONDERVAN™

GRAND RAPIDS, MICHIGAN 49530 USA

WWW.ZONDERVAN.COM